LUCRETIUS
AND HIS INFLUENCE

BY

GEORGE DEPUE HADZSITS

COOPER SQUARE PUBLISHERS, INC.
NEW YORK
1963

Published 1963 by Cooper Square Publishers, Inc.
59 Fourth Avenue, New York 3, N.Y.
Library of Congress Catalog Card No. 63-10292

DIIS MANIBUS SACRUM
W. D. H. et H. H. B.

CONTENTS

[vii]

CONTENTS

[viii]

LUCRETIUS AND HIS
INFLUENCE

LUCRETIUS AND HIS INFLUENCE

I. LIFE OF LUCRETIUS

WHILE we know the exact dates of birth and death of many of our Roman authors, those of Titus Lucretius Carus are curiously obscured. From statements, conflicting as they are, in Donatus and Jerome, who lived about four hundred years after Lucretius, it would appear that our poet was born *ca.* 99 B.C. and that he died forty-four years later, on the fifteenth of October, 55 B.C.[1] It is surprising that such a veil of mystery covers the life of one whose importance, as thinker and as poet, was so very great to the Rome of his own day. It might be difficult to discover an analogue to this strangely anomalous situation. The discovery of records is revealing to us facts in the career

---

[1] Cf. Merrill Edition, Int., pp. 11 seq., for a convenient discussion. I cannot credit the Codex Monacensis nor the Borgian *Vita*.

of Shakespeare, but the recovery of details of Lucretius' life on earth seems most unlikely. We are, therefore, in ignorance and are likely to remain in the dark about Lucretius' birthplace, his social status, his place of residence, his activities, political, military, or otherwise, his private life, his personal appearance.[2] All of this is in strange contrast with the fullness of our knowledge of Catullus, Caesar, Cicero, Virgil, Horace, or Ovid. No external evidence exists that throws light upon any of these problems; the poem, the *De Rerum Natura*, has been scanned over and over again with a view to discovering some internal evidence that might be recognized as valid. But scholars have drawn diametrically opposite conclusions from the same passages, maintaining and denying that Rome was his home, affirming and denying that Lucretius was an aristocrat, claiming the highest moral standards for him and arguing that he was a voluptuary. It is idle to speculate any longer, on most of these questions, until other evidence should appear. This much we know — that of Latin he was a master and that he called it his native, his ancestral

---

[2] We should, however, not forget the likeness of the poet, appearing on a black agate, which Munro accepted as ancient and authentic.

tongue.[3] I have no doubt that he was a *civis Romanus* [4] and that he knew Rome. But Rome, with all of its splendors, did not intrigue him. To which branch of the illustrious Lucretian gens he belonged remains uncertain; whether he came from the North or the South remains unknown.

The remarkable statement of Jerome about Lucretius' insanity and suicide has ofttimes been quoted, perhaps far too often if it has unduly influenced opinion:

Titus Lucretius poeta nascitur qui postea amatorio poculo in furorem versus, cum aliquot libros per intervalla insaniae conscripsisset, quos postea Cicero emendavit, propria se manu interfecit anno aetatis quadragesimo quarto.

Titus Lucretius, the poet, was born (*i.e. in* 95 B.C.). *Later he was driven mad by a love-philtre, after he had written several books in the intervals of insanity; Cicero subsequently corrected these books; Lucretius died by his own hand in the forty-fourth year of his life.*

We can affirm nothing of the truth of this.[5] It is altogether likely that the tradition, how-

---

[3] I. 832, III. 260, V. 337 (all references are to Munro's text).

[4] It would require a long note to prove this, but I. 41 and V. 36 should be borne in mind.

[5] Cf., *e.g.,* Giacomo Giri, *Il Suicidio di T. Lucrezio,*

soever it started, was current at least as early
as the days of Suetonius — perhaps, even earlier
in the first century after Christ. The story,
whether true or false, has clothed the name of
Lucretius with a romantic halo and the uncriti-
cal Tennyson was swift to seize upon the tale, as
though veridic: that a wife Lucilia [6] had secured
a philtre

> To lead an errant passion home again;

that this love potion

> Confused the chemic labor of the blood,

and that, in consequence, the unhappy Lucretius ended his own life. Sensation flies through
the centuries. Long ago Virgil told us how true
it is that stories grow, and Ovid knew perfectly
well that human nature loves to believe the
worst:

> Sed nos in vitium credula turba sumus. [7]

Palermo, Clausen, 1895, who thinks the story of suicide an
invention of the Empire period, while Ettore Stampini, " Il
Suicidio di Lucrezio " (1896), in *Studi di Letteratura e
Filologia Latina,* Torino, Bocca, 1917, hesitates to dismiss
the story, as legend. The greatest variety of opinions has
been held, both on the subject of insanity and suicide, by
students of Lucretius.

[6] ' Lucilia,' wife of Lucretius, may be pure fiction.

[7] *Fasti,* IV. 312.

At the most, we can admit that Lucretius may have suffered from intermittent insanity, but neither the case of Pascal who wrote his *Pensées* in intervals of suffering, nor the reputed epilepsy of a Caesar proves anything about Lucretius. Stories told about the death of Lucian, experiences of Tasso, sensitive and high-strung as he was, may or may not be analogues to the life and the end of Lucretius.[8] Lucretius' *mind* we shall come to know, its intensity and its passion, its melancholy and its brooding, its pessimism and its optimism, its marvelous mastery and its lapses. These are important considerations that may or may not indicate abnormality. But the traditions of insanity and suicide, although they may lie within the realm of legitimate inquiry, are apt to remain beyond all possibility of proof or disproof.

[8] The same may be said of other so-called (partial) parallels: those, for example, of Samuel Johnson, Voltaire, Ruskin, Nietzsche, Bergson.

II. EPICURUS AND EPICUREANISM
IN ATHENS

ALTHOUGH the major purpose of this little book will be an analysis of the work and a study of the influence of Lucretius, some slight account of the rise of the Epicurean school may seem permissive and, indeed, necessary.

The main facts of Epicurus' life have been elicited from a tangled mass of conflicting testimony and it may be safe to say that Epicurus was descended of a noble Athenian family, that in 342/1 B.C. he was born on the island of Samos, probably, to which his father Neocles had gone as one of the earliest colonists; that he became a teacher of philosophy in Mytilene and in Lampsacus; that in 306/5 B.C., he established, in Athens, a school which was destined to become famous for all time, known as the "Garden of Epicurus," and that he died in 270 B.C. Epicurus stamped his own personality upon this school and exercised such authority that his doctrine was accepted by his followers as virtually final. At the time of the establishment of the school, the Platonic Academy had been in existence for some years; Theophrastus was head of the Lyceum of Aristotle; Zeno was expounding his Stoicism to his own circle in the Porch. The Epicurean school took its place in the group of Four and, for many hundred years, in their various, respective ways these assessed life, interpreted the ideals of life, and, to a large extent, formulated Greek and, later, Roman philosophic speculation.

The Epicurean and Stoic schools became bitter enemies; Epicurus and his contemporaries wrote attacks on Platonism, polemics against Aristotle and Theophrastus; nor did these attacks remain unanswered. Epicurus' diatribes spared no head and his shafts were levelled against Protagoras, Heraclitus, even Democritus and Aristippus, in spite of his great indebtedness to the last two. It is not surprising that calumniators of Epicurus were numerous, and for long the scandalous stories told especially by Stoics and by Timocrates, the " Judas of the Society," were accepted at their face value. All of this *chronique scandaleuse* has been discounted in our own

[9]

time by competent scholars,[1] and the many fine qualities of the man are cited in his defense, as well as his many, known acts of kindness, gratitude and piety, to say naught of the extraordinary honors that were bestowed upon him.

Within the school, however, remarkable harmony prevailed. The value of friendship [2] became a tradition, and veneration of the founder, in his own life-time, found eloquent expression, later, in the verses of Lucretius. Epicurus was looked upon as a Redeemer. A unanimity of opinion held the members of this Epicurean society together, so that it is not strange that it has often been compared to the early Christian Church. Differences of nationality, of sex, and of social status constituted no barrier; cosmopolitanism, which was taking the place of the old nationalism in Greek life, found natural expression here. Not a philosophic or scientific society in any profound sense — not comparable in this respect to the Academy or to the Lyceum, not greatly troubled by the work done at the Museum and Library of Alexandria, whether in natural history or in literary

[1] Cf. Cyril Bailey, *The Greek Atomists and Epicurus,* and A. E. Taylor, *Epicurus,* who, however, blames Epicurus for his " inexcusable ingratitude " toward his teachers.

[2] Cf. No. 27 of the Κύριαι Δόξαι.

criticism, or, a little later, by the great mathe-
maticians and astronomers, as Euclid and Aristarchus — the Epicurean school was largely
concerned with the practical problems of individual conduct. The study of philosophy
fell under three heads, of Canonics, Physics,
and Ethics, but the first two were subordinated
to the paramount importance of the third. The
claims of Logic could not be wholly denied and
rules of inductive logic were formulated (called
'Canonics') demonstrating how true infer-
ences may be drawn from the data of sense-
perception. Studies in ' Physics,' *i.e.,* of natural
science, were not pursued for their own sake [3]
but as a means to escape superstition and fear
of angry gods, to demonstrate the mortality
of the soul and to secure release from fear of
death, and to learn the limits of pain and desire. The egoistic hedonism of the Epicurean
school sought, above all else, a life of blessed
tranquillity, of imperturbability (ἀταραξία),
with a body free from pain and a soul free
from care. No statement could be franker:

καὶ διὰ τοῦτο τὴν ἡδονὴν ἀρχὴν καὶ τέλος
λέγομεν εἶναι τοῦ μακαρίως ζῆν.[4]

[3] Cf. No. ii of the Κύριαι Δόξαι.
[4] 128 (Letter of Epicurus to Menoeceus).

[11]

And for this reason we call happiness the beginning and the end of the blessed life.

Happiness was regarded as the first good, innate in us. But 'pleasure' did not, of course, mean sensual enjoyment; [5] and one of the Κύριαι Δόξαι (or 'Principal Doctrines') put the matter so distinctly that confusion should never have followed:

Οὐκ ἔστιν ἡδέως ζῆν ἄνευ τοῦ φρονίμως καὶ καλῶς καὶ δικαίως (οὐδὲ φρονίμως καὶ καλῶς καὶ δικαίως) ἄνευ τοῦ ἡδέως.[6]

It is not possible to live pleasantly (happily) without living wisely, nobly, justly, nor to live wisely, nobly, justly without living happily.

Happiness was unthinkable without wisdom, without virtue; and the three were inseparable.

Whatever the imperfections, weaknesses, or faults of this system of philosophy, its appeal was so great that the school enjoyed a long life, for in the third century after Christ it still flourished as a distinct sect. There is evidence that in the fourth century it was moribund.[7]

---

[5] 131 (*ibid.*).

[6] No. 5.

[7] Refuted by Dionysius, Bishop of Alexandria, and by Lactantius, it was still a dangerous rival of Christianity; Julian the Apostate (360–363) forbade Epicureanism; for St. Augustine, see Chapter X.

All matters of dispute aside, 'Epicureanism' soon came to mean to all men (1) a physical doctrine of atomism; only a few, relatively, of high intelligence could comprehend this; (2) an ethical philosophy that regarded 'pleasure' as the *summum bonum;* many might find themselves inclined to such a doctrine, even while there would be wide variation in the definition of 'pleasure'; (3) a denial of immortality, from which many would shrink; (4) a new interpretation of religion that conceived of gods as far removed from this world and, far from exercising Providence toward mankind, as quite indifferent to our happiness or to our suffering; such a dogma, very different from orthodox notions, might repel many although it might draw carelessly-minded people, sincere skeptics, and even genuine idealists.

It was this philosophy that Lucretius embraced, but as it filtered through his mind it acquired a new temper. Lucretius undoubtedly meant to reproduce the philosophy of his master, faithfully, with the zeal not only of a disciple but rather that of an apostle; and all students of the text of Lucretius and of the surviving work of Epicurus must be struck with the fidelity with which the Roman reproduced the leading principles of the philosophy of the Greek. Lucretius shared Epicurus' hostility to other schools; he never mentions Plato or Aristotle by name; he opposes some of their dogmas as well as of the Stoics, without naming the other schools; he believed the Epicurean doctrine to be true and final. But the scattered lights of Epicurean doctrine were strangely fused into one bright, hard light, as the Roman with a Roman's genius for organization sought to harmonize, more closely, the more loosely organized material of a Greek who lived in a decadent age. Epicurus' literary style utterly lacked distinction; Lucretius bestowed upon the system the gift of poetry, at times extraordinarily brilliant and, again, of haunting beauty. Benn [8] has made the shrewd suggestion that Lucretius had probably had a lawyer's education. "He certainly exhibits great forensic skill in speaking from his brief." The good will and the genial amiability exhibited toward his associates by Epicurus, the physical invalidism and the winning personality of the Greek, who certainly does not rank among the great thinkers of antiquity, are fol-

8 A. W. Benn, *The Greek Philosophers,* London, Smith, Elder & Co., 1914,[2] p. 400.

lowed by a strength, a vigor, a dogmatism, a relentless driving to logical conclusions that belonged to the new Power in the West of which Lucretius, whatever the facts of his personal life, was an incarnation. The negative Epicurean philosophy of flight, of escape from intolerable political and social conditions became, in the mind of Lucretius, an instrument of reformation. The utter disillusionment, the timid humanitarianism of Epicurus were succeeded by the positive ardor of Lucretius' evangelism.

Approximately two hundred years elapsed between the foundation of the school by Epicurus and the birth of Lucretius.[9] The school had enjoyed an uninterrupted history, and, when Lucretius was born, Zeno of Sidon was head of the school in Athens; Cicero regarded him as 'princeps Epicureorum.'[10]

---

[9] We learn of pupils of Epicurus and of his successors in the School: among his disciples and intimate friends were Metrodorus, Colotes, Polyaenus, and Hermarchus; other members of this cultivated society were Herodotus, Menoeceus, Pythocles, Idomeneus, Leonteus. Hermarchus became second president of the school upon Epicurus' death; Polystratus, Dionysius, Basileides were leaders of the school in succession and, towards the close of the second century B.C., Apollodorus was the conspicuous exponent of this creed in Athens, while Zeno of Sidon, a pupil of Apollodorus, appears as the next distinguished leader. Menander should also be mentioned as an intimate friend of Epicurus.

[10] *De Nat. D.,* I. 21. 59; cf. *T. D.,* III. 17. 38.

III. LUCRETIUS AND THE ROMAN EPICUREANS

PHAEDRUS and Patro were subsequent shining names in the later, illustrious Greek succession, and their names were distinguished in the first half of the first century before Christ. Epicureanism was known in Rome in the days of Ennius:

Ego deum genus esse semper dixi et dicam caelitum,
Sed eos non curare opinor, quid agat humanum
genus;
Nam si curent, bene bonis sit, male malis, quod
nunc abest.[1]

In the second century B.C., Gaius Amafinius[2] was conspicuous among those who were popularizing the philosophy in Italy. Cicero, whose opposition to Epicurean doctrines is expressed frequently enough in his essays and in his letters, knew, to his chagrin, how large the accessions to the sect had been from its first appearance in Rome down to his own day.[3]

[1] Cic., De Div., I. 58. 132; II. 50. 104; De N. D., III. 32. 79; cf., also, Plautus' Mercator (prol.).
[2] Cic., T. D., IV. 3, 6–7.
[3] Cic., De Fin., I. 7. 25, ibid., II. 15. 49; T. D., II. 3. 7; cf. pro Caelio, 17. 41.

[16]

We know that there were many in Italy, in Rome and in the vicinity of Naples, who were regarded as 'Epicureans,' men with closer or looser affiliations with the Epicurean doctrine or with Epicurean circles. We wonder, naturally, what relations Lucretius had maintained with leaders of the sect in Athens or in Italy; but complete and utter darkness enshrouds the figure of Lucretius, though he was the greatest literary champion of Epicureanism throughout the active history of the school from the beginning to its close in the fourth century after Christ.

Cicero certainly does not enlighten us and his complete silence on the subject of Lucretius, the man, is baffling. If Cicero, because of his strong disapproval of the tenets of the Epicurean school, had shunned Epicureans, we might, perhaps, understand this mystery. But, in spite of his uncompromising hostility to the Epicurean principles, Cicero enjoyed cordial relations with such proponents of Epicureanism as Phaedrus [4] and Patro, [5] and he expresses his

---

[4] (Phaedrus) *De Fin.*, I. 5. 16; V. 1. 3; *N. D.*, I. 33. 93 (nam Phaedro nihil elegantius, nihil humanius; sed stomachabatur senex etc.); *Ep. ad Fam.*, XIII. 1; etc.

[5] (Patro) *Ep. ad Fam.*, XIII. 1. 2 (Cum Patrone Epicurio mihi omnia sunt, nisi quod in philosophia vehementer ab eo dissentio); cf. *Ep. ad Att.*, V. 11. 6; etc.

[17]

respect and, even, deep affection for these men: the former he held in high esteem as a philosopher and he had regard for him as a man, because he was honest, amiable, and obliging; no one, in fact, was more polished or more cultivated than Phaedrus, while with Patro, Cicero says that he was in complete accord, except on philosophic grounds. Similarly, Cicero writes, handsomely, of Siro and Philodemus that they were gentlemen of highest quality and very learned men.[6] But of Lucretius — his life, character, behavior — not one word, although there were many opportunities to do so.

It was in 51 B.C. that Cicero[7] wrote Memmius begging him to restore to Patro, as head of the school, the property that had come into Memmius' possession and upon which there stood some ruins of Epicurus' house. Of course the ruins of this house appeared a sacred place to the mind of Patro and to his sect. Although not friendly to the Epicurean doctrine, Cicero — for love of Patro, his predecessor Phaedrus,

---

[6] Cic., *De Fin.*, II. 35. 119 ('familiaris nostros, credo, Sironem dicis et Philodemum, cum optimos viros, tum homines doctissimos.') ; cf. *Ac. Pr.*, II. 33. 106 (et omnia meminit Sciron Epicuri dogmata) ; *Ep. ad Fam.*, VI. 11. 2 (Siro, our friend) 45 B.C.

[7] *Ad Fam.*, XIII. 1.

and especially for the sake of Atticus, and for his own sake — begs Memmius to yield and to restore to the school a property which Memmius does not require. Cicero's letter is most gracious and tactful. It was only a few years before this date that Lucretius had died. And it was to Memmius that Lucretius had dedicated his work which, of course, was known to Patro. Whatever the personal relations, at the time, between Memmius and Patro, between Memmius and other Epicureans, it certainly appears that there was every reason to mention the *De Rerum Natura,* as one of the strongest arguments why Memmius should grant this favor. Lucretius' dedication of his poem to Memmius constituted the latter's most likely title to fame and immortality, and Cicero must have known that. Yet no mention of Lucretius, here.

Perhaps it will be maintained that Cicero was not intimately acquainted with that poem. We shall probably never know, with any certainty, the extent to which Cicero was familiar with the *De Rerum Natura.* Scholars [8] have held the most widely different views on this

---

[8] Cf. W. A. Merrill, *Cicero's Knowledge of Lucretius's Poem,* University of California Publications in Classical Philology, 1909.

debatable subject. But Cicero's one reference to Lucretius, by name, in his letter of
54 B.C., to his brother, once and for all establishes profound admiration for the poem. The
several scornful statements in Cicero[9] to the
effect that he did not read the Epicurean philosophical works, written in Latin, refer, plainly,
only to a body of literature that, to his mind,
was superficial in character and repellent to
him, personally, because utterly and apparently
intentionally lacking in literary merit. Amafinius, Rabirius, and others, unnamed, are rejected. But the letter to his brother, to which
I have just referred, seems to me to place
Lucretius' poem, very definitely, in that other
category of great literature which Cicero was
so eager to see grow in Italy. Cicero's pleasure
in fine exposition, even of Epicurean doctrine,
is unmistakably expressed in praise[10] of Velleius and of Zeno, as distinguished speakers. A
man, so minded, could have had but one view
of the literary merits of Lucretius' *De Rerum
Natura*. But, curiously, Cicero failed to refer

[9] *T. D.*, II. 3. 7; *T. D.*, IV. 3. 6–7; *Ac. Post.*, I. 2. 5–6;
De Fin., I. 5. 14.
[10] *N. D.*, I. 21. 58–59. Cicero did read contemporary
Epicurean literature; cf. *Ep. ad Att.*, XIII. 39. 2. (Phaedrus' book ' On the Gods ').

to Lucretius even in his memorable letter to
Memmius.

Even if Cicero was following Greek sources
in writing his *De Natura Deorum, De Finibus,*
and the *Tusculan Disputations* (expositions of
religion, ethics, and immortality of the soul),
his failure to mention Lucretius, to refer to him
in some way or other, remains inexplicable.
Velleius of Lanuvium was the exponent of Epicurean philosophy of religion in the first book
of Cicero's *De Natura Deorum,* which, alone,
is sufficient to indicate his rank and reputation.
But Cicero pays him, besides, a fine compliment, as a scholar and speaker of highest
rank.[11] Again, no mention of Lucretius, at a
point where we might have expected it.

Our rather full knowledge of the Epicurean
garden-school of Siro, in the vicinity of Naples,
as well as of Siro's famous friend, Philodemus
of Herculaneum,[12] further sharpens our curi-
osity about Lucretius. But neither Ciceronian
nor Horatian references to these Epicureans,
nor the Herculanean rolls, nor the documents

[11] *N. D.,* I. 21. 57–58 (the statement tacitly places Velleius ahead of Lucretius) ; at the time of composition of the
De Nat. Deorum, Velleius was a senator and the ranking
Roman Epicurean (I. 6. 15) ; a slight criticism of his art appears in Cic., *de Or.,* III. 21. 78.

[12] Of course he *came* from Gadara (in Palestine).

[21]

that inform us of Virgil's association with this
school in South Italy ever or at any time throw
any light on the life or work of Lucretius. In
that school and company which may well have
drawn to it many distinguished Romans, Lucretius' name must have been held in highest
honor.

Zeno, Phaedrus, Patro — Siro and Philodemus — Velleius and Lucius Manlius Torquatus — the latter, exponent of Epicurean
ethics, defender and sturdy champion of Epicurus' theory of happiness in Cicero's *De Finibus* — are not phantoms but real personalities;
other 'Epicureans,' to mention but a few, Piso,
father-in-law of Caesar, and Caesar — Crassus,
the orator, and Cassius, the conspirator — Titus
Pomponius Atticus — move across the stage.
Their paths often crossed. Friendship among
Epicureans was a by-word; Torquatus had put
it rather magnificently:

sunt autem qui dicant foedus esse quoddam sapien-
tium, ut ne minus amicos quam se ipsos diligant.[13]

Did any of these Greeks and Romans know
Lucretius? Can it be that Lucretius was
known to none of them? Credible or incredible, as you like! Did Lucretius live the life of

[13] Cic., *de Fin.*, I. 20. 70.

[22]

a recluse and a hermit? We do not know. We stumble across no reference to Lucretius, the man. But in the present state of our knowledge, or, better, ignorance, Lucretius appears an elusive wraith, or, if you prefer, a lonesome pine.

Cicero, as we have seen, was friend of Zeno, Phaedrus, and Patro, and Atticus, in no lesser degree. Cicero was friend of Philodemus and Siro. Virgil was an intimate associate of Siro, and, no doubt, of Philodemus, as well. The Herculanean rolls and Probus' *Life of Virgil* make it appear altogether likely that Lucius Varius Rufus, Plotius Tucca, and Quintilius Varus, those loyal friends of Virgil and Horace, belonged to that congenial group that met, near Naples, in Siro's garden. Lucius Calpurnius Piso,[14] father-in-law of Caesar, was, it is said, Philodemus' patron. And in his argument against infliction of the death-penalty upon the Catilinarian conspirators, Caesar [15] had spoken

[14] Cicero's oration *In Pisonem* makes Piso's interest in Epicureanism clear enough; 9. 20, 16. 37, 18. 42, 25. 59, 28. 68–70; similarly, the oration, *Post Red.*, 6. 13–14. But it is Epicureanism on a very low level. Cicero abuses Piso, Epicureanism, and the Greek philosopher-friend, whom Asconius identifies as Philodemus; but I am doubtful about this identification. Asconius says of Philodemus: Epicureus illa aetate nobilissimus, cuius poemata . . . lasciva.

[15] Sall., *Bell. Cat.*, 51. 20: de poena possum equidem

as an Epicurean when he had said that ' death is a relief from suffering and not a torment; it annuls all human woes; beyond it there is no place for sorrow or for joy.' Crassus, the orator, was closely associated with Velleius.[16] Lucius Manlius Torquatus [17] and Cassius [18] defended hedonism. These men met and discussed Epicureanism but we do not know that Lucretius, in person, touched the lives of any of them, at any point. I do not believe that a parallel to this exists in the history of philosophy.

The names of other ' Epicureans '[19] might be mentioned to emphasize, still further, the apparent isolation of Lucretius from the lives of his contemporaries. But sufficient has been

---

dicere, id quod res habet, in luctu atque miseriis mortem aerumnarum requiem, non cruciatum esse; eam cuncta mortalium mala dissolvere; ultra neque curae neque gaudio locum esse. Cf. Cic., *Cat.*, IV. 4. 7.

[16] Cic., *de Or.*, III. 21. 78: quid enim meus familiaris, C. Velleius, adferre potest quam ab rem voluptas sit summum bonum, etc.

[17] As spokesman in Cic., *De Fin.*

[18] Cf. Cic., *Ep. ad Fam.*, XV. 16 (45 B.C.) and 19 (Cassius to Cic.).

[19] *E.g.*, Gaius Catius, the Insubrian Gaul, and Marcus Pompilius Andronicus, a Syrian by birth, are two very interesting cases. We shall hear of Catius, later (p. 178). For more names, cf. Zeller, *The Stoics, Epicureans, and Sceptics* (tr. by Reichel), pp. 413–15; N. W. De Witt, " Notes on the History of Epicureanism," in *T. A. P. A.*, LXIII. 166–176 (1932).

said to make it clear that in the 60's and in the 50's of the first century before Christ, Epicureanism exerted a wide influence in Rome. In thought, at least, Lucretius was not solitary. Of course the extent of attachment to an Epicurean 'school' or to a body of doctrine called 'Epicurean' varied greatly according to many different circumstances. Atticus, perhaps, was not counted an Epicurean [20] in any real or full sense of the word, but he says of himself: [21]

at ego, quem vos ut deditum Epicuro insectari soletis, sum multum equidem cum Phaedro, quem unice diligo, ut scitis, in Epicuri hortis, . . . sed veteris proverbii admonitu vivorum memini, nec tamen Epicuri licet oblivisci, si cupiam, cuius imaginem non modo in tabulis nostri familiares, sed etiam in poculis et in anulis habent.

But I, whom you are wont to reproach as being devoted to Epicurus, spend much time in the gardens of Epicurus in the company of Phaedrus whom, as you know, I love . . . but reminded by the old proverb I remember the living, though I do not forget Epicurus, even if I should choose to do so, because our intimate friends not only have his picture upon their walls but have his image engraven on their cups and finger-rings.

[20] Cicero, *Ep. ad Fam.*, XIII. 1. 5, says of him: Is (non quo sit ex istis; est enim omni liberali doctrina politissimus, sed valde diligit Patronem, valde Phaedrum amavit) etc.

[21] *De Fin.*, V. 1. 3.

[25]

Epicureans assuredly were 'intimate friends' of Atticus, but, as we learn abundantly from Nepos' *Life of Atticus,* all men were inclined in friendship and bound by ties of friendship to Titus Pomponius 'Atticus.' Without affiliating himself with any political party, Atticus was friend of and friendly and generous to men of widely different political views. He was, in short, a friend to mankind, although, from conviction, he held aloof from affairs of state; [22] this non-participation was as much an expression of his own temperament as it was, at the same time, a conscious or unconscious exhibition of Epicurean doctrine. Nepos gives us no reason to believe that Atticus was, in philosophy any more than in political life, anything but an eclectic, always guided, to be sure, by the highest personal motives: [23]

nam principum philosophorum ita percepta habuit praecepta, ut iis ad vitam agendam, non ad ostentationem uteretur.

for he had so completely mastered the precepts of the leading philosophers that he employed them not for display but for the guidance of his life.

[22] *Atticus,* Ch. 6, especially § 5 (Qua in re non solum dignitati serviebat, sed etiam tranquilitati) ; 7. 3; 8. 4; 9. 5 (se non fortunae, sed hominibus solere esse amicum) ; 11. 3; 15. 3 (ex quo iudicari potest non inertia, sed iudicio fugisse rei publicae procurationem).   [23] *Ibid.,* 17. 3.

And we learn, from another passage, in Cicero,[24] that Atticus did not subscribe to the Epicurean denial of divine providence, although he calls Epicureans his 'fellow-disciples.' Atticus' personal relationships with members of the school were such that he was eminently qualified to figure in the effort to secure a return of the property in Athens, from Memmius, to the School of Epicurus.[25]

Perhaps very few of the many 'Epicureans'[26] owed or acknowledged such complete allegiance and adherence to the school as did Lucretius, to whose mind Epicurus' doctrines were dogma. But time has drawn an impenetrable veil over the personal relations that existed between the other Epicureans in Rome or elsewhere in Italy and the foremost exponent of the Epicurean doctrine in the West.

[24] *De. Leg.*, I. 7. 21.
[25] Cic., *Ep. ad Fam.*, XIII. 1.
[26] Catullus should be mentioned. I do not think that the problem of Catullus' relations with Lucretius or *vice versa* has been solved. The latest article that I have seen, Professor Frank's " The Mutual Borrowings of Catullus and Lucretius," in *Cl. Phil.*, *XXVIII*. 249–256 (1933) is too hypothetical to be convincing. It is well to remember Catullus 3 and 101, and the striking parallel between C., 51 and L., III. 152 seq.

IV. THE *DE RERUM NATURA* AND ROME OF THE FIRST CENTURY B.C.

IT HAS often been said that Lucretius made his way slowly. It has even been claimed that he was overwhelmed by a " conspiracy of silence " on the part of his contemporaries and successors. While there is no reason for believing that the *De Rerum Natura* was at once acclaimed with popular enthusiasm as was the *Aeneid* or that its appearance was eagerly anticipated, as was the poem of Aeneas, such a welcome could hardly await Lucretius' poem on Nature whatever its high merits. But I think that it can be shown that the *De Rerum Natura* at once took its proper place, in the minds of the discerning, in the growing body of Roman literature, and that it was speedily recognized as a work of genius. The profound influence it exerted upon the mind of Virgil, the knowledge of it betrayed by Horace, the esteem in which it was held by Ovid, the *testimonia* of the first century B.C. and immediately after are clear evidences of immediate and permanent appreciation.

The comment of Cicero in a letter to his brother, Quintus, is as remarkable as it is brief. We have no right to regard the brevity of the statement as an indication of lack of interest in the poem; Cicero's pre-occupation in other affairs is quite sufficient explanation, if explanation be needed, why the orator did not write at greater length. His few words fully expressed great admiration for this new contribution to Roman literature, — all the more noteworthy because of Cicero's established habit of not quoting from contemporary authors and, especially, because of his well-known and deep-seated opposition to the Epicurean school and his professed refusal to read the books of Latin writers of that school.[1] In spite of this, in February of 54 B.C., shortly after the poet's death, Cicero hailed the poem in these memorable words:

Lucretii poemata, ut scribis, ita sunt: multis luminibus ingenii, multae tamen artis.[2]

[1] *T. D.,* II. 3. 7.
[2] *Ad Q. fr.,* II. 9. 3; I am, of course, familiar with discussions of this text and the numerous interpretations that have been proposed.

The work of Lucretius abundantly displayed original creative genius and, at the same time, literary art, a rare and unexpected combination of the qualities of vigor of the old school of Ennius [3] and Accius with the artistic qualities of the new, as illustrated, it may be, by Catullus. In the broadest sense, this estimate is eminently just. Without committing himself on Epicurean doctrines with which the poem was concerned, Cicero, in the only passage in which he mentions Lucretius,[4] pays a fine tribute to the poet, and this prompt recognition of a new star in the Roman literary firmament was as creditable to Cicero as it was fair to Lucretius.

Conington had found almost two hundred reminiscences of Lucretius in the *Aeneid,* and

[3] Ennius' influence on Lucretius must have been evident to all readers, and Cicero's admiration for Ennius is well-known; cf. *T. D.,* III. 19. 45.

[4] Jerome's statement that Cicero had edited the poem (*emendavit*) remains inexplicable to me. That was just about the last thing Cicero would do. Whether Cicero knew his Lucretius well or not is another question. If Lucretius studied and followed Cicero's verse translations of Aratus, that fact might have established a certain bond of sympathy between Cicero and Lucretius. But scholars have entertained diametrically opposite views on this question. (Cf. W. A. Merrill, *Lucretius and Cicero's Verse,* University of California Publications in Classical Philology, 1921 and 1924).

editors [5] have repeatedly, since his day, added to that number and called attention, as Conington, also, had done before, to numerous phrases, cadences, and instances of imagery in the *Eclogues* and *Georgics*, as well, that recall the *De Rerum Natura*. The Virgilian poetry, over and over again, echoes the language of Lucretius who exercised a mighty spell over the sensitive nature of the Mantuan.[6] Lucretian phraseology is woven into the fabric of Virgil's verse, and, whatever the metamorphosis, it became an integral part of the new poetry. Sellar goes so far as to say that Lucretius was Virgil's chief example in technical execution.

The ancients were not unaware of Virgil's debt to Lucretius. Aulus Gellius and Servius recognized the fact. We shall consider the latter, later; the former said: [7]

[5] This is true of all of the great editions of Lucretius and of Virgil. Munro believed that Virgil's " mind was saturated with the verses of Lucretius " (see note on III. 449). Cf., further, W. A. Merrill, *Parallels and Coincidences in Lucretius and Virgil*, University of California Publications in Classical Philology, 1918.

[6] I cannot call attention to many similarities, here: but cf.

Lucr. I. 136 and 926 with *Georg.*, III. 289 seq.,
Lucr. I. 78   with *Georg.*, II. 492,
Lucr. VI. 743   with *Aen.*, VI. 19,
Lucr. VI.   with *Georg.*, III. (account of plague).

[7] Aul. Gell., *Noct. Att.*, I. 21. 7 (Macrobius, too, was fully aware of this fact).

Non verba autem sola, sed versus prope totos et
locos quoque Lucreti plurimos sectatum esse Ver-
gilium videmus.

*We see that Virgil not only adopted single words
of Lucretius but also closely followed very many
verses and passages, almost in their entirety.*

Namque canebat, uti magnum per inane coacta
semina terrarumque animaeque marisque fuissent
et liquidi simul ignis; ut his exordia primis
omnia et ipse tener mundi concreverit orbis;
tum durare solum et discludere Nerea ponto
coeperit et rerum paulatim sumere formas;
iamque novum terrae stupeant lucescere solem,
altius atque cadant summotis nubibus imbres;
incipiant silvae cum primum surgere, cumque
rara per ignaros errent animalia montes.

*"For he sang how throughout the vast void were
gathered together the seeds of earth and air and sea,
and withal of fluid fire; how from these originals
all the beginnings of things and the young orbéd
world itself grew together; then began to harden its
floor and set ocean-bars to Nereus and gradually
take shape in things: while now earth in amaze sees
the new-born sun rise shining higher, and the rains
fall as the clouds uplift; when the forests first begin
to spring, and when live creatures roam thinly over
the unknowing hills."* [8]

[8] *Ecl.,* VI. 31–40; Tr. of Mackail, Longmans, Green &
Co., London and New York, 1915.

The world has long since recognized the relationship of these sweeping, soaring verses to the splendors of the Lucretian account of creation.[9] It is not merely the verbal and rhythmic similarities that hold our attention, it is not merely the distinctly Epicurean framework common to the two poets, but the identical spirit of awesome wonder at the marvel of evolution that dominates the two minds; a kinship of spirit is proclaimed that prepares us for belief that Virgil was a profound student of the *De Rerum Natura.*

Me vero primum dulces ante omnia Musae,
quarum sacra fero ingenti percussus amore,
accipiant, caelique vias et sidera monstrent,
defectus solis varios lunaeque labores;
unde tremor terris, qua vi maria alta tumescant
obicibus ruptis rursusque in se ipsa residant,
quid tantum Oceano properent se tinguere soles
hiberni, vel quae tardis mora noctibus obstet.

" Me indeed first and before all things may the sweet Muses, whose priest I am and whose great love hath smitten me, take to themselves and show me the pathways of the sky, the stars, and the divers eclipses of the sun and the moon's travails; whence is the earthquake; by what force the seas swell high over their burst barriers and sink back into them-

---

[9] V. 416–508.

[33]

selves again; why winter suns so hasten to dip in Ocean, or what hindrance keeps back the lingering nights." [10]

Even more clearly than before, Virgil announces his deep personal interest in the grand phenomena of Nature and the desire that undoubtedly held him for a while to be a poet of science and philosophy. These verses do not necessarily prove an inclination or, it may be, a longing to follow in the footsteps of Lucretius, alone,[11] because Empedocles, among others, may well have inspired Virgil; but the famous verses that follow close upon these refer to Lucretius, and, I think, to Lucretius alone, or, at least, to Lucretius before all others:

Felix, qui potuit rerum cognoscere causas,
atque metus omnes et inexorabile fatum
subiecit pedibus strepitumque Acherontis avari.[12]

Happy he who had the intellectual strength to comprehend the causes of things in Nature and who laid under foot all fears of death, pitiless fate, and the roar of greedy Acheron.

[10] *Georg.,* II. 475–482; Tr., Mackail (as before).
[11] The Lucretian reminiscences in vss. 323 seq. are, however, extraordinary.
[12] Cf. the obvious reminiscences of verses in Lucr., I. 78–79, III. 37, 1072; perhaps, V. 1180. The interpretation of Cumont seems to me unjustified; p. 210, *After Life in Roman Paganism,* Yale Press, 1922.

An apostrophe to Lucretius, who more than any other Roman had preached the doctrine of annihilation and the conviction that his doctrine might result in happiness (voluptatem liquidam puramque). While Virgil could not and did not accept the Epicurean philosophy, his own brooding melancholy over death, his own brave pageant of souls in another world did not exclude appreciation of Lucretius' contrary, dogmatic denial of immortality. Nay rather, a wistful yearning for that proud victory over the grave and its limitless sadness pervades these verses.

For a third time, Virgil allows himself to write of the wandering moon, eclipses of the sun, the origins of man and beast, of rain and fire, of the reasons for the long winter nights, and the short days, as he presents Iopas the bard at the banquet of Dido.[13] But Virgil does not expand the theme and he knew only too well that Lucretius had preëmpted the field with his didactic poem on the philosophy of Nature.

Felix, qui potuit rerum cognoscere causas,

and

Fortunatus et ille, deos qui novit agrestes,

[13] *Aen.,* I. 740 seq.

[3 5]

represent two ideals, two states of mind that are as far apart as the poles, but Virgil could, in imagination, build a bridge across the wide chasm. In spite of his own deep piety, Virgil does not shrink from the mad protests of Lucretius that there is no providence. Unable to subscribe to the doctrine, none the less he was able to enter, with extraordinary sympathy, into the mood of those who were driven by the cruelties of this world to question the protection of heaven and of the gods. The example of Iarbas is not alone; skepticism seizes upon Aeneas himself!

If not at Rome, as used to be believed, then in the vicinity of Naples, as seems altogether likely now,[14] Virgil studied his Epicureanism under the distinguished Siro in the remarkable garden-school which Siro conducted in company with Philodemus, there. Whatever the date of the *Catalepton* which expresses a joyous farewell to rhetorical studies (perhaps 48 B.C. may be accepted as the approximate date), Virgil looked forward eagerly to his studies with Siro:

---

[14] See Tenney Frank, *Vergil,* Henry Holt and Co., N. Y., 1922, and H. W. Prescott, *The Development of Virgil's Art,* The Univ. of Chicago Press, 1927, and the recent critical literature.

[3 6]

Nos ad beatos vela mittimus portus,
magni petentes docta dicta Sironis,
vitamque ab omni vindicabimus cura,[15]

and these studies may have continued until Siro's death which occurred about 42 B.C. Here, let us assume, Virgil pursued his Epicurean studies in delightful companionship and gained that understanding of Epicureanism which affected his thinking all the rest of his life. Philodemus' liberal interpretation of his philosophy may have counted for much. Lucretius' text had been available since early in the year 54 B.C. Lucretius, Siro, and Philodemus were Virgil's teachers in Epicureanism which, somehow, by a magic or mysterious process that psychologists cannot explain lay side by side, later, in Virgil's mind with his accepted Stoic and Pythagorean doctrines. Though these superseded the earlier Epicureanism, the influence of Lucretius, as thinker and writer, exerted a powerful fascination over Virgil's entire speculative and artistic life.[16]

[15] *Catal.*, V. 8–10; cf. VIII. 1: Villula Sironis, etc.
[16] The belief of some that 'Sironem' should be read for 'Silenum' in the sixth *Eclogue*, as Servius suggests, is confirmed by Servius' other statement (*Aen.*, VI. 264) about Siro's influence on Virgil; cf., too, *Catal.*, VIII. Cf. a very suggestive article by N. W. De Witt, "Vergil and Epicureanism," in *The Classical Weekly*, XXV. 89–96 (1932).

There can, I think, be no doubt about Horace's intimate acquaintance with Lucretius' *De Rerum Natura*. An epic of such majesty compelled attention. Since the days of Lambinus and Bentley, editors of the two poets have diligently sought for marks of influence of the older poet upon the work of his successor. These traces of influence, of imitation, of echoes of Lucretius are numerous and varied, and, while scholars may disagree about the genuineness or the validity of some of these which will necessarily remain under dispute, the residue of certain evidence is all too great to ignore.[17] Professor Merrill's conclusions deserve quotation, as they appear to me to come very close to the truth: "in early life when Horace wrote his Satires, Lucretian influence was strong upon him; during his more mature years, as shown by his Odes, direct Lucretian influence is for the most part absent. In the first book of the Epistles the influence of Lucretius again revives, but afterwards in the second book of

[17] Cf., *e.g.*, A. Weingaertner, *De Horatio Lucretii Imitatore*, Diss. Inaug., Halis Saxonum, 1874; Weingaertner makes out Horace as "studiosissimus atque amantissimus Lucretii." W. A. Merrill, "On the Influence of Lucretius on Horace," in *University of California Publications, in Classical Philology*, I. 111–129 (1905). Porphyrio does not seem to comment, anywhere, on Lucretian influence on Horace (cf. Teubner text).

[38]

the Epistles, the fourth book of the Odes, and in the Ars Poetica, it is practically non-existent." It is not my intention to pass under review the very many passages [18] that have been scrutinized by scholars and which establish the literary debt of Horace to Lucretius. While we may take it for granted that Horace had read and re-read, with admiration, the many majestic verses that he found in the *De Rerum Natura,* none the less a great gulf, represented by their differences in temperament, separated the two men. The literary relationship was not accompanied by any genuine spiritual affinity.

Lucretius was not, in any real sense, an inspiration to Horace. Horace does not mention Lucretius, by name, a single time, although he might well have done so on several occasions.[19] His mention of and admiration for Homer, Ennius, Lucilius, Pollio, Varius, Virgil and others are well-known. Lucretius might easily have been included in more than one chorus of praise, had Horace willed it so. The *argu-*

[18] I wish that space permitted a review, here, of these passages; the evidence is, I think, absolutely conclusive and shows Horace's acquaintance with all six books of Lucretius. Cf., *e.g., Sat.,* I. 1. 119 and L., III. 938; *Odes,* II. 16. 20 and L., III. 1068.

[19] *E.g., Satires,* I. 10; *Epistles,* II. 1, II. 3 (*Ars Poetica*).

mentum ex silentio [20] is not always effective and may be deceptive; but Horace's generosity prompted him to speak frankly enough of his friends or of those who had aroused his sympathy. He does not, to be sure, condemn Lucretius for his philosophy; but he does not commend him, as a poet. This is the surprising fact; patriotism might have led him to do that. In a certain sense Horace stood aloof from Lucretius, whose language and ideas he repeatedly borrowed or modified without, however, any acknowledgment of indebtedness. He could hardly have written of Lucretius: animae dimidium meae.

Horace's affiliations with Epicurean philosophy were not sufficiently strong to bind him to Lucretius. His own philosophy was a blend of Epicureanism, Stoicism, and of his own good practical sense, an independent sum total of his own reflections; and at no time did he acknowledge the leadership of Lucretius in thought. He followed him neither in his rejection of divine providence, nor in his denial of immortality; he was not greatly interested in "natural questions," nor was he a student of social evolution.

[20] Euripides, for example, is not mentioned.

We have Horace's own words for it, that Epicurus and Lucretius were not his guides in philosophy:

> Ac ne forte roges, quo me duce, quo Lare tuter,
> nullius addictus iurare in verba magistri,
> quo me cumque rapit tempestas, deferor hospes.
> nunc agilis fio et mersor civilibus undis,
> virtutis verae custos rigidusque satelles;
> nunc in Aristippi furtim praecepta relabor,
> et mihi res, non me rebus, subiungere conor.

Do not ask me, pray, who my leader is, what Lar protects me. I am not bound to swear allegiance to any master; wherever the storm carries me, I put into port and seek shelter. Now I become the man of action and plunge into the waters of civil strife, the guardian and stern escort of true virtue; again, I slip back, secretly, to the precepts of Aristippus, and try to adjust life to myself, not myself to life.[21]

This gives us the key to the "carpe diem" poetry![22] Wisdom, as Lucretius understood it, philosophy, as Lucretius expounded it, one great systematic, logical system, with all the constraints and implications, was not to Horace's liking. The "wise man" of the schools might be inferior in wisdom only to Jupiter,

---

[21] *Epistles*, I. i. 13–19.
[22] Of course there are many points of contact, on this score, between Horace and Lucretius.

rich, free, honored, fair, a king of kings,[23] conspicuously sane; but all of this was lost, when a troublesome cold beset him! With such light banter, Horace dismisses the ideal that a Lucretius had set before himself.

The Epicurean theory of gods and denial of divine providence certainly had not commended itself, *seriously,* to the mind of Horace, despite the seeming testimony of a few lines to the contrary:

>   dein Gnatia lymphis
> iratis exstructa dedit risusque iocosque,
> dum flamma sine tura liquescere limine sacro
> persuadere cupit. credat Iudaeus Apella,
> non ego: *namque deos didici securum agere aevum,*
> nec, si quid miri faciat natura, deos id
> tristis ex alto caeli demittere tecto.
> Brundisium longae finis chartaeque viaeque est.

Then Gnatia, built under the displeasure of water-nymphs, afforded us laughter and jests, while eager to persuade us that incense melts on the sacred threshold, without fire. Apella, the Jew, may believe it, but not I; for I have learned that the gods spend their life, all free from care, and, if Nature effects wonders, gloomy gods do not send such

    [23] *Epistles,* I. 1. 106–8. Ad summam, sapiens uno minor est Iove, dives, Liber, honoratus, pulcher, rex denique regum, Praecipue sanus, nisi cum pituita molesta est. Cf., also, *Satires,* I. 3. 124–142.

miracles down from their lofty, heavenly home.
Brundisium is the end of my story and of a long
journey as well.[24]

Of course this recalls Lucretius, and the verbal
similarity may even *prove* that Horace had his
Lucretius in mind:

Nam bene qui didicere deos securum agere aevom.[25]

And if Horace had with any kind of consistency
shown that he had accepted this doctrine as
true, we might well believe that he had learned
this great lesson directly from Lucretius, its
chief expositor in Rome, and that he was announcing the fact, here. But there is no real
reason for believing that the doctrine had captured Horace's mind, except momentarily and
as a passing fancy in his earlier years. The
very many verses, throughout his poetry, at-
testing his allegiance to orthodoxy, are evidence, rather, that Horace belonged to that
larger category of souls, whose timidity Lucretius laments: men, who had learned what
Lucretius believed to be true but who had
proved faithless to their emancipation and who
had fallen back on their old faith and fear.

[24] *Satires,* I. 5. 97–104.
[25] V. 82, VI. 56. Editors commonly accept it as true
that Horace is quoting Lucretius.

If Horace had genuinely believed this iconoclastic doctrine — so contrary to his conservative and conformist nature — he could not but have left traces of it in his poetry and must have reflected something of the Lucretian protests and indignation. In place of that, we have the innumerable expressions [26] of belief in gods and their providence, and no one, I think, would venture to deny their essential sincerity. Besides this, we have the later specific repudiation [27] of Epicurean philosophy of religion, in

> Parcus deorum cultor et infrequens,
> Insanientis dum sapientiae
> Consultus erro, nunc retrorsum
> Vela dare atque iterare cursus
> Cogor relictos: namque Diespiter, etc.

A worshipper of the gods, infrequent in my worship and ungenerous, was I, while I wandered — an adept in a mad philosophy; but now I am constrained to spread my sails and return and retrace courses I had abandoned; for Jupiter, etc.

[26] *E.g., Odes,* I. 2, 3, 9, 10, 11, 12, 14, 17, 18, 19, 21, 24, 30, 31, 34, 35, 36; II. 7, 10, 17, 19; III. 1–6, 13, 18, 22, 23, 28, 30; IV. 1, 2, 5, 6, 13, 14, 15; *C. S.; Satires,* I. 1. 15–20, II. 4. 88; *Epistles,* I. 4. 6–7, I. 11. 22, I. 12. 3.
[27] *Odes,* I. 34. 1–5.

Thus Horace declares his freedom, his release from Lucretian control.

The third book of Lucretius, with its vehement denial of life after death, had touched Horace even less. Whatever uncertainties attended Horace's reflections [28] upon the possibility of a life after death, he did not accept the Epicurean doctrine of nihilism, he did not close the door, and deny himself the hope of extension of this world's happiness beyond the grave. The language of Horace, as he refers to the future of the soul, is, in the main, that of orthodox belief and there is no trace of the Lucretian atomic argument, of dissolution of the soul like smoke, of nothingness.

There is no reason to think that the magnificent structure of the Lucretian atomic theory captured Horace's imagination; indestructibility of the atom, its swiftness of motion, its shapes and combinations, upon which Lucretius [29] expended such a wealth of argument, illustration, and eloquence — these do not figure in the Horatian poetry; and there is little of reference to the great problems of the

[28] *E.g., Odes,* I. 4, 10, 24, 28; II. 3, 13, 14, 18; III. 3, 11, 27, 30; IV. 7; *Epistles,* I. 6. 27.
[29] Books I, II, IV.

world's creation and dissolution, to which
Lucretius had devoted such extended, sustained,
and brilliant discussion.[30]

> hunc solem et stellas et decedentia certis
> tempora momentis sunt qui formidine nulla
> imbuti spectent:

*Yon sun and stars and the seasons retiring at fixed
periods — there are those who can view them with
no taint of terror* [31]

might refer to the astronomical discussions of
the fifth book of the *De Rerum Natura* and
Lucretius' repeated and eager call to escape
fear of natural phenomena and of divine control; but if these lines were written with Lucretius in mind, as very likely they were, we have
but a pale reflection of the passionate vehemence of the earlier poet. At most there is
but an echo of Lucretius here.

> Nil admirari prope res est una, Numici,
> solaque quae possit facere et servare beatum.[31]

Marvel at nothing, Numicius, for that is well-nigh
the one and only way to become happy and remain so.

This is neither true Stoic ἀπάθεια nor Epicurean ἀταραξία; it is not genuine philosophic

[30] Book V.
[31] *Epistles*, I. 6. 3–5; cf. vss. 1–2; vss. 15–16.

[46]

calm but, at most, an exhortation to *avoid excess,* to achieve a wise indifference to the bounties of earth and sea, to material blessings, or to fame, and, even, to Virtue:

insani sapiens nomen ferat, aequus iniqui,
ultra quam satis est Virtutem si petat ipsam.[31]

The *nil admirari* Epistle is the very antithesis of the Lucretian insistence upon the importance of this problem, of escape from fear of natural phenomena and divine wrath; the problem is mentioned only casually, here, and not elaborated elsewhere. The Epistle is as far removed as can be from the dogmatism of Lucretius and the latter's confidence that there was only one way of life and of happiness. Of course, Horace and Lucretius were in agreement in the belief that the externals of wealth and power could not secure permanent happiness or virtue, but the *nil admirari* doctrine, with its implications of carelessness and of indifference, was in utter conflict with the Lucretian deeper earnestness and singlemindedness. Horace's greater tolerance would even have offended the inflexible sternness of Lucretius, and these few lines on the wonders of the firmament, in the midst of an ethical *Epistle,* so different from the

Lucretian temper, certainly suggest, at most, some knowledge of the Lucretian discussion of natural phenomena. Horace was not deeply interested in these problems and Lucretius had not affected him profoundly.

The same can be said of another allusion to these questions in the *Epistle* to Iccius,[32] who is represented as interested in these lofty themes, although opportunities for gain as procurator of Agrippa's estates in Sicily might have diverted him:

adhuc sublimia cures:

quae mare compescant causae, quid temperet an-
    num,
stellae sponte sua iussaene vagentur et errent,
quid premat obscurum lunae, quid proferat orbem,
quid velit et possit rerum concordia discors,
Empedocles an Stertinium deliret acumen.

*You still care for these high themes: what causes
bind the sea, what may make the year hot or cold,
whether stars wander and stray in their courses, of
their own free will or under some law; what shrouds
the moon in darkness, what brings it forth to our
view, again; what Nature's harmony in discord
seeks and effects; whether Empedocles or Stertinius'
wit is mad.*

[32] *Epistles,* I. 12. 15–20.

Far from demonstrating any real influence of Lucretius, as has been maintained, these lines look rather in another direction; Empedocles and the Stoics are in Horace's mind. Empedocles,[33] one of Lucretius' great admirations, is hardly referred to with awe; Stertinius counted as a Stoic, while Iccius, we know, was a student of Panaetius and Socratic lore.[34] These lines do not necessarily even suggest Lucretius; every problem, mentioned here, was discussed by Stoics as well.

It is commonly claimed that Horace had Lucretius before him and that he modelled certain verses of the third of the *Satires* of Book I, on Lucretius. That Horace knew his Lucretius must be admitted; the great Lucretian passage, V. 925–1457, was the outstanding discussion, in Latin literature, of the theme of the development of human society. But the magnificent march of the Lucretian arguments and the mighty rush of that roaring torrent left no deep marks on Horace, as poet or as thinker.[35] He might have written the verses in question, about twelve in number, even if Lucretius had never written at all — expressing, as he did,

[33] Cf., also, *A. P.*, 465 seq.
[34] *Odes*, I. 29. 14.
[35] Cf., *e.g., Odes,* I. 10. 1–4; I. 16. 13.

a commonplace interpretation of man's emergence from barbarism and giving utterance to ideas that must have had wide currency among the educated:

Quis paria esse fere placuit peccata, laborant,
cum ventum ad verum est: sensus moresque repugnant
atque ipsa utilitas, iusti prope mater et aequi.
    Cum prorepserunt primis animalia terris,
mutum et turpe pecus, glandem atque cubilia propter
unguibus et pugnis, dein fustibus, atque ita porro
pugnabant armis, quae post fabricaverat usus,
donec verba, quibus voces sensusque notarent,
nominaque invenere; dehinc absistere bello,
oppida coeperunt munire et ponere leges,
ne quis fur esset, neu latro, neu quis adulter;
nam fuit ante Helenam cunnus taeterrima belli
causa; sed ignotis perierunt mortibus illi,
quos venerem incertam rapientis more ferarum
viribus editior caedebat, ut in grege taurus.
iura inventa metu iniusti fateare necesse est,
tempora si fastosque velis evolvere mundi.

Those who like to believe that all sins are virtually equal, have difficulty in proving their creed in the face of facts: feelings and customs rebel, as well as Utilitas, *the mother — almost — of justice and right.* [Horace rebels against the Stoic doctrine that all sins are on a par.]
When living creatures first crawled over the surface of the earth, dumb, brute beasts, they fought

[50]

for their acorns and their lairs with nails and fists, and then with clubs; next with weapons which need had later fashioned for them, — until they discovered language (e.g., verbs and nouns), by which they defined their cries and feelings; from that time they abandoned war and began to build strong towns and lay down laws, that there should be neither thief, robber, or adulterer among them; for even before Helen's day, love of woman was war's most shameful cause; and a man of superior might, like the bull in the herd, struck down those who after the manner of wild beasts seized their love recklessly, and these died deaths unknown to fame. If you choose to consult the records of the world and study its history, you must needs confess that right and law were born of fear of injustice.[36]

The verbal similarities, great as they are, between the two poets are sufficient evidence of the literary indebtedness of the one to the other, and the undeniably genuine clue to Horace's use of and knowledge of Lucretius lies in his employment of the Lucretian phrase:

fateare necesse est.

For a moment, Horace catches something of the Lucretian earnestness, or, perhaps, even this was but mock earnestness. It was not like Horace to impose his beliefs on others and the

[36] *Satires,* I. 3. 96–112.

entire satire is an exposition of his belief in mutual tolerance. The *fateare necesse est* phrase leaps forth from the page as ironical and Horace did not need to mention Lucretius by name to indicate his own smiling disapproval of the extreme dogmatism of his predecessor. He must have missed, in Lucretius, the element of humor with which he himself was so richly endowed, and that constituted one effective bar to his own full enjoyment of, or, it may even be, proper appreciation of the *De Rerum Natura*.

To be sure, the verses that introduce the whole passage are Epicurean enough:

atque ipsa utilitas, iusti prope mater et aequi,[37]

but Horace shows no real knowledge of the significance of this Epicurean social doctrine, although he is, for the moment, arguing against an old, abandoned Stoic argument that all faults are equal; his brief survey of the development of human society is intended to show the truth of the utilitarian theory of the origin of law. The claim that this passage is based on Lucretius, both in expression and substance, can be accepted as true, but other literature

[37] Cf. Lucr., V. 1019, 1023, 1029, 1147, etc.

could have supplied Horace with every idea, expressed here. Horace, we take it, knew the grandeur of the Lucretian passage, its scholarship, its earnestness, and its human sympathy; but, even so, he betrays that knowledge but slightly, in his slurring quotation of the genuine Lucretian, grim and determined phrase:

> fateare necesse est.

Perhaps no admission of Horace's more sharply defines the difference in temper between the two men than the following:

> Inter spem curamque, timores inter et iras
> omnem crede diem tibi diluxisse supremum;
> grata superveniet, quae non sperabitur, hora.
> me pinguem et nitidum bene curata cute vises,
> cum ridere voles, Epicuri de grege porcum.

"In a world of hope and care, of fears and angry passions," hold to this belief that the day that has dawned, is your last; whatever hour that comes, unhoped for, will give you joy. As for me, you will find me, fat and sleek, well-cared for, a pig of Epicurus' sty, whenever you seek a laugh.[38]

An Epicurean of a sort, perhaps, and for a little while, as the mood held him. Even granting that these verses express, as Sellar puts it, an

[38] *Epistles,* I. 4. 12–16; cf. the different tone of *nobilis* libros Panaeti, *Odes,* I. 29. 13.

" ironical self-disparagement," even so, no such confession could have fallen from Lucretius' lips at any time.

On the one hand we observe the intense fire of Lucretius' earnest enthusiasm, on the other, the lesser fires of Horace's charming urbanity and dilettantism. Even the language of Lucretius has something of his own inflexible nature; and as Horace borrowed from the elder poet, that language underwent a transformation in the crucible of his mind and method of composition. But the literary debt is unmistakable.

Ovid, it is thought, knew his Lucretius perfectly well.[39] It is unnecessary, in this place, to dwell upon the details of the evidence that shows acquaintance with and indebtedness to the language and the thought of all six books of *De Rerum Natura*. But the careless poet of love, the poet of wayward mythologies, the romantic poet of Roman festivals, the poet of lamentation could hardly follow closely in the footsteps of the scholar and scientist who had preceded him. The entire attitude toward life that so largely controlled the student and

[39] The truth of this has long been recognized. Cf., *e.g.*, A. Zingerle, *Ovidius u. sein Verhältniss zu den Vorgängern und gleichzeitigen Römischen Dichtern*, Innsbruck, Wagner, 1869–71.

thinker, was alien to Publius Ovidius Naso. In spite of possible verbal reminiscences in Ovid's hymn of creation, the differences in tone and conception are all too great to admit any real obligation, in thought, to the great Lucretian passages.[40] The poet in Ovid, however, responded to the poet in Lucretius and the poet's admiration was great, as the following well-known passage [41] amply proves:

Carmina sublimis tunc sunt peritura Lucreti,
   exitio terras cum dabit una dies

The verses of Lucretius, the sublime, will perish only When one day will give the world over to destruction.

Prophecy of Lucretius' fame is coupled with a graceful adaptation of a Lucretian verse (V. 95). These two lines come in a brief survey of

[40] Lucretius' invocation and Ovid's hymn to Venus in the *Fasti* (IV) have often been compared. Munro thinks that Ovid was " doubtless " thinking of Lucretius in *Met.*, II. 204 (Lucr., V. 1205).

A. A., I. 637 seq.:
   Expedit esse deos, et, ut expedit, esse putemus;
      dentur in antiquos tura merumque focos;
   nec secura quies illos similisque sopori
      detinet; innocue vivite, numen adest.
The frivolous cynicism of this famous passage and the fling at Epicurean conception of gods more clearly, perhaps, than any other passage, reveal the distinction between Ovid and Lucretius.

[41] *Amor.*, I. 15. 23–24.

literary immortals: Homer, Hesiod, Callima-
chus, Sophocles, Aratus, Menander, Ennius,
Accius, Varro (Atacinus), Virgil, Tibullus,
Gallus are mentioned, and in this company
Lucretius belonged — Lucretius "the sublime,"
whose verses only then would die, when destruction befell the world. Ovid confidently
predicted his own inclusion in this company
of those whose literary fame was of the fairest.
He does not mention Horace, here, nor, for that
matter, Catullus, either; but both received his
tribute elsewhere.[42] Lucretius, however, re-
ceives unqualified and enthusiastic praise.

Lucretius is again mentioned, by name, in
the *Tristia*.[43] Ovid is defending himself as a
poet of love and he enumerates others who had
written no less freely than he on this dangerous
theme, without suffering punishment: the wan-
ton Catullus, Calvus, Memmius, Cinna, Varro
of Atax, Gallus, Tibullus are among these; —
contrasted with them all are Ennius and Lucretius. Ovid might well have included Lucretius
in the other category because of his fourth
book which discusses the subject of love with
such extraordinary frankness; but, instead, it

[42] *Tr.*, IV. 10. 49 (numerosus Horatius); *Tr.*, II. 427.
[43] II. 425–6.

[56]

is, as before, Lucretius, the prophet of the world's ultimate destruction who hovers before Ovid's imagination:

Explicat ut causas rapidi Lucretius ignis,
casurumque triplex vaticinatur opus,

Lucretius the causes of the scorching flame unfolds,
And fall of that triple world he prophecies,

the triple world of earth and sea and sky.[44] Early in life and later, when writing the *Amores* and when in banishment, it was this aspect of the work of Lucretius that strangely captivated the gay and, later, the saddened Ovid.

Cicero, Virgil, Horace, and Ovid show us plainly enough that Lucretius' position in Roman letters was secure before the close of the Augustan age. Failure of Virgil and of Horace to name him does not affect the truth of this statement. Scholars [45] have by careful scrutiny shown that Lucretius may have influenced Tibullus, Propertius, and, even, Livy; but more important for our purposes are the ringing *testimonia* of Nepos and of Vitruvius.

[44] An echo, again, of Lucr., V. 95.
[45] Cf., *e.g.*, Lucr., IV. 1018 and V. 1158 and Tib., I. 9. 27; Lucr., V. 95 and Prop., III. 5. 25 seq., but IV. 7 expresses belief in spirit-life (sunt aliquid Manes, etc.); Prop., II. 34. 29 (perhaps); S. G. Stacey, "Über Spuren des Lucrez bei Livius," in *Archiv für Lat. Lex.*, X. 52 (1898).

The former grouped Lucretius and Catullus, as the two great poets by whose work that of successors might be judged. The position of Lucretius is anything but equivocal; his reputation is fully established and Calidus is honored by the comparison. Nepos is telling of Atticus' kindness to Lucius Saufeius and Lucius Julius Calidus whose properties had been proscribed but were rescued by Atticus:

Idem [*i.e.,* Atticus] L. Iulium Calidum, quem post Lucretii Catullique mortem multo elegantissimum poetam nostram tulisse aetatem vere videor posse contendere, neque minus virum bonum optimisque artibus eruditum . . . expedivit.

Atticus was, likewise, helpful to Lucius Julius Calidus. I think that I may truthfully claim that Calidus is by far the most elegant poet our age has produced since the death of Lucretius and Catullus. Calidus was, besides, a good man and endowed with the highest culture.[46]

I do not know whether the last statement was meant to contrast Calidus' private life with that of Lucretius and Catullus, or not, but Lucretius' position as a poet seems fully assured.

In an eloquent argument on the values, to society, of the work of philosophers and other

[46] Nepos, *Atticus,* 12. 4.

writers, Vitruvius mentions Lucretius' name in an illustrious company. Pythagoras, Democritus, Plato, Aristotle, Archimedes, Archytas had been discussed, and Vitruvius' summing up includes these words:

Ergo eorum virorum cogitata non solum ad mores corrigendos sed etiam ad omnium utilitatem perpetuo sunt praeparata.

The thoughts of these men are, thus, an everlasting possession not only for improvement of character but also for the practical good of all men.[47]

Those, he continues, whose souls are steeped in the delights of literature, carry, enshrined in their hearts, images of their favorite authors. Ennius, Accius, Lucretius, Cicero, Varro live and will live, their judgments gaining in weight with the passing of years.

Item plures post nostram memoriam nascentes cum Lucretio videbuntur velut coram de rerum natura disputare, de arte vero rhetorica cum Cicerone, multi posterorum cum Varrone conferent sermonem de lingua latina, . . .

Likewise, more, after our death, will feel that they are discussing Nature with Lucretius, as though he were face to face with them, with Cicero the art of

[47] *De Arch.,* IX. *Praef.* 15.

rhetoric, and many of our posterity will confer with Varro on the subject of the Latin language.[48]

There is no uncertainty in these remarks: Ennius is revered as a god, Accius' vigorous language is admired; Cicero and rhetoric, Varro and the Latin language are inseparably associated, and Lucretius is hailed as the great scientist.[49]

Poet and scientist — the dual rôle that was his by right, the dual rôle that has continued to be his to the present day: a commanding poet in ancient Rome, whose influence was mighty; a commanding scientist, whose immediate influence, as scientist, was less. Science — whether the science of cosmology, geology, biology, anthropology, psychology — had yielded in the Greek schools of philosophy to a study of ethics, of life, here and in some hereafter, with related studies of religion; and Rome, too, stressed these elements. Science had not gripped the Roman people's imagination and I cannot believe that Lucretius' exposition of atomism, dogmatic, intense, and confident as it was, made a deep impression on

[48] *De Arch.*, IX. *Praef.* 17.
[49] It is at least possible that Vitruvius' language implies knowledge, in his day, of Lucretius' physical appearance.

his own age. The invisibility of the atom gave it an appearance of unreality, that was too great for the practical Roman mind to permit acceptance of the atomic theory. Vitruvius' prophecy of Lucretius' later influence, as scientist, was verified to an extent and to a degree far beyond the possibilities of Vitruvius' imagination. Lucretius, as a man of science, in spite of his errors, as a searcher for the laws of Nature, was to become a great figure in later days. In his own century, it was the poet who loomed so large. We cannot determine the extent of the influence of Epicureanism in Rome and in Italy in the 40's (B.C.) and immediately after, but the philosophy of 'pleasure,' with its denials of divine providence and of immortality of the soul, was undoubtedly winning converts and it gained a strong hold in the Empire period. In the first century before Christ, Lucretius was the recognized outstanding exponent[50] of that philosophy, and his brilliant poetry won the honor of applause and the greater homage of sincere imitation from the foremost writers of his age.

[50] See p. 178, for estimate of Catius.

[61]

V. LUCRETIUS AND THE ATOM

LUCRETIUS, as scientist,[1] would explain the phenomena of Nature purely and entirely by reference to natural laws. This, at once, put him in opposition to all the orthodox teleological theorists who found ultimate refuge in divine creation and in divine control. His dogmatic denunciation of this old belief rings like a trumpet-blast at the very beginning of his scientific exposition. The opposition between the two schools of thought is sharply proclaimed.

First, then, comes the fundamental, thorough-going, searching thesis that *nullam rem e nilo gigni,* naught is created from nothingness. The world of nature establishes this dogma, as we see that all living creatures and fruits of the earth come from definite sources that remain unchanged; and that all products cannot spring from all or any sources; furthermore, growth of earth's bounties in certain seasons also refutes the hypothesis that things

[1] I. 146 seq.

can come from nothingness, and, no less, the fact that time is essential for that growth; we do not see children develop, of a sudden, into youths; no less impressive is the fact that attendant circumstance of rain and cultivation of the soil are essential for fruits of the earth and food for living creatures — which would not be the case if things could come from nothingness; why, besides, cannot nature produce giants and men of vast age? All of these phenomena are marshalled in defense of his belief that there exists a definite source for each and every product that we see, and Lucretius' confidence finds expression in triumphant exclamation:

nil igitur fieri de nilo posse fatendumst (205)

we must, therefore, admit that nothing can come from nothingness.

All of this is true argument and it is a logical exposition of the *Reign of law* in Nature which Lucretius would prove.

The reverse of this first principle is equally important — that nature resolves naught back into nothingness — and that she could do so must also be proven false by argument and by illustration: the most cogent of these is the obvious truth that infinite time and days of the past would long since have reduced all to nothingness, if that could be the destiny of matter. On the contrary there is, on every hand, the evidence of a constant renewal, of a constant cycle of death and life, — and Lucretius could not possibly have chosen a more valid, and at the same time, a more poetic defense of his position that all things are resolved, back again, at the time of their death, to some form of indestructible matter. That cycle is constant and Lucretius was fully aware of its poetic implications.[2] But, more important than that, is his great certainty, as before; he excludes, absolutely, all possibility of the reverse being true; belief in the *indestructibility of matter* is the essence of this eloquent and poetic outburst, and Lucretius, of course, believed that this was proven. The way was thus prepared for a discussion of the atom.

But how prove the existence of the invisible? There is at hand the phenomenon of the wind, which, though unseen, works havoc as great as that wrought by a flood, and with an impetuosity as mighty as that of the rush of waters that

[2] ' Father Ether ' and ' Mother Earth ' are not merely mythological terms to his mind; cf. pp. 340–342.

he describes, Lucretius argues, by analogy, for the existence of his atoms. The same dogmatic boldness characterizes this argument as before and appears as one of the striking qualities of Lucretius' mind; escape from his conclusions or from his conviction is an impossibility and his confidence would accept no denial (270, 277, 290, 295). The corporeality of odors, heat, cold, voices is asserted with the same vigor (302), as inescapably true. Further illustrations are piled up to prove that invisible matter is functioning on every hand: clothes, hung up by the sea-shore, absorb dampness, and dry in the sun; finger-rings are gradually worn away, as is the curved plough-share; dripping water gradually hollows out the rock; stone pavements are worn, and the hands of bronze statues grow thin as worshippers touch and kiss them; rocks are eaten away by the salty brine, but a jealous nature does not allow even the keenest sight to observe the gradual additions or subtractions of matter. Invisibility, therefore, is no barrier to acceptance of Lucretius' great theory of the atom (328).

Still, the way is not fully prepared, as yet, for convincing demonstration. Besides the atom, there must be void, which is essential for motion, and knowledge of void is essential for a real comprehension of matter (*i.e.,* the atom), as we shall see, later. Therefore, Lucretius, at this point, plunges with characteristic confidence into demonstration of the existence of void. Motion without a void is regarded as unthinkable; and substances that seem so solid, are porous — water oozes through rocks, food is assimilated by the body [3] and by trees, voices travel through walls and closed houses, cold penetrates to the bone; objects, of similar bulk, as of wool and of lead, do not weigh the same — all of these illustrations are convincing demonstrations that void does exist:

est igitur nimirum id quod ratione sagaci
quaerimus, admixtum rebus, quod inane vocamus.
  (368–369)

therefore that which we are seeking with shrewd reason does exist, intermingled in the composition of substances, and we call it void.

Lucretius could hardly be more dogmatic. Two more illustrations, of hoary antiquity, are treated with an assurance that brooks no contradiction. Motion is impossible without void,

---

[3] Lucretius' knowledge of ' assimilation ' is, of course, crude enough.

and Lucretius could not entertain the conception of the ' fullness ' of things. (Parmenides and the Eleatics, Aristotle and the Stoics are not even honored by mention of their names.)　A brusque rebuttal is what we expect (377, 382, 393). The *indestructibility of matter* has been announced (221, 236, 239, 245), and Lucretius' argument for motion is a form of argumentation for the *conservation of energy!*

In the midst of this furious rush of arguments, Lucretius pauses a moment, and his lordly confidence asserts itself proudly.　Comparable to Robert Browning's fine phrase,

W*hile I triumph o'er a secret wrung from nature's
close reserve,*

is Lucretius' intense eagerness to drag the truth from its hiding-places, and his sincere belief in his own victory and ability to persuade.

Now, then, existence of matter (*i.e.*, the invisible atom) and of void has been established; and, resuming his argumentative mood, Lucretius utterly denies the possibility of any third reality; this is really essential for his demonstration of the character and behavior of the atom.　There is no third; neither senses nor reason could establish the existence of a ' third

[67]

nature' and all experience could be interpreted only in terms of Matter and Void. Matter and Void alone have reality, they alone are, and they are the absolutes: all other things that come within our knowledge are either essential properties (*coniuncta*) or accidental properties (*eventa*) of these two: time does not exist *per se* and all events of history and all experiences of life are the results of the action and interaction of the two great, fundamental, physical essentials. We are quite prepared for the materialistic universe and for the materialistic philosophy of Lucretius! Matter and Void! all else is ephemeral. Acceptance of this great fundamental truth is regarded as inevitable (462, 479), and the didactic power of this passage is equalled only by the hard and brilliant poetry of the lines that tell of the fall of Troy as one of those ' eventa ' of Matter and Void!

Immediately there follows Lucretius' insistence that the atom must be solid and this statement made in advance of demonstration or proof shows, conclusively, the importance of this contention to his mind. Most things seem to argue against the existence of the utterly solid, anywhere, and Lucretius has, before, recognized the presence of void in all composite things. But, as he sees it, *vera ratio* (498) compels belief in the existence of these solid and eternal (500) atoms which are of so much moment to him.

In perfectly logical sequence, there follows the demonstration that matter and void, the two great underlying factors of existence, are mutually exclusive, and whatever has not void in itself, is, necessarily, solid. This argument, resting upon pure reason, was quite unassailable, and, Lucretius believed, finally and forever established the truth of his contention. The evidence of the senses plays no part here, and Lucretius argues his point with legal exactness. If solid, matter is indestructible and imperishable, it cannot be dissolved by blows from the outside, nor can its texture be unwoven as if it were a composite thing; it cannot be crushed, broken, or split; it cannot yield to moisture, nor cold, nor heat, nor any other comparable force; it is therefore *eternal;* it always has been and it always will be (*aeterna, immortalis*) (500, 519, 539, 545). This is a brilliant conclusion and Lucretius seems to feel the significance of it; his language has the tone not only of certainty (510, 526, 538/9, 548) but also of triumph.

[69]

The nature of the atom is proclaimed unto Rome and the Romans, as important as the news of a great military victory; it remains to be seen what effect it had on Roman thought, after the death of the great exponent. The argument for the imperishability of the atom is linked up with his initial argument about matter coming from nothingness or returning to nothingness. No! all comes from the atom and to the atom all returns! The singleness of the solid atom guarantees renewal of all through the ages.

After the tension of this passage, Lucretius clearly relaxes and before he comes to his demonstration of what we may call the 'molecule,' he repeats arguments that have appeared before; these arguments and their accompanying illustrations simply show a mind filled to overflowing with enthusiasm and earnestness. The most significant argument he advances for the existence and functioning of unchangeable atoms is that suggested by the invariability of species: birds illustrate his point. The *reign of law* is hereby again emphasized, that law that decrees what can and what cannot be in Nature. While Lucretius is not a biologist in our sense of the word, with full knowledge of spermatozoa and of evolution, he is deeply aware of the laws of heredity (586, 592, 598).

An astonishing argument follows, with a fresh start, after this brief interlude, which can, I think,[4] be interpreted only in one way: atoms are single and uncompounded, but they cannot and do not exist, individually, by themselves; rather, they exist in clusters, which alone provide the necessary conditions of entanglements, blows, and clashing motions, which creative matter must possess. An amazing argument this is, anticipating the molecular theory or, even, the chemistry of to-day with its theory of nuclei and electrons!

> quae nullis sunt partibus aucta,
> non possunt ea, quae debet genitalis habere
> materies, varios conexus pondera plagas
> concursus motus, per quae res quaeque geruntur
> (631–634).

In all three cases, the Lucretian cluster, the molecule, and the 'atom'—or, indeed, the 'nucleus' of some atoms, as understood, to-day—the pattern is much the same.

---

[4] Even if Lucretius is arguing for minimal parts of the 'atom,' that notion approximates our notion of the atom, as consisting of nuclei and electrons.

Such was Lucretius' exposition of the nature and behavior of the atom — appearing, early, in the first book and thus occupying the important position that it deserved. Lucretius' enthusiasm has been obvious throughout, and his ·deep belief no less manifest, here, than in the subsequent refutation of the views of Heraclitus, Empedocles, and Anaxagoras. The wonders of the atomic theory and of the scientific system, of which it was the basis, deeply stirred Lucretius, the scientist, and inspired the poet; and in his dual rôle he invited [5] Memmius to learn, and, through Memmius, Rome — to master the obscurities of science and, thereby, secure the exultation of emancipation from false religious beliefs.

The Rome of Lucretius' day may have had a certain interest in science, but that interest was relatively limited. Wars, politics, wealth, religion were far more beguiling, and, in addition, in Augustus' day, other forms of literature and the architectural splendors of the capital. Why pay heed to an atomist? The atom could not seem vital in the scheme of life, whatever the appeal of other aspects of Epicurean philosophy. And the open conflict of

[5] I. 921–950, etc.

Epicurean science with orthodox religion constituted a barrier, all too great for many. The Stoic Seneca's *Natural Questions,* in spite of its gross errors, might enjoy a far greater vogue in pagan Rome and exert a far greater influence in the Middle Ages than Lucretius' *De Rerum Natura:* the Stoic, of course, accepted the principle of divine influence.

But for Lucretius, belief in the atom was of fundamental importance. The second book was devoted, largely, to discussions of movement of the atoms, downward and swift, or swerving; to the shapes of atoms and their combinations. The third book denies the immortality of the soul, because of its atomic structure. The fourth book explains sense-perceptions as the result of corpuscular activity. The fifth book presents the brilliant exposition of creation of our world and of its dissolution: a universe filled with atoms, falling in parallel lines until some swerved from their directly downward course and caused a collision among themselves, whereby followed creation of earth, sea, air, sky, and heavenly bodies — as atoms sought out their affinities. In similar fashion and with equal consistency, Lucretius conceived of biological origins and biological evolution, as due to atomic activity — a vast experimental, quasi-evolutionary process that resulted in the creation of the first specimens of all organic species and genera, whether of plant or of animal life: a gradual creation of species, fit to survive, that have remained invariable ever since. The atomic theory became the physical basis of Epicurean ethics of pleasure, and, as all else, the gods, too, were atomic in structure.

Lucretius wrote in the tradition of the ancient atomists, Leucippus, Democritus, and Epicurus; he repeated some of the errors of his predecessors and he made no important contribution to the theory.[6] His science is often at fault: his geology is insignificant; his astronomy, at times, absurd; his biology and anthropology, inadequate. But his science, none the less, is presented with fervor, although a true scientific method was lacking; and the atomic theory had, in Lucretius, an eloquent exponent, who deserves all credit for affirmation of and defense of a scientific theory, as significant and as fertile as any proposed by the human mind. The ancient atomists were

[6] Cf. H. F. Osborn, *From the Greeks to Darwin*, N. Y., The Macmillan Co., 1902. I cannot discuss their agreements and disagreements, here.

[74]

engaged in their merciless search for the ultimate in Nature, and their answer to the problem was far more penetrating than another ancient theory of four elements, associated with Empedocles' name and honored for centuries. The ancient atomists, for lack of scientific instruments, could not go beyond a theory of mechanical mixtures or compounds; this limitation was fatal to any proper development of the theory. The atomic theory was revived by Gassendi (1592–1655) and received the powerful support of Isaac Newton (1642–1727). But the world waited on scientists, like Robert Boyle (1627–1691) and John Dalton (1766–1844), and their successors, for demonstration of the genuine validity of the corpuscular theory, for scientific explanation of molecules, of chemical compounds, of the law of atomic weights, and of the chemical ' elements,' as a cardinal and basic explanation of Nature and of life itself. Not that the debt of the new chemistry to the ancient atomists is direct, but the imagination of the ancients, like flashes of insight, and their logic are none the less startling and of importance to the world!

Lucretius could not know the chemistry of soils, of food, of the blood — but none the less, he thought of Mother Earth as atomic, and he knew, as well as we, that trees may burn or decay and that, in either case, the tree returns to Mother Nature all the matter and the energy that it had originally borrowed; that there is a constant endless cycle of creation and destruction and that, despite the disintegration of matter, nothing is lost.[7] Lucretius could not know the modern theory of the atom, as a solar system, or of the nucleus of some atoms, as a small, fierce world, but his conception of the inevitable cluster of atoms, somehow, anticipates that theory, imperfectly, to be sure, but clearly enough. Lucretius could not know of radium and of radio activity, but, none the less, he had a strange adumbration of matter (as of the bodies of the gods), that poured forth substance ('films') from its surface forever, with no, or with little, appreciable loss of weight. Epicurus had arbitrarily assumed the swerve of the atom[8] from its straight-line fall, and Lucretius repeated the doctrine; with what joy they would note the 'jump' of an electron into a new orbit — a discovery that bids fair to affect our own physics and biology, pro-

---

[7] *E.g.*, II. 991 seq.
[8] To refute the Stoic dogma of necessity.

foundly, and, perhaps, our psychology, also. Lucretius would hail Newton as a fellow scientist, but, because of his own unyielding faith in natural laws, would scoff at Newton's form of belief in God, as the final cause. " It seems probable to me that God in the beginning formed matter in solid, massy, hard, impenetrable, moveable particles; of such sizes and figures, and with such other properties, and in such proportions to space, as most conduced for the end for which He formed them; and that these primitive particles, being solids, are incomparably harder than any porous bodies compounded of them; ever so very hard, as never to wear or break in pieces; no ordinary power being able to divide what God himself made One, in the first creation." [9] He would marvel at empirical progress, but, with perfect right, he would claim certain parallels between ancient and modern thinking:

(1) that the tiny ' atom ' is the ultimate in matter (if it be true that the ' atom ' is a microcosm and consists of a nucleus and one or many more electrons, the term ' atom ' should be applied to a smaller component unit — we should say, one of the component parts of the

[9] *Optics,* Bk. III.

nucleus); (2) that this ultimate is indestructible and has existed from everlasting; (3) that shapes, sizes, and weights are important characteristics of the 'atom' and that these are limited in number; (4) that matter is not continuous but discrete (little could Lucretius imagine the void, the relatively vast amount of empty space now predicated of the 'atom' and thought to lie within it, between its electrons); (5) that all substances differ according to their atomic (chemical) structure; (6) that the 'atom' (we would add, the 'electron') is in constant motion and that it has a veritable passion for almost incredible velocity.

VI. LUCRETIUS AND THE SOUL

STEP by step Lucretius undertakes to prove the Epicurean theory of the Soul, as the only true and tenable thesis and explanation of its existence, its nature, and its functioning. It is surprising, perhaps, that neither Plato nor Aristotle is even mentioned in this discussion, nor any member of the Stoic school. All three schools had argued for the existence of the 'Soul' and, so far as the Epicurean school also held to the belief that the Soul was an entity, a reality, it was in line with the Greek philosophic tradition which, in due course, became established in Rome, too. But the Epicurean school, alone of these four, unhesitatingly and systematically, undertook to demonstrate the Soul's mortality.[1] This was of utmost importance and this was the one point which the world at large, at the time and after, would comprehend, even if the great majority

---

[1] The Stoic school wavered, as is well-known, and Panaetius all but abandoned hope in immortality while the Peripatetic Alexander Aphrodisias denied immortality. But these individuals do not represent the thought and aspiration of their 'schools.'

neither followed the argument nor understood it, either for lack of interest or for lack of intelligence.

It is, however, essential that we follow Lucretius' argumentation, in order to realize more fully both his own intense earnestness [2] and the significance of the doctrine which he flung at Rome and upon the world for all time. I should like to present that argument, as fully and faithfully as possible.

First of all, then, the 'Soul' is as much a part of man as the hand, the foot, or the eye. Any argument that represented the thing 'Soul' as a 'harmony' of the whole, or a vital state of the body, that claimed that this unsubstantial 'harmony,' which might be likened to 'good health,' was responsible for sensation and life, seemed to Lucretius an egregious error, which he rejected with characteristic scorn (94, 105, 131 seq.). Other theories, besides that of Aristoxenus, are not analyzed or mentioned, and the rejection of this theory must have seemed to Lucretius' mind sufficient for his purposes. The Soul could not be thought of in terms of music; that 'harmony,' whether music or a harmonious adjustment of all, de-

[2] Cf., *e.g.*, vss. 94, 105, 130, 135, 136, 166, 175, 179.

pended, too much, upon the perfection of the instrument (119). 'Soul' Lucretius defined as *animus* and *anima*. Now *animus* was the same as *mens* or mind, and proof that *animus* was an organ of the body lay in such obvious phenomena as the simultaneous ill-health of the body and the abounding vitality of the mind, or the reverse, the wretchedness of mind that might be accompanied by physical well-being of the entire body. No one would contradict this truth and, so far, the existence of the 'Soul' is proven. An analogue might be found in the simultaneous but contrary conditions of health of the foot and the head, or in the interesting simultaneous but again contrary conditions of the body as a whole, relaxed in sleep, and the lively emotions of joy and fear of the 'Soul.' If we associate *animus* with mind and call mind, part of the 'Soul,' no one could quarrel with Lucretius. But the existence of an organism called *anima* was more difficult to prove. Belief in its existence resided, primarily, in the difference between the body in life and in death — in the presence of warmth and breath in the living body. This required, for him, a postulate of a life-principle or, rather, a life-giving organism — which pervaded the body, which carried (in itself) heat (*calor, vapor*), air (*aer*), and the breath of life (*ventus vitalis, aura*). Lucretius knew, of course, of heart, lungs, and liver; he knew naught of the brain structure, of the spinal-cord, of nerves, of the circulation of the blood. In the absence of that fuller knowledge, the assumption of *anima* was reasonable enough, dogmatic as it was, and was, I think, forced on him by the astounding difference between the living body and the corpse. Thus *animus* and *anima* were proclaimed as the constituent parts of the mysterious thing that the Greeks called Ψυχή and which we are wont to call 'Soul.' Lucretius had no doubt about the truth of its existence. A vague 'harmony' it certainly was not. The phenomenon of life, *i.e.*, just living, the no less mysterious phenomena of thinking, of reasoning (95, 139), of feeling, of all of the emotions (116, 141, 288, 290, 293), of willing (95, 164) demanded the dogmatic assumption, in the ancient world, of 'Soul.'

Anima was the center, the organ of life itself, *animus,* the seat of reason, feeling, and of will. In the next place, what Lucretius has chosen to call *animus* and *anima* make up one *unity;* the two constituent parts of the 'Soul' are conjoined, although they may function separately. The *animus* (or *mens*) is the ruling principle, that ultimately governs not only the entire soul but the body as well. It was located in the breast, as Peripatetics and Stoics also agreed. The reason for this belief lay in recognition of the fact that emotions of fear and of joy are often conspicuously felt to reside here. This is equivalent to a recognition of the ever-close functioning of reason and of feeling. Although the Epicureans were in conflict with some other schools and although to-day we know far more about mind and brain, this error of location is of minor consequence in the whole scheme. Of more importance, was the idea of unity of soul, which Lucretius labored to prove. Although *animus* and *anima* might, at one and the same time, be variously affected, although the one might be disturbed by sensations of pain or of joy, while the second was not affected at all, even as other parts of the body might simultaneously be variously disturbed, as the head or the eye, tortured with pain, while the rest of the body was free, yet, a sufficiently powerful impulse proved the essential one-ness of this *animus-anima* structure. Without knowledge of the nervous-system,

Lucretius knew or believed that he knew that *animus* (or *mens* = mind) and *anima* were, essentially, one. A remarkably vivid pen-picture of great physical distress, arising from mental terror and transmitted to the whole body, shows knowledge, clearly enough, on Lucretius' part, of physical disorders and of the intimate relations of all parts of the body. No other conclusion was open to Lucretius but that *animus* and *anima* are united, and the conclusion seemed to him an obvious one, which anyone must recognize (158). The unity of the two is, therefore, confidently proclaimed!

The next step follows logically — *i.e.,* statement of his conviction that *animus* and *anima* are corporeal in nature. *Animus* and *anima* are realities, *animus* and *anima* are functioning organs, and they must be made of the same stuff or substance that made all else. The transmission of effects from mind to the rest of the body, or vice versa, from body to mind, implied inescapably (166, 175), Lucretius thought, interaction of atoms, the blows of atoms upon atoms. Had he not proven, in the first book —

tangere enim et tangi, nisi corpus, nulla potest res
   (304)

[84]

at facere et fungi sine corpore nulla potest res
    (443).

These are fundamental beliefs of his materialism. A second description of great physical agony, no less detailed and powerful than the previous one, is given, as demonstration of this fundamental truth, and in it we realize there lies an unconscious anticipation of all of our present knowledge of the nervous system.

If atomic in nature, the *animus* and *anima* are naturally believed to consist of atoms, the smallest, the smoothest, the roundest, the most subtle in the human body. Lucretius is particularly eager that the reader should grasp this, and his insistence that the reader pay heed (181), his didactic claim that this knowledge is of greatest importance (206), and his dogmatic assertion that it is true (203, 208, 216, 228) — all express the vehement and sincere nature of the expositor. But how prove this? Lucretius believed that the incomparable swiftness of thought proved this extremely subtle character of the atoms of the *animus*. The many various terms used to express the ideas of small, smooth, and round, the repetitious statements of the mobility of such atoms express an intense eagerness to establish a

[85]

claim, that could, perhaps, not be proven at all, but Lucretius' conviction cannot be questioned that explanation of the swiftness of thought lay in the assumption of such atomic structure. For him, the comparison with the fluidity of water, the stickiness of honey, the lightness of the poppy, the heaviness of stone was conclusive evidence. The marvellous phenomena of swift thought admitted of no other explanation and, not having knowledge of the nervous system, Lucretius argued, logically enough, that the atoms of the *animus* (or mind) could not be heavy, could not be rough! The same must be true of the atoms of the *anima* that exist, interlaced, amid all the complex structure of veins, flesh, and sinews. Comparable to the bouquet of wine or to the aroma of perfumes, the *anima,* at death, left the body that had been warm — chill and cold. But though *animus* and *anima* were fled, there was no appreciable loss of weight of the body nor was its external contour altered. *Anima,* therefore, was likewise composed of atoms of similarly fine texture.

Having established, as he thought, the existence of *animus* and of *anima,* having demonstrated, as he believed, the atomic structure of

[8 6]

these two component parts of the 'Soul,' Lucretius ventured, without timidity (237, 241, 260, 282), upon explanation of the mysteries [3] of sensation and of reason. Some discussion was certainly called for. The heat (*calor,* or *vapor*), the air (*aer*), and the breath of life (*aura,* or *ventus*) that entered into the composition of the *anima* (as we have already seen) and of the *animus,* were not sufficient to explain sensation and thinking (238–240). Therefore a fourth nameless 'natura' was arbitrarily predicated of the *animus,* as a 'necessary' and altogether sufficient factor.[4] Naught was more mobile than this nameless substance, naught composed of smaller or smoother atoms, atoms more mobile or tenuous. It originates sensations and transmits them to heat, breath, and air, and, in turn, to blood, flesh, bones, and even marrow, whether sensations of joy or the reverse. Eager to explain these phenomena, it was the poverty of the Latin language, *i.e.,* its imperfect philosophic vocabulary, alone, that prevented full demonstration and imposed brevity upon this discussion (260). These four factors, *viz.,* of heat, air, breath, and the fourth

[3] Cf. use of *caeca,* 247, 269, 316.
[4] This doctrine of Epicurus reminds one of Aristotle's 'quintessence.'

nameless substance, were essential for explanation of emotional and rational life, of all psychic processes; they were inseparably united, and the dance of their atoms explained all. This may seem naïve, but, as before, we must recall that Lucretius had no knowledge, as we understand it, of brain, ganglia, or nerves, and his assumption was a perfectly natural and logical step, after the argument that preceded. Lucretius very properly argued that all four constituent parts made up one unity. Separate or disparate function of one, apart from the rest, was absolutely denied. The nameless fourth element, which lay most deeply hidden in the recesses of our physical being, he called the 'soul of the soul.' It, in fact, dominates all the rest, and life itself depended upon its security. No uncertainty attends this argument, and the way was prepared for his theory of soul-mortality; as *animus* and *anima* made up one unity and its functioning was a possibility only in the body, separate soul-existence was excluded.

Before coming upon discussion of the relation of 'Soul' to 'body,' we find a brief explanation of what we may call behavior, habits, and character. *Calor* (heat) is responsible for anger, *aura* (breath), for fear, *aer* (air), for tranquillity in human nature. Lucretius has argued consistently, and these three elements of the *animus,* according to their quantitative amount, determine our predisposition to the violent nature of the lion, to the trembling character of the stag, or to the placid disposition of the ox. Such is man. Curiously, not a word is said of the fourth, nameless element. But Lucretius maintained that learning (*doctrina, ratio*) can so far affect our predispositions, *i.e.,* affect those physical factors of heat, breath, and air (and the fourth nameless substance) in the soul, as to leave only the slightest traces of original evils in us and enable us to live lives worthy of the gods. Stronger claim for education could hardly be made. Lucretius is fully aware of the enormous difficulties involved in his thesis (314–318), but he is content to state what he believed to be the fact, that reason can miraculously influence physical structure. As an Epicurean, he has, of course, in mind atoms of very numerous varieties which he holds responsible for the variations of human nature. Crude as it may be, the argument is in harmony with his premises and Lucretius has brought to a close an amazing

[89]

exposition of his belief. It is straightforward and logical, it is emphatic, it is vehement, it was a challenge to Rome and his contemporaries. Nothing has been absolutely proven — not even existence of *animus* or of *anima* — the skeptic would remain skeptical still — Lucretius was neither biologist nor chemist in our sense of these words — but the argument remains enormously impressive and its influence was no doubt very great. Strangely enough, it approaches closely to our own knowledge of brain and nerves, and comes as close as was possible, in the ancient world, to our conception of those ultimate chemical changes which we accept as the true explanation of psychosis!

After this interlude, it remained for Lucretius to insist upon the *organic unity* of 'soul' and body. And insist he did! Soul and body exist together from the moment of conception; they are bound together, their atoms are woven into one web, and from the beginning to the end they are endowed with a common existence — which is true enough of body, brain, and nerves. Through contacts, soul and body 'learn' those vital motions that spell life and sensation. Sensation is the flame that flesh and soul kindle

between them. Their roots cling together, and
soul and body cannot be torn asunder without
destruction of the whole organism, without dissolution and decay. Repetition of his conviction, over and over, expresses the vehemence of
his belief and, while analogues are not proof,
they are offered as clarification of his thesis:
pluck the perfume from lumps of frankincense?
Everyone would say 'no.' And at the end —
the frank, the naïve (it may be), yet the certain belief that no one could doubt the great
fact of the one-ness of soul and body. Life,
sensation, reason — the product of ceaseless
atomic activity. Argument had preceded and
this was his conclusion. Proof? proof lay in
that earlier argument for the existence and behavior of atoms. There was no other 'matter'
to which argument could be referred. And if
the mysterious conjunction of atoms of 'soul'
and body resulted in the greater mystery of life
and sensation, of reason and of will, at least the
fact was there, and to Lucretius' mind that fact
admitted of no other explanation.[5]

[5] Lucretius has spent much of his strength, and before
proceeding to his long list of arguments or proofs (vss. 417–
829) to establish the *mortality* of the soul, he argues, briefly,
for the *combined* activity of soul and body to establish
sensation. Verses 350–416 lack the close-knit character of
the long previous passage (94–349). The united activity of

In spite of the finality of his conclusions, Lucretius rushes into a long series of arguments and illustrations to convince his readers that the 'soul' *is* mortal. He gathers himself together for a fresh assault.

Argument 1, if we can dignify the discussion with title of 'argument.' At least Lucretius is in deadly earnest and believes that his verses,

the two, however, seems to Lucretius so obvious that extended argument was hardly necessary. To illustrate, he refutes the Platonic notion that the soul sees and that the eyes are but windows of the soul. His remarks are very much to the point but he dismisses the whole problem abruptly. Lucretius then refutes a thesis of the revered Democritus that atoms of soul and body lie alternately next to each other. On the contrary atoms of soul are not only smaller than those of the body but by no means so numerous. We are not always aware of dust adhering to the body, of the impact of chalk that rests upon us, of mist, of slender spider-webs, of feathers of birds, nor of the feet of small crawling creatures — these illustrations are his proof; a slight knowledge of nerves would have helped him greatly; but this paragraph, as the preceding one, has the appearance of a certain lack of finish, as though the final touch had not been put to it. The important point is the relation of atoms of 'soul' to those of body, their mutual functioning to produce sensation, the utter impossibility of their separate activity or existence. The dualism of Plato is as a tale that is told. The following paragraph is either out of place, having been removed by some chance from its proper setting, or it represents an afterthought: it dwells upon the unity of *animus* and *anima,* the subject of earlier discussion; it repeats the conviction that the *animus* is the more essential for life; an illustration of the eye and its 'pupil,' though graphic and vivid, unfortunately is wholly unsound. But Lucretius could not know this. These verses are, certainly, far from complete; they represent a pause, before the furious rush of arguments that follow.

the product of long, sweet labor, deserve serious attention. *Animus* and *anima* are one, we are again reminded; they are composed of the minutest atoms; these atoms are much smaller than those of water, mist, or smoke; the soul has the greatest mobility of motion and it may be stirred by the slightest cause. These are facts, as Lucretius sees it! (The theory of *simulacra*, which was at the basis of his epistemology, was true beyond all doubt.) Therefore, his illustration was altogether valid and seemed to him a conclusive parallel: as water flows away when the vessel that contained it is shattered, as mist and smoke disperse, so soul could not, possibly, maintain its existence, in air, when once it had withdrawn from the protection of the vessel, the body that had held it.

Argument 2. The mind (*mens,* or *animus*) grows strong with the body and grows feeble as age comes on. To this all of us would, in general, subscribe and, as an argument for the mortality of the 'mind,' Lucretius is arguing on safe grounds. Now, he has, of course, identified *mens* with 'soul,' and if 'soul' is, in part at least, mind, the fate of the soul is clear. Lucretius again shows his knowledge of physical disturbances and disease in a passage of extraordinary power — it is all pitched on a plane of intense feeling — and the conclusion is certain that the 'soul'[6] may be dispersed like smoke.

Argument 3. This passage, too, is one of great passion and power. Diseases of the 'soul' inevitably prove its mortality. Lucretius' language leaves his readers no room for doubt:

quare animum quoque dissolui fateare necessest (470).

Lucretius is speaking from the bitterness and sadness of personal experience (473) and sympathy pervades every line of this dramatic account of human suffering. The effect of wine upon the system is another parallel, and a third description of (it may be) a stroke (or epilepsy) is detailed, as previous descriptions of physical disorder have been, and shows intimate knowledge of the dreadful disease, and is further proof of the mortality of what Lucretius regards as the 'soul.' Cures of physical ills of mind as well as of body similarly prove the mortality of that 'soul.' How, then, be-

[6] Now called *anima*. The terms *animus* and *anima* are interchangeable throughout this discussion, as Lucretius himself plainly says (421–423).

lieve that *animus* and *anima* can possibly hold their own, outside the body, in the open air, battling with mighty winds? Diseases are the result of the disarrangement of atoms, and cures result from the restoration of their normal positions; but immortality has naught to do with such changes, additions, or subtractions of atoms. Diseases and cures, alike, give us the grim foreboding of the soul's mortality. Lucretius concludes with characteristic assurance that his is the *ratio vera*.

These three methods of approach are typical of the modes that Lucretius employs in the parade of arguments that follow. In brilliant verses (526–829), about three hundred in number, Lucretius hammers away to establish, as he believes, finally and forever, belief in the *mortality* of the 'soul.' He pleads, like an advocate in defense of justice or, even, of life itself; he argues furiously. The entire passage (417–829) is one of extraordinary sustained vigor and vehemence, and, if we ask for the motivating reason for such passion, we must grant that it lies, in part, in the conviction of the pleader, and, in part, in his profound belief that fear of death was one of the haunting evils of Roman society. Granted his premises,

[95]

that the 'soul' consists of atomic *animus* and *anima,* the conclusions [7] are rational and logical enough. There is much of repetition; the effect of diseases plays a conspicuous part in this recital, and, possibly, suggests personal suffering; the idea that the 'soul' could enter a living body, after birth, is held up to infinite scorn; the phenomenon of heredity and of inherited qualities is a powerful argument on his side; the fact that we have no real recollection of earlier times is not ignored; mind and soul and body are *one,* as we have learned before. 'Soul' in Acheron, equipped with the five sense-organs of the body, becomes an absurd conception. Everything is in its own proper place and the reign of law in Nature excludes the possibility of the separate existence of body and soul. Naught is more incongruous than thought of union of mortal body with immortal soul!

These successive arguments are flung together; they are not arranged in logical sequence but show a mind working at fever heat, ignoring the desirability of orderly arrange-

[7] With one exception, perhaps; escape of *animus* and of *anima* was not the only possible hypothesis. Chemical change, or something analogous to it, within the body after death, seems not to have occurred to Lucretius.

ment. They are heaped up, one upon the other, they are marshalled in rapid array, and, in their totality, they are breath-taking. Lucretius all but sweeps the reader [8] from any earlier moorings of belief or conviction, of faith, or prejudice. Reason, logic, scorn, ridicule, mockery, derision combine in creating this amazing argument of destruction.

quapropter fateare necessest (470, 593, 677, 766, 799)
quod fieri totum contra manifesta docet res (686)
quapropter neque natali privata videtur
esse die natura animae, nec funeris expers (711–712)
deridiculum esse videtur (777)
tanto magis infitiandum (796)
mortale aeterno iungere . . . desiperest (802)

are a few of the vehement, dogmatic assertions hurled at us, as we read, until, at last, this insistence upon mortality concludes with a dramatic plunge into the black waters of forgetfulness (829). Yet all of this, we must remember, is intended as an exposition of reason — which Lucretius, himself, regarded as the supreme quality of human nature (753).

This is Lucretius' impassioned reply to the

8 For a startling illustration of this, see p. 356.

dualists, his denial of Platonism and of Stoicism. The argument remained the most important, in Latin literature, on the subject of the mortality of the soul. No subsequent writer could possibly ignore it. Cicero and Virgil must, I think, have read it; the *Tusculan Disputations* (Book I) and the sixth book of the *Aeneid* are their reply. At least the issue was fairly drawn in Rome.

Lucretius was arguing counter to the cherished beliefs of the Graeco-Roman world and an instinctive longing of the human race. His third book is a monument to his audacity as well as to his courage, as a scientific thinker; the ideas were borrowed ideas, but he had made them his own and proclaimed them with the assurance of sincerity and conviction. No other school, no other individual went so far. Plato's *Phaedo* was the work of a poet and a seer; it remained a comfort for the pagan and even the Christian world. Seneca, Quintilian, Tacitus, Hadrian, Marcus Aurelius, neo-Pythagoreans represented the desire of the great majority to believe in immortality, if possible.

Lucretius was, relatively, a solitary thinker. 'Epicureans,' if at all consistent, were bound to the doctrine; and the Elder Pliny, as we shall see, though not an Epicurean, shared Lucretius' views on soul-mortality. But the Lucretian argument could not prevail over instinctive human hopes and, therefore, Platonic reason, that supplemented that hope, Stoic persuasion and Christian faith won the victory over the European heart and mind. While it might seem true, as Lucretius argued, that there is no Hell for sinners because of soul-mortality, of course, there could be no Heaven, either, for the virtuous; that gave readers pause.

The "Hymn to Death," as the concluding reflections [9] of the third book have been called, evoked the spectre of death and sought to banish the fear that spectre had always inspired. Lucretius' courage cannot be questioned. The grim fortitude of Ennius lived, again, in him, and Lucretius might have written: "Let no one dishonor me with tears, let no one conduct my funeral with weeping." The courage that Lucretius preached had all the sublimity of Socrates.

Courage was not lacking and sympathy for family-sorrow appears, but there are strains of impatience that weaken the appeal to humanity which requires compassion and consolation in

[9] Vss. 830–1094.

the midst of the sorrows of death. Nature is personified and she taunts the weak for their weakness; she reviles the old for their cowardice; such language offends sensibilities and must have disappointed sincere Epicurean readers; such speech makes no converts to any creed. Lucretius argues that death is the great leveler who respects no rank. There was cold comfort in the reflection that the good, the powerful, the great had died, as well as the lowly; that Ancus, Xerxes, Scipio, Homer, Democritus, and, above all, Epicurus had not escaped the law of Nature. Their example might stir others to emulation but the fact of their death would move few to resignation. It was splendidly said of Epicurus:

Epicurus himself has died, the light of his life has run its course; he surpassed the human race in genius and extinguished all other lights, as the ethereal sun, on rising, extinguishes the stars.

But that Lucretius weakened his appeal to man with scornful epithets and expressed indignation that man should resent the inevitability of death is astonishing in an evangelist, even in a defiant and haughty mood. The Christians were much wiser in their appeal to the lowly, the humble, and, even, the wicked. Lucretius, on the contrary, flays the irresolute and resorted to the sting of satire.

With all of his courage, Lucretius does not summon ecstasy as an ally to his earnestness; and to claim that Lucretius, like Keats, was "half in love with easeful Death," [10] misses, entirely, his love of life, the emphasis he places on the pathos of the brevity of life, and his exhortation to *live* nobly. Plato and Cicero were spellbound by the prospect of eternal happiness, and rapture appears in their phrases quite as much as in the language of Christian Fathers. Lucretius' sincerity carried with it brave acceptance of his own reasoning and of its conclusion, but, certainly, no exultation. The belief in an inexorable fate that dooms all that is great, good, and beautiful to Death might inspire resignation and courage, but, hardly, joy. Yet the belief in annihilation does not exclude hope of survival in fame and in the fond memory of followers — as Epicurus demonstrated by the terms of his will asking that the day of his birth be commemorated; his disciples observed the request for several hundred years. Nor does that belief in destruction exclude hope

[10] Duff, *Lit. Hist. of Rome*, p. 286; cf. Lucr., III. 977.

of survival of influence [11] — a hope which Lucretius cherished.

Most interesting of all, however, is the strange anticipation we find, in Lucretius, of modern belief that psychosis rests on neurosis. Using a different language, Lucretius came very near the argument and, hence, the conclusions of the biologist, the chemist, and the psychologist of to-day. Whether argument will, in the twentieth century, conquer ancient hope and faith, deeply rooted in the heart and in human institutions, remains to be seen.[12] For almost two thousand years, however, Lucretius' argument had fallen on deaf ears.

[11] Cf. C. H. Moore, *Ancient Beliefs in Immortality,* 1931 (in the " Our Debt " Series).
[12] Cf., *e.g.,* p. 345.

VII. LUCRETIUS AND RELIGION

THE origins[1] of religion, Lucretius felt, admitted of easy explanation, and dread and fear lay at the root of the ancient psychology. The orthodox Graeco-Roman concept of god, Lucretius held, was born of fear and of ignorance. In waking moments and in dreams, primitive man had caught glimpses, as he thought, of immortal gods of might and majesty whom no force could conquer. Observation of various, grand natural phenomena, explanation of which lay beyond his ken, and, especially terror of appalling forces of lightning and thunder had suggested gods of illimitable strength, who controlled all these manifestations of nature about him. These gods had continued to hold the human mind, abject, in slavery of dread and cowardice. Lucretius recognized that the thunder rolling through the heavens, the lightning smiting the earth, storms and shipwrecks at sea, and earthquakes naturally inspired this reaction of terror and this

[1] V. 1161–1240.

[103]

belief in gods whose power was thus conceived to be absolutely limitless. Ignorance of natural laws held proud kings, admirals, whole races and peoples in continued terror of gods who not only controlled natural forces but often scornfully ignored human suffering. The sad fact remained, as Lucretius knew only too well and repeatedly admitted, the world was still in the grip of the old fear and ignorance; all-powerful gods ruled relentlessly, as harsh task-masters, over humbled and humiliated souls. The old legacy was one of tears, that would be handed down to children's children and the old conception of *pietas* would prevail. Worship, prayers, vows, and sacrifices to these false gods of anger and of savage wrath would continue, accompanied by fearful anxiety.

Courage of the reformer, passionate zeal of the iconoclast, sympathy and sadness inspired these magnificent lines. His own knowledge of natural law caused Lucretius to abandon, utterly and finally, any such false notions of divine control or of divine providence. Lucretius did not seem to feel that proof for the existence of gods was required.[2] At least he

---

[2] The Epicurean theory of epistemology proved it; cf. Cic., *De N. D.*, I. 16. 43 seq.

nowhere stops to give such proof or proofs. But the false notions about gods, as gods of might and wrath, an old conception at the very base of the whole structure of Roman religion and the product of human ignorance and fear, provoked the fury and the scorn that carried Lucretius along on this wave of indignation. We shall realize the truth of this more fully when we read his account of gods and their Heaven, as the Epicureans conceived them, and of Epicurean prayer to these gods.

No less impassioned is another outburst,[3] against the idea of divine creation, which was bound up with the theory of divine control and of divine providence. Lucretius' irony, scorn, and ridicule are poured forth with all the vehemence of his passionate nature to proclaim the utter folly of this old belief. Divine creation or no might not disturb Rome so deeply. This was not, I believe, an original Italic notion. It was borrowed from Greece, but Romans, with Stoic or Platonic inclinations, had come to accept it and, a little later, Cicero eloquently voiced such a conviction. Perhaps, many untutored Italians, too, had come to the same belief. But a divine universe! Others

[3] V. 146–234.

might maintain such foolish platitudes. Though this were heresy, Lucretius, undaunted, railed at the imperfections of a natural universe that in so many respects even he recognized as sublime: mountains, forests, wild beasts, rocks, marshes, the 'estranging' sea, the tropics and the arctics, barren soil that caused the farmer endless toil, inclement and unseasonable weather, heat, and cold, frosts and whirlwinds that ruined his best efforts were proofs of a cruel Nature that showed no divine interest. More than that, the tragedy of untimely death that stalked abroad was final, absolute proof of absence of divine providence. Such contradictions were not divine! Aye, instinct made even the babe weep, when, as a sailor tossed by savage waves, it lay, helpless, at birth, upon the new shore, conscious of the evils of life, — a thought, repeated later by Lear:

Thou know'st, the first time that we smell the air,
We wawl and cry; . . .
When we are born, we cry that we are come
To this great stage of fools.

The three ideas of divine creation, divine control, and of divine providence stood together or fell together.

An earth-goddess,[4] for example, who in very truth controlled the bounties of the earth — she was born of ancient but false fancies; she was the creation of idle imagination that conceived the earth as divine. All of the awe-inspiring and terrifying ceremony of her worship rested upon a false assumption, and with solemn denunciation of that basic principle, the goddess was toppled from her throne. Let us recall, however, that Augustus restored her temple. Magna Mater, whose worship had stirred emotion to the depths, was haughtily denied. The concept of this great earth-goddess grew out of a natural wonder at the rich variety of manifold products of the earth. But an earth-goddess, a Mother-goddess, ancient and noble as that concept might be, who brought these bounties to us — no! The earth was atomic and its richness was due to the great number and variety of atoms that made it. And in one superb, sweeping outburst of rationalization, her ritual is described as allegory, and the Roman conception of such a goddess, the product of false reason.

The same would be true of Neptune, Ceres, Bacchus and, for that matter, of any other

---

[4] II. 581–660.

divinity in the Roman pantheon whether gods of childbirth [5] or of the fields,[6] Diana, for example, Faunus, Satyrs, Nymphs, or, again, of Janus, Vesta, Jupiter. Any intelligent ancient reader of Lucretius must have realized that. Magna Mater here served Lucretius' purpose, to prove that no gods exercised control in the spheres with which orthodoxy had associated them. This longer passage was sufficient to illustrate his argument; and the briefer references to the natural laws of conception and childbirth, to the futility of prayer to gods for children, to the beloved divinities of field and stream and the naïve belief in their presence, simply constitute a confirmation and extension of the denial of the presence and the power of Magna Mater, here. The great earth-goddess and the great sky-god and the host of other divinities, great or small, on earth or between heaven and earth had absolutely no power over any natural laws. Worship Jupiter, an irrational and a wicked god? [7] who destroyed his own images and temples, or withdrew into the desert spending his rage in hurling thunderbolts that oft did not touch the guilty but

[5] IV. 1233 seq.   [7] II. 1090–1104; VI. 379–422.
[6] IV. 580–594.

destroyed the innocent! As we read Lucretius' breath-taking lines of supreme contempt for this great sky-god of the Mediterranean basin, we marvel, as we wonder what effect such lines had upon his position in Rome. To be sure, religious belief was shaken in the first half of the first century before Christ by the crises of war and of bloodshed, by the terrors of proscriptions, by the commotions of civil discord; and this judgment might have found an echo in many a wondering soul. Long before Lucretius' day, as Job and Euripides remind us, and, many times since, as even Christ in Gethsemane is our witness, the thoughtful have been perplexed at the apparent irreconcilability of divine wisdom and human suffering. But here we have an attack of unmitigated fury upon the accepted concept of Jupiter, the god of thunder and of lightning, the god of gods, whom many had been taught to call the 'Mightiest and the Best.' His temples were a visible symbol of his invisible majesty and they had been erected in gratitude for his favor and protection. It is hardly thinkable that at the time of his religious revival Augustus would have tolerated such scornful ridicule. But this god, capricious and irresponsible!

[109]

Lucretius would have none of him or of his mythologies.[8]

The gods of Rome and their providence were proudly rejected. A childish imagination had begotten them and error had for centuries ruled the world. Whatever other notions Lucretius might have held of divinity and of divine behavior, it was especially in his rejection of the old, favored notion of divine Providence that he must have appeared to some as the boldest iconoclast. For it was out of an ancient belief in divine Providence that the whole institution of Roman religion had grown. The theory had given comfort to countless silent multitudes for ages. The theory had supported the state through innumerable crises. Educated and uneducated, alike, had subscribed to it. Platonists, Aristotelians, and Stoics had not rejected this principle, whatever other modifications of orthodox religion they had proposed. Yet, in the first half of the first century before Christ, Lucretius had the audacity to fly in the face of the orthodox, with this bitter denial. His great admiration, Epicurus,[9] is sketched as a leader of utmost courage, a veritable Titan

[8] Cf., *e.g.*, Lucr. I. 199–204; V. 14–37, 395–406 seq., 878 seq.; Cic., *De N. D.*, I. 16. 42.

[9] I. 62–79.

who defied the wrath of gods, an Ajax who had no fear of their most terrifying weapons, thunder and the lightning. The old orthodoxy had kept human life crushed under the weight of false fears. Knowledge of natural law had taught Epicurus what could and what could not be. The victory of the great emancipator had raised man to the threshold of Heaven and Lucretius rejoiced in the victory!

The intelligent and eager searcher for god, in Rome, in the first century before Christ, must have scanned the *De Rerum Natura* with impatience for Lucretius' exposition of his own conception of the truth about god or gods. Unfortunately, the passages, dealing with religion, appear in various places through the course of the poem. If Lucretius had gathered all of his arguments, destructive and constructive, into one book, with full explanation, so that any reader could have seen with ease what the real nature of his gospel was, I cannot help but think that the result would have been sensational and the ultimate effect, far more profound. As it is, all of these passages are scattered and, thereby, much of their force was undoubtedly lost. Besides, the positive side of the subject was not fully treated by Lucretius, who gave promise of much fuller treatment ⌐ ⌐t, obviously, did not live to re-write his poem and to redeem this particular promise.[10] But, even as it is, it is possible to discover from Lucretius' own language [11] the broad outlines, at least, of his own belief, *i.e.*, the Epicurean belief regarding the true gods, and catch the glow of his enthusiasm. In ecstasy, Lucretius [12] acknowledges his debt to Epicurus himself, for this revelation, while a careful reading of other Epicurean sources [13] supplements this knowledge and protects us from the errors of contemporary and later critics.

In their Heaven, situated in the lucid interspaces between the worlds, vision of which Lu-

---

[10] V. 155. The subtleties of the "physical constitution of the Epicurean gods," for example, have troubled ancient and modern students. While this is an important problem for the philosopher, it need not, I think, have worried the average 'Epicurean' worshipper very much.

[11]
V. 146–155, 165–175,	V. 1161–1240,
II. 646–651, 652–660,	V. 146–234,
II. 1093–94,	II. 581–660,
III. 14–24, VI. 56,	IV. 1233, IV. 580–594,
VI. 43–68–95; cf. V. 1194–	II. 1090–1104 (1095),
1203 (on *pietas*),	VI. 43–65,
I. 1–43 (Invocation),	V. 82–90,
	I. 146–158, 75–77.

[12] III. 1–15.

[13] *E.g.*, Philodemus; Velleius in Cicero, *De N. D.*, I; and scattered references in Epicurus and Diogenes of Oenoanda.

[112]

cretius had caught in his inspired moments, the gods dwelt, quiet, tranquil, and serene:

> *Where never creeps a cloud, or moves a wind,*
> *Nor ever falls the least white star of snow,*
> *Nor ever lowest roll of thunder moans,*
> *Nor sound of human sorrow mounts to mar*
> *Their sacred, everlasting calm!*

Cloudless ether covered the gods, whose every need Nature supplied. Naught disturbed their peace of mind at any time, and joy reigned in this Heaven of light. The blessed and immortal gods enjoyed supreme peace, free from care; far removed from our affairs, they were free from every pain, from every peril free; self-sufficient in their own resources, they had no need of us, and were not won by our favors or merits, nor moved by wrath. This was the truth about the gods! These were the true gods! Haughty, angry taskmasters they were not, gods of limitless power they were not, and fear of gods was banished for ever and ever. On the contrary, adoration might mount, unmolested, toward these gods, who, as bodying forth the Epicurean ideals of everlasting beauty, happiness, and perfection, inspired the sincere Epicurean worshipper with most enthusiastic devotion and allegiance. True Epicureans —

Epicurus (at least as Lucretius represented him) and Lucretius of a certainty [14] — reserved ultimate aspiration and veneration for these gods, who were revealed to man's mind through high intelligence, who represented the incarnation of all that was holy, and whose supreme felicity human life through imitation sought to attain.[15] It goes without saying that the Epicureans took over the old pantheon, because no religious system is created *de novo*. The old gods were re-created, in accordance with Epicurean ideas of divinity; ignoble ideas of mythology about gods were abandoned, only ideas and associations worthy of divinity were retained; particular Epicurean ideas of peace, serenity, and happiness were stressed. A new Ceres emerged from this transformation; Neptune and Bacchus were idealized, anew; Magna Mater with all her graciousness was in the new Heaven; the goddess of beauty and love was there, whose victory over Mars was the burden of Lucretius' prayer; Calliope remained, solace of men and delight of gods; Jupiter, transformed and exalted by terms of Epicurean philosophy, ruled over this divine court where he

[14] The same is true of Velleius, of Philodemus, of Diogenes of Oenoanda.
[15] III. 322; cf. VI. 79 seq.

reigned and ruled from everlasting to ever-lasting, because the gods seemed to have es-caped the law of the atom, the law of dissolu-tion. Epicurean philosophy of religion had discovered the truth about the gods, and re-ligion, with worship and prayer, was placed on a nobler basis.

The gods were, of course, atomic, as all else in the universe. The abodes and the bodies of the gods were, of course, of the finest atomic structure. This made apprehension of the sub-tlety of their nature difficult for the senses and, even, for the mind. This approaches mys-ticism, yet the gods awakened in the thoughtful soul of the genuine worshipper, the sugges-tions that were theirs to convey. From their holy bodies there emanated a constant, unfail-ing stream of finest films, as swift as light, heralds of their divine form, which could stir, in the hearts and minds of those who knew, suggestions of their perfection and an uplift-ing adoration.[16] This was the new *pietas,* in-telligent, free from all alarm, pervaded with peace at the altar, and content with admiration and the inspiration that accompanied this heaven-sent gift. Of course this gift was not

[16] Cf., also, VI. 750, 753, on Pallas.

bestowed upon man, as the orthodox believer had for ages imagined that favors came from Heaven, bestowed by gods conscious of man's deserts and with the will to reward; this gift could come into man's life only through his apprehension of that constantly flowing stream of atomic films which, coming from the divine bodies of gods, filling the universe, awakened in man consciousness of the perfection of their divinity.

Prayer brought its own response and reward, through the atomic contact that it established between god or gods and the worshipper. Worship and prayer are taken for granted, as the only medium of communication between man and gods, and the *De Rerum Natura* opens, naturally enough, with an invocation that represents, very clearly, Lucretius' adoration of divinity. The glow of language that pervades the Lucretian invocation is the surest token of the rapture of the poet, philosopher, and worshipper whose upturned face has beheld the effulgence of Venus. An authentic vision of divinity, no less genuine than that vouchsafed to Aeneas,[17] no less true than that which inspired the soul of the artist to whom we owe

[17] *Aeneid,* I. 402 seq.

the Venus of Melos, confirmed the inner longing for beauty and for peace. Though far removed in space, Venus was none the less near
at hand, because atoms fly as swift as light, a
companion, a consolation, the delight of gods
and of men, and, in a new, spiritual sense, the
Mother of the Aeneadae. There is present all
of the exaltation of religious belief. Venus was
no mere symbol of Nature's creative force; she
was that,[18] to be sure, but much more. Venus
was a radiant goddess. She carried over from
the old orthodox belief all of the old romantic
suggestions of creation, of love, and of loveli-
ness; beauty and repose flowed into the soul
of the worshipper of this sublime divinity, and
Lucretius very properly, as an Epicurean,
prayed to her for her gift of beauty to him
as poet and of peace to the Roman world in the
midst of its misery.[19]

[18] II. 652–660 explains this very clearly and in many
passages in the *De R. N.* the word 'Venus' is simply a
symbol or a metaphor for 'love.' Such use of proper names
of gods is common enough in Latin poetry.

[19] I. 1–43. All of the language of this prayer must be
taken with the mental reservations, with the re-interpreta-
tions that were inescapable for Epicureans as long as they
availed themselves of the old machinery of worship. The
only difficulty I can find lies in the use of *voluisti* (27) and
Lucretius, alone, I fear, could explain what seems to us an
enigma; perhaps his use of the word *numen* (III. 18, VI. 70,
I. 154, IV. 1233, cf. also *vis*, VI. 71) may throw some light
on this. The power of Venus and her inspiration of the

These, then, were the new gods whom Lucretius invited Rome and the Romans to worship. They were not the gods of the Roman soldier and of the Roman army, of the peasant, of the politician or of the statesman, nor yet of the Roman economic world; they were not the gods of the untutored orthodox. They were the gods of the philosopher and idealist, whose imagination was aflame with a new spiritual consciousness. Whether Lucretius believed that this new gospel could finally triumph, remains beyond our knowledge, though pessimism rings in some despairing lines.[20] Could any one who had had a glimpse of the new Epicurean truth of gods and their heaven, worship the old haughty taskmasters? Of course, they could, and, of course, they did, and, therein, lay the greatest irony. Even those who had learned the truth might prove deserters from the new faith.[21] Yet for Lucretius a great revelation was hovering in the air and it was his hope that Memmius, at least, might comprehend the sig-

common man and of beasts of the fields cannot be reduced to exact terms either of science or philosophy; emotion is too strong for both.

[20] E.g., V. 1194–1197, 1164–1167, 1204–1209; V. 82 seq., and VI. 56 seq.

[21] VI. 43–56–67; V. 82–90.

[118]

nificance of this message: [22] a harmonization of
science and religion. Rome, however, was en-
slaved by her ritual and did not realize the nature of her bondage.[23]

Rebellion against the old gods, resentment
at the old fear of gods, pity for a betrayed
humanity are expressed most eloquently. Lucretius knew full well that his own day and
generation would shrink from his religious
iconoclasm and he expressed the fear that
Memmius might think that he was guilty of impiety and of crime.[24] Yet he was not, so far
as we know, writing under the scrutiny of any
court of inquisition. Freedom of criticism was
allowed. It is as an implacable foe of the old
orthodoxy that Lucretius appears in the bitter
lines that he has left us, and words like *respuis*
(VI. 68) and *turpis* religio (II. 657) epitomize
that utter scorn. In these passages he attacks
not so much the externals of cult and of ritual,
or of festivals; there is, to be sure, the rationalization of the worship of Magna Mater and
there is the savage attack [25] on the idea of hu-

[22] I. 50–53; 80–82; 140–145; 146–158, etc.
[23] It is obvious that I place Lucretius with all of the
earlier Greek Protestants.
[24] I. 80–82; cf. 50–53, 102, 945.
[25] I. 80–101.

[119]

man sacrifice; the burning fury of this passage is difficult to understand unless we assume that Lucretius felt that the old Graeco-Roman concept of gods and their domineering control of the Universe might make renewal of this supreme sacrifice of human life to angry gods a possibility in any generation. Lucretius does not attack corrupt priesthoods; [26] if he had done so, many a later reader and admirer would have seized upon his artillery and used it again, in later ages, against such recurring evils. No, — it is, primarily, the orthodox concept of gods, gods of supreme might, gods of anger, gods who controlled all natural processes, that Lucretius sought to destroy and thus, through knowledge of natural law, banish [27] one of the great evils of contemporary human society — as he thought — a base, cowardly fear of gods. Perhaps Lucretius exaggerated that element of fear, but Lucretius knew, as well as we do, that Roman religion was born of fear and that, despite triumphs of the intellect and of sentiment, fear had continued throughout its history and had

[26] There is a brief reference to priests, I think, in I. 102–109, and there are several references to contemporary cult, *e.g.,* III. 52, V. 1161–1167, 1194 seq., IV. 1237, VI. 75, etc.

[27] I. 146–158.

not died. Epicurus' reasoned conclusions about gods and their Heaven carried conviction and exaltation; reason and emotion were blended in Lucretius' enthusiasm.

Lucretius certainly realized that the religious experience is, fundamentally, emotional in character. Mind or intelligence plays upon an instinctive belief and modifies, with time, the concept of God or gods. This is implicit in everything that Lucretius says. The Epicurean Velleius, more specifically, says, in Cicero's *De Natura Deorum*,[28] that the religious belief in gods is instinctive and universal, and Philodemus puts it, exactly, when he says that while the gods do not need man, man does need god. Furthermore, Philodemus[29] wrote what Lucretius unquestionably felt to be true, that prayer, with its resulting contact with gods, gave man his highest rapture.

To deny Providence, however, was a mighty challenge. Lucretius' courage bordered on recklessness. Stoics charged the Epicurean school with atheism — a denial of gods — a wholly unjust charge but a natural one, which

[28] *De N. D.,* I. 16. 43 seq.
[29] Cf., too, Cic., *De N. D.,* I. 19. 49–50.

[1 2 1]

denial of Providence had prompted. This erroneous conception died hard and Mrs. Browning gave it new life:

> Lucretius, nobler than his mood,
> Who dropped his plummet down the broad,
> Deep universe, and said ' No God,'
> Finding no bottom; he denied
> Divinely the Divine . . .

Denial of gods! Not the faintest suggestion of that appears in Lucretius. Denial of Providence, on the other hand, was an essential in this philosophy and it was a dogma that the world at large heard and readily understood without in the least troubling to understand the steps by which Epicurus had arrived at his conclusion. The Epicurean school, alone, in the Graeco-Roman world proclaimed this doctrine. Lucretius' spear had writ upon its point ' No Providence ' and with heroic force and fury he hurled it. He had written ' No Providence ' in flaming letters across the skies. But neither his energy nor his earnestness prevailed. His threat was no real menace to the old Roman religion. Men were reluctant to surrender the fond belief that the gods might move among them and bestow their divine favors upon mortals. In pagan comment on Lucretius, this central doctrine of 'No Providence' was either ignored or met with contradiction,[30] while Christian Fathers caught at this very doctrine and made it their chief weapon of attack against a philosophic system often but poorly understood. Many a scholar, since the Renaissance, has, because of the same prejudice, manfully resisted any temptation that he might have had, to understand Lucretius' religion. The old problem has remained to plague many a present-day commentator on Lucretius and only recently has there appeared a true understanding, as I see it, of the Lucretian denial of Providence combined with worship of God.[31]

[30] Cf., *e.g.*, Cic., *De N. D.*, I. 42. 117: horum enim sententiae omnium non modo superstitionem tollunt, in qua inest timor inanis deorum, sed etiam religionem, quae deorum cultu pio continetur. Lambinus and many after him have agreed.

[31] Cf., further, " The Lucretian Invocation to Venus," in *Classical Philology*, II. 187–192 (1907), " Significance of Worship and Prayer among the Epicureans," in *Tr. Am. Phil. Assoc.*, XXXIX. 73–88 (1909), " Lucretius as a Student of Roman Religion," in *T. A. P. A.*, XLIX. 145–160 (1918), " The Personality of the Epicurean gods," in *The Am. J. of Ph.*, XXXVII. 317–326 (1916). I see no reason for abandoning conclusions which I reached some years ago. Cyril Bailey, *Phases in the Religion of Ancient Rome,* University of California, 1932 [Ch. VII admits the presence of contemplation, adoration, communion, and imitation, here]. It is all too easy to caricature the Epicurean gods, as indifferent and as *nihil agentes;* this facile label has caused endless mischief.

[123]

VIII. LUCRETIUS AND ETHICS

LUCRETIUS presents no systematic treatment of the subject of ethics any more than he does of religion. Yet we can assemble his reflections and discover, clearly enough, his attitude toward certain problems of right and wrong, toward virtue and vice. Even though we have no specific treatise, here, on ethics, as that of Aristotle or like Cicero's *De Officiis,* the problems of conduct had, of course, impinged themselves upon Lucretius' mind and his acute awareness to their existence appears in many places.

Does he give us what might be called a genuine 'Epicurean' interpretation of ethics? Do the old catch words and phrases appear here, such as ἡδονή, λάθε βιώσας, ἀταραξία? Epicurus had certainly made 'pleasure' the end of existence, and the aim of his philosophy was to attain that goal. Was the refined, regulated pleasure of Epicurus' early school Lucretius' ideal? *i.e.,* a happiness of tranquillity, that was the Greek's compensation for the Greeks' loss of political prestige, a quietism, an intellectual refuge from the storms and wreckage of more active life. Is hedonism proclaimed as a moral theory, even in spite of Plato's *Protagoras?* Is *voluptas* enthroned and what does it mean? We shall see.

The beginning of the second book[1] gives us the first suggestions of importance. (1) Lucretius attached the utmost importance to detachment from life for a proper appraisal of true and permanent values. The exhortation to withdraw, for the sake of observation of life, is no selfish gospel of individualism, as might appear on the surface, but is acknowledgment of a necessary means to an end — in order to "see life steadily and see it whole." The ultimate value of Lucretius' words lay in his recognition of the rights of the individual and his profound belief that salvation of the individual meant redemption of society. It was a wholesome exhortation in ancient Rome where the State still absorbed the individual. Life is compared to the trials of the mariner on the stormy sea and it was sweet to realize, from the shore, what ills one escaped. Life is compared to the contests of the battle-field, and

[1] II. 1–61.

sweetness and happiness certainly did not lie out there. Not that this detachment was a selfish end, sought for its own sake; on the contrary, discovery of wisdom was not attainable otherwise. From his lofty sentinel, the "ivory watch-tower" of Walter Pater, the thinker could gaze upon the scene with the eye of the philosopher, without prejudice; and the philosopher-spectator might become the preacher and fulfil his rôle of sympathetic adviser. Neither here nor elsewhere does Lucretius undertake an organization of human society; nowhere do we find anything comparable to the elaborate consideration of social and economic problems such as we find in Plato's *Republic*. Lucretius does not discuss these problems in detail. But for the individual to be engulfed in the mad maelstrom of Roman life and society afforded hope neither for the individual nor for the State. Collectivism, in all its forms, depended upon the guiding light of individualism. And as he gazed upon the scene, what a scene the Roman world presented to Lucretius: men wandering and searching in vain for the path of life, struggling with all the power of genius and of noble birth, by day and by night striving for resource and dominion! That life was enveloped in the darkness of error and involved in peril:

O *miseras hominum mentes, o pectora caeca!*

Language of pity and of sympathy, words of yearning and compassion. Aloofness of individualism, deliberate enough, — to re-engage itself in social reformation! [2] (2) First of all, then, the call to the simple life: the two great imperative demands of Nature being a body free from pain and a soul free from care and fear. This was no idle repetition of Epicurus' words, but the clarion call of an earnest evangelist who knew that all the splendid externals of wealth and the pomp of power assure neither the necessity of physical well-being nor the other requisite of peace of soul. With extraordinary skill and with sensuous feeling, Lucretius drew his picture of the Rome of his day, of its wealth and its brilliance; but these did not dazzle, and even all the glory of kingship could not guarantee freedom from bodily pain any more than the supreme power of general or of admiral secured release from the

[2] The complete withdrawal from active, political life, exemplified by Epicurus, had a selfishness that does not appear in Lucretius who, for example, recognized Memmius' duties to the State.

great terrors inspired by gods and by death. The natural is sharply set over against the conventional, the simple life contrasted with the complexities, the fallacies, the charms, even, and the allurements of wealth and power, in order to prove the adequacy of the former — an old theme, to be sure, but neither Theocritus before, nor Horace or Rousseau, later, felt the conviction more sincerely than Lucretius that health of body and of soul depends little on an environment of luxury and power. Lucretius' exhortation might well have been a command, and it would have been well for Rome if he had had the authority to order and to direct society. (3) Now, in particular, two great haunting fears, of gods and of death, beset the world as Epicurus had taught and as Lucretius believed, observing Roman life. They made mockery of man and all his shams of armor and of purple. What could provide liberation? Reason (*ratio*) alone, as Lucretius saw it, could save — the wisdom of Epicurean science and philosophy, which was thus enrolled in the interest of ethics. Denial of providence and of immortality of the soul, as we have seen, were essentials of this Epicurean speculation, and Lucretius used these *principia,* solemnly, in his ethical discussions. Here, and conspicuously again, — in all, three times, — Lucretius repeats the conviction that all the terrors of the soul and the shadows that enveloped it could be scattered only by Epicurean interpretation of Nature and her laws.

Thus the second book begins with a mere sketch, brilliant and arresting, of ethical import, and with very great significance: Epicurean, in its individualism, in its search for happiness, in its sensuousness, in its acceptance of Epicurean dogmas; Stoic, in its simplicity and its acceptance of responsibility; human and eternal, in its discovery of the values of the simple life. An Epicurean formula is implied, here, which becomes clearer as we proceed: that salvation can come through wisdom alone, that wisdom secures and fortifies the end of our existence, namely happiness, and that justice and virtue inevitably follow in the train of such wisdom and happiness. It will be well to remember this formula, which was expressed by Epicurus as follows:

Οὐκ ἔστιν ἡδέως ζῆν ἄνευ τοῦ φρονίμως καὶ καλῶς καὶ δικαίως (οὐδὲ φρονίμως καὶ καλῶς καὶ δικαίως) ἄνευ τοῦ ἡδέως.[3]

[3] See p. 12, for translation.

[129]

Entirely in keeping with this initial statement of his belief is the passage [4] of grim character at the beginning of that third book which is devoted to a denial of immortality. Fear of death and dread of gods had been singled out as the most terrifying to the human soul, and, here, the former is held responsible for many, if not most, of the evils of society, whether public or private:

> haec vulnera vitae
> non minimam partem mortis formidine aluntur.

Therefore, that dread of Acheron must be driven forth;
it disturbs human life, utterly, from its deepest depths,
overspreads everything with the blackness of death,
and leaves no joy clear and pure.

Lucretius' conviction was accompanied by a passionate belief that Epicurean speculation, alone, would guarantee emancipation from the two root evils that were primarily responsible for so much misery in contemporary life; so he repeats:

This terror of the mind and the shadows that surround

[4] III. 31–93 (cf. I. 102 seq.).

[130]

*neither the rays of the sun nor the bright shafts of
    day
can dispel, but only a study of the outer aspect and
    the
inner law of nature must do it.*

Whether the fears that gods and death inspired
were as great as Lucretius believed,[5] whether
they, actually, were responsible for social evils,
as Lucretius maintained, is for us, at present,
beside the mark; such, at least, was his diag-
nosis; whether the cure lay in Epicurean science or in any other scientific knowledge is,
also, not our present concern. We do know Lucretius' conclusions and his aspirations; we
realize the intensity of his horror, as the moralist observed and recalled some of these cancers
of the social structure: avarice; blind passion
for honor, power, fame, wealth; civil war, mur-
der, poisonings and envy; all of this struggle,
to fortify oneself against the fear of death;
all of this cruel competition, to build up de-
fenses against death and win a temporary victory over the spectre, to withdraw from the
portals of death. But the awful dread of death
finally drove mortals, in a vicious circle, through

[5] I hardly need to cite the many discussions of this problem.

a deep hatred of existence, into the arms of death, and such virtues as sense of shame, friendship, filial devotion to country and to family were put to rout. This argument is sufficiently original to be impressive and its repetition, in later literature, may quite certainly prove indebtedness to Lucretian ways of thinking. All of life was awry; the whole political, social, military, financial struggle was in vain — its ambitions false in their inception, and self-destruction, their end. No wonder we have this satiric tirade, as savage an arraignment as we find in any other Roman moralist, — one that places Lucretius with Sallust, Juvenal, and Tacitus, with Swift and with Carlyle. We discover the devotion of Lucretius, the Epicurean, to virtue; we discover the devotion of Lucretius, the Epicurean, to happiness: dread of death that seared the soul left no room for *voluptas, liquida puraque;* we discover the devotion of Lucretius, the Epicurean, to the wisdom that Epicurus had proclaimed; Epicurean wisdom, he repeats from the second book — denial of providence, denial of immortality — alone, could save! Epicurean wisdom could and must expel fear of death; that fear banished, happiness and virtue might return.

[132]

This was a bold and a stunning proclamation, — for freedom from fear (of gods and of death) meant, to Lucretius' mind, intellectual and spiritual freedom. It was, in the Epicurean school, a *fiat* against Stoic determinism. Fear of gods was fundamental in Graeco-Roman religion; [6] fear of death was fundamental in Mediterranean notions of any hereafter. This release from fear signified a new freedom in life, an emancipation from slavery, a freedom that might be easily misunderstood, but without which there could be, Lucretius held, no sound ethical thinking and no nobility in human lives. It is an Epicurean statement of individualism, and expresses a sense of human rights versus any and all capricious tyrannies, whether political, religious, or social; and Lucretius certainly had in mind the good of all. Freedom from fear — a germinal doctrine, certainly, and one that no one had a better right to expound than Lucretius.

Epicurean scientific interpretation of nature, and especially of the soul, was one hope of the world. Hence we have the vigorous, the passionate argument that follows which proves

[6] Cf. Chapter VII, on ' Religion '; freedom from fear of gods also meant release from all of the evils of superstition and of orthodox religion.

[133]

the mortality of the soul. Pell-mell, as we have seen,[7] Lucretius rushes madly and furiously through his long series of arguments and illustrations to prove his thesis. It was established, as he thought, beyond all cavil or doubt, and a superb passage of about three hundred lines (830–1094), that concludes the third book, picks up, almost, it would seem, at random, certain situations and problems of life, presenting them briefly in order to suggest the manner of human behavior, if fortified by the Epicurean doctrine of mortality, and to indicate some of the ethical implications of this belief.

In unforgettable phrases, Lucretius states his belief that, as we have no consciousness of even one of the greatest cataclysms of history, the Carthaginian wars, so, after death, consciousness on our part is ended, and we should have no awareness of commingling, even, of earth and sea, of sea and sky. Even if time should gather together, again, what we know as our soul and body, the union of matter would not be the old ego, once the thread of self-consciousness has been snapped, because memory could not be restored. A former, precisely

[7] Chapter VI.

similar collocation of atoms, altogether like
that making up the individual of to-day, is acknowledged as a possibility, but memory, consciousness, any kind of recollection of such a
former existence, — no, we have none. All of
this is uttered with intensest earnestness. The
remote past and the future, after our death, are
in the same psychological category, and, as far
as our personal existence and personal consciousness are concerned, both are reduced to
absolute zero. They concern us — the one, as
of historical interest, and the latter, only in so
far as our personal influence and ideals may be
carried forward. The ego, the self, is ended by
the visitation of death and, therefore, that utter
nihilism removed, once and for all, *fear of
death*.[8] This is the first victory of the Epicurean doctrine and the second, a *new courage*
to meet death.

Thus the way is prepared, with great solemnity, for the reflections on life and death that
follow. First, then, it is the question of the
disposition of the dead body that engages Lucretius' attention. With utmost scorn, he dismisses as inconsequential the fate of the body,

[8] Lucretius does not discuss, here, the need of adjustment to the idea of nothingness; he does at vss. 972 ff.
(which ought, I think, to follow here).

—burial, cremation, embalming, a rending asunder by wild beasts or birds—it matters not. And if one has embraced the Epicurean doctrine of annihilation and still fears, such a one does not ring true. Lucretius has little patience for that continued solicitude which betrays only lack of courage. His appeal to reason is equally an appeal to courage and sincerity.

The virtues and happiness of family life found a noble and eloquent exponent in Lucretius and the deepest sympathy pervades every line of his argument that we should not grieve. The family mourns the death of the father, and Lucretius voices the sorrow of the survivors that death seems to rob the parent of his sweetest family ties. But recall! death means annihilation and the father has no conscious longing for the joys of his former life. In that conviction we must find our comfort. If mankind could only realize the truth of this, anguish and fear might cease. But still there remains the mourning of those who survive, because of the enforced separation:

aeternumque
nulla dies nobis maerorem e pectore demet.

Could any other words express the desolation, the devastation of death more truly? Lucretius makes the only reply possible for one of the Epicurean faith: why continue to mourn for one who has but fallen into eternal sleep and who has returned to rest? Such a belief brought a real balm and *courage*.

The Epicurean doctrine of annihilation necessarily brings into sharp relief the idea of the brevity of life, and Epicureans, as Epicureans, may have been particularly sensitive to the pathos of that idea. *Carpe diem* becomes a proper definition of Epicurean eagerness to seize life before it slipped away. Of course interpretation of the phrase would vary according to individual taste, inclination, or character. Some might look upon life as a feast and therefore sigh that soon the feast would be over. For such interpretation of life and its purpose, Lucretius has only ironical scorn: banquet scenes are not a proper symbol of life or a dramatic version of real living. We may, I think, see in this brief fleeting picture a scornfully abrupt rejection of a type of Epicureanism that expressed itself in the "eat, drink, and be merry" phrase of vulgar misunderstanding of Epicurean ideals; in the nothingness of death, longing for these scenes or participation in them has no place. This may seem a curt dismissal of a natural love of life; far from it; Lucretius, as Epicurean and as individual, loved life, but his personal Epicureanism placed life on a far higher level.

Nature herself is personified; a real drama unfolds; she taunts those who are guilty of the crime of wasting opportunity; her words are words of indignation and she rebukes the careless, the heedless, the reckless for their crime against herself and their own lives. He who wastes his opportunities deserves no pity; even if he should never die, life would remain the same for him. And the old man who complains that death stands by his side all too soon, is held up to ridicule for not having learned the true significance of life. "Fools" they are, "buffoons" and "bleeting sheep" for not having seized this precious gift of life and thus being unprepared for death when that visitor arrives. Here we have one of the deepest implications of the Epicurean doctrine of nihilism — the moral obligation laid upon us by the brief span of our existence to live a rich and abundant life of sense and spirit, of the body and of the soul, that one might withdraw, at the appointed hour,

plenus vitae conviva,

with equanimity, and even nobly and proudly. Lucretius' vehement spirit runs through these lines and his impatience with those who do not know and who will not know gives a strange force to the entire passage. Death should teach us the great lesson of life — how to live and how to die! As though life were ours for the keeping, forever, and not given to us for briefest use! Use it before the sleep of death falls upon you, and meet the end, bravely! As for dread of annihilation, that state, upon reflection, cannot cause terror or appear sad; it signified greater freedom from care than any sleep.

The soul was mortal; the finality of death was absolute! This had been proven. The doctrine of soul-mortality carried with it, as Lucretius presents it, two ideals of far-reaching consequence: (1) release from fear of death and far greater courage to meet death; (2) recognition of the brevity of our existence here on Earth and a nervous insistence on the need of making the most of Nature's gift. The old illusion that death might signify a continuation, an extension of existence, with rewards or with

punishments, with opportunity to carry out un-
fulfilled hopes and desires, however great its
prestige and great the authority of those who
had sponsored it, was rejected as utterly un-
tenable on scientific grounds. The generally
accepted ethical implications of that belief in
immortality, with its hopes of Elysium and fear
of Tartarus, were held false by Lucretius.
While he actually dwells only on the second
of these two ethical aspects of the theory of
immortality, the two were bound together; but
Lucretius has left us no doubt of his belief that
fear of death had been responsible for much of
the evil in Roman social and political life. A
tide of feeling mounts, here, a crescendo of
moral indignation such as we do not find, elsewhere in the poem, or, perhaps, anywhere else
in Latin literature. Of course there was no
Hell, as commonly believed, where souls suffered in torment, forever. But actually,
through error and blindness, selfishness and
cruelty, man transformed this life into a veritable Tartarus. Fear of death and of continued, eternal punishment drove men through
mad careers on earth, in the hope that power
would bring forgetfulness of that dread doctrine; thus it became directly responsible for

innumerable social injustices. The doctrine
was a hideous one, which belief in the soul's
mortality might amend. The Epicurean theory
held promise of purification of the human mind
and heart, of human conduct. Plato was in
error, and Lucretius was arguing against Plato
as well as any successor, as St. Augustine,
Dante, John Calvin, Milton, or Jonathan Ed-
wards, who held the opposite view. Little could
Lucretius, in fact, anticipate the diseased im-
aginations and the cruelties imposed upon later
centuries by fears of everlasting punishment.
Tantalus and fear of gods; Tityus and unholy
love, lust, passion and all its agonies; Sisyphus
and insane craving for political and imperial
power; the Danaids and failure to seize the
sweeter joys of the simple life were here, not
there; and the tortures of Hell, the fear of punishment for crime, the horrors of the guilty conscience piled up around us and made Rome and
Italy and the world a Purgatory. Such is
the unsparing condemnation that Lucretius,
in a moment of pessimism, wrote in verses of
singular vehemence and power, that are immortal. Exaggeration, of course, you will say
is present here — the exaggeration inherent in
satire — in spite of the well-known record of

wars, proscriptions, and crimes committed in the names of finance, religion, and patriotism. But his satire is born of pity not of malice, and the important thing to remember is that an Epicurean is the *moralist;* not an Epicurean moralist, mild-mannered as Epicurus, in whose footsteps Lucretius professed to follow, but an Epicurean of Roman strength of character, — an Epicurean, none the less, to whom ideals of wisdom, happiness, and virtue were of supreme importance. A Roman who, perhaps, wrote his own death-sentence as *moralist,* in these lines of extreme, bitter accusation, but a Roman and a patriot, none the less. Nowhere does Lucretius express his horror at sin more passionately than in this denial of Tartarus as an abode to which spirits of dead were said to depart; nowhere do we discover, more clearly, his longing for peace and happiness in a world that had for so many become a Hell on Earth,

hic Acherusia fit stultorum denique vita,

where blind ignorance, vice, and unhappiness, with all of their ruinous effects, prevailed. We have reached the climax of Lucretius' succession of passionate utterances — one of the boldest in the entire course of the poem.

Lucretius might well have concluded his third book with this powerful passage. The doctrine of mortality had been proved and all of his conclusions drawn from it. But Lucretius chose to write a few more paragraphs. With unsparing irony, Lucretius flays the irresolute who drift in wayward wandering because the finality of death had laid no compelling hand upon them and had not constrained them to learn the purpose of life. His mood continues to the end. The ennui of Roman society of wealth and fashion stirs Lucretius profoundly. Disquietude, because of fear of death and of suffering after death, lay at the heart of things and caused all this waste of precious life. The futility of trying to escape self points the moral. And, again, with the earnestness of the preacher, this Roman Epicurean exhorts men to leave all and learn from him that wisdom that might prove their salvation — to conquer fear of death, for social ethical reform! Lucretius clearly believed that Epicurean philosophy was of utmost importance to all eternity. The storm of his soul is almost over as he gazes out upon the eternity of time we shall be gone. That endless, boundless stretch of ages, when we shall be no more, calls eloquently

to us to live as he would have us live, before immortal Death (*mors immortalis, mors aeterna*)
claims us! In such fashion Lucretius enlisted
his doctrine of soul-mortality in behalf of and
in defense of his ethics. His *rendezvous* with
Death leaves us, perhaps, trembling, but not
him.

We come upon the eloquent eulogy of Epicurus, as an ethical leader, at the beginning
of the fifth book. Lucretius had, as Epicurean,
dogmatically insisted that fear of gods and fear
of death must be wiped out if there was to be
an ethical reform in the world; he had vehemently maintained that Epicurean philosophy
of religion and of the soul, which denied divine
providence and denied the immortality of the
soul, alone could prepare the way for the rich
life and the good life. Live fully — *plenus
vitae conviva* — without fear and with tranquillity — shines forth as an ethical ideal; live
nobly and free from sin — this was the Epicurean's exhortation. Ancient readers and
modern have, by attentive reading, discovered
the truth of the Lucretian-Epicurean ethical
gospel, but disappointment awaits one who
hopes to find, in the course of the *De Rerum
Natura*, explicit account of what constituted

right to this Epicurean's mind and what, from his Epicurean view, was wrong; what the proper bounds of *virtus* were and what *voluptas* signified; what duties one owed to society and what the inalienable rights of the individual might be; what principles differentiated Epicureanism from Stoicism! Epicurus is extolled as a god, who had served human society better than Ceres, Liber, or Hercules. He had taught how to conquer, or, rather, he had conquered the perils and disasters of cares and passions, fears, pride (*superbia*), lust (*spurcitia*), and wantonness (*petulantia*), luxury and sloth; by his philosophy (*ratio, sapientia*) he had lifted life out of floods and darkness, and placed it in tranquillity and light; he had, thus, left mankind rewards of living (*praemia*), and the sweet comforts and solaces of life (*dulcia solacia*); all of these victories were in the moral field but Lucretius is content to speak in general terms, confident, possibly, that his own generation understood:

at bene non poterat sine puro pectore vivi

one cannot live well without a pure heart

might have been the dictum of a Stoic, as well, or the words might have fallen from the lips

[145]

of an ancient prophet. But all this is eulogy
of an *Epicurean moralist*, abhorrent of evil and
consecrated to his ethical ideal, whose disciple
Lucretius regarded himself. *Virtus* certainly
was not neglected by this exponent of Epicureanism; but Lucretius is far more interested
in concrete virtues than he is in the meta-
physics or the logic of ethical theory. A second eulogy of Epicurus, the divine, at the beginning of the sixth book, presents him, again,
as the champion of virtue and the enemy of
vice — Athens' most precious gift to humanity
for his ethical teaching: the master had taught
the *solacia dulcia vitae*, truthfully, that nature
demands the simple life, that wealth, honor,
and fame are *per se* insufficient in securing escape from anxiety, that the heart must be pure
for out of it came all the issues of life; he had
taught the limits of passion and fear; he
had defined the *summum bonum* toward
which all eagerly strain, and he had demonstrated the folly of most human cares. This
is all very well as eulogy and Lucretius
believed it to be true; but mention of the
summum bonum is not, unhappily, definition, and we must be content with the third
re-statement, in exactly the same words as

before, of the supreme importance of Epicurean philosophy:

Even as children tremble and, in dark, are in dread awe of all things, so we even in the light are afraid, betimes, and our fears are as little justified as the children's fear and trembling, in the dark, at what might befall; this terror of the mind and all the shadows that beset us, neither the rays of the sun nor the bright shafts of day will necessarily dispel, but only a knowledge of the outer aspect and of the inner law of nature.

At the close of the first important ethical discussion these words appear; at the close of this final paragraph on conduct they re-appear. Epicurean philosophy it was that might secure release from fears of superstition and of death, and Epicurus' philosophy was Lucretius' sole and only guide; that philosophy might, by expulsion of fears, purify the heart, overcome passions of evil ambition and of lust, it might teach the folly of artificial desires, it would secure a strange peace and content. As presented by Lucretius, Epicurean ethics acquired a new austerity which Epicurus' easy life of placid enjoyment did not vouchsafe to human affairs. Lucretius' discussions have all included fervent protests against forms of evil, and the Rome of his day was his sombre background. Lucretius had a new sense of human dignity and *virtus* has loomed large; Lucretius has appeared as satirist and reformer. But he did not depart from the essentials of his master's teaching and *voluptas* had its proper place in his scheme, as we all see.

The virtues have played such a large part in these ethical discussions of Lucretius that they gain, almost, a Stoic importance and quality. One phrase emerges, so genuinely Epicurean in character, that we must recall the words, *plenus vitae conviva,* to realize the Lucretian appreciation of the Epicurean's hedonism. Epicurus had called ἡδονή the ἀρχή (the beginning) and the τέλος (the end) of all existence, human and animal alike. But ἡδονή had been inseparably united, for man, with wisdom or intelligence, as Epicurus defined the term, and with justice, which is virtue. Lucretius held to the same beliefs. Lucretius did not stop to dogmatize on 'Pleasure,' to insist on its importance or significance in human affairs, but many passages in which the word *voluptas* appears make it abundantly evident that to his mind, too, 'Happiness' was a human instinct, for which, however, defense or justification was hardly required. In all of the discussions we have considered, longing for happiness is implicit; it becomes explicit, as we pursue the word *voluptas* in its flight through the course of the poem.

dux vitae, dia voluptas [9] (divine pleasure, the guide of life) is innate in us; it is that immemorial law of Nature or urge to re-create the species, fundamental and ultimate, that might, of course, be debased, by excesses, but became exalted in the name of a goddess. Frankly used of sexual pleasure, yet it deserves to be called *pura voluptas, blanda voluptas.* 'Voluptas' defines other physical and sense pleasures,[10] and the Epicurean world subscribed to their validity. Aesthetic pleasures of the dance, the cithara, and of the stage are also defined by the word *voluptas,*[11] and the span of interests that the word covered was very wide, reaching into the realm of friendship; [12] Memmius' manliness (*virtus,* as it is called) and the hoped-for joy of his sweet friendship were sufficient to inspire the poet to utmost labor of finest poetic creation; this *voluptas* of friendship had no tinge of selfishness but carried ideas

[9] II. 172; IV. 1075, 1081; 1263; (cf., also, IV. 1057, 1114, 1201) (VI. 389, of the reputed irrational use of thunder by Jupiter).

[10] II. 966, 968; III. 251; IV. 627, 629.

[11] IV. 984.   [12] I. 140.

of intellectual comradeship. *Voluptas* is used
of the philosopher's joy in emancipation [13] from
error; and the thinker's profound rapture at
the revelation of Nature's secrets is called
divina voluptas.[14] Assuredly, *voluptas* is as
truly enthroned in Lucretius' poem as in Epicurus' arguments: Lucretius does not debate
the limits of pain and desire, though he is fully
aware that man is ever perplexed by the problem of the proper bounds of *vera voluptas.*[15]
Human fear of death had called forth the vehemence of the third book and the arguments
to prove the soul's mortality — but the motive
of all this energy was to free mankind from such
fear and secure *voluptas, liquida puraque.*[16]
Otherwise, life were not worth the living! And
we care to live only as long as *blanda voluptas*
coaxes and enthralls; if we may not taste the
love of life, why be born? [17] The poem begins
with the description of Venus, as

Aeneadum genetrix, hominum divomque voluptas.[18]

Voluptas possessed all of human life and en-

[13] II, *init.*
[14] III. 28.
[15] V. 1433; cf. III. 1081.
[16] III. 40.
[17] V. 178; cf. III. 1081.
[18] Cf., also, VI. 94 (Calliope). Joy in Nature and in the
Arts should be added, though Lucretius does not use the
word *voluptas* of these delights.

tered into the kingdom of heaven. *Voluptas*
— permanent, secure, and lofty! Lucretian
ethics were hedonistic, but Lucretius felt no
necessity of defending *voluptas!* It was a happiness of sense, of mind, of spirit — a balance
and a harmony of the three — it was joy, it was
happiness, it was *gaudium* and *laetitia*. It was
a universal law. And as the virtues were secure only under the Epicurean's interpretation
of Nature and her laws, so happiness, too, was
safe only under the same enlightenment. No
conflict was recognized or felt between *voluptas,*
as defined by wisdom, and the *virtues,* personal
or social, to which Lucretius attached so much
importance. If Epicurus' ethics and his hedonism were, in essence, individualistic and selfish
in character, there is nothing in the *De Rerum
Natura* to indicate Lucretius' contemplation of
individual perfection for its own sake. It is
society at large, always, that is the object of his
brooding; and, I believe, the nature and behavior of the atom were, to his mind, the authentic parallel, in the natural universe, to the
individual in the social world. That atom was
the ultimate, upon the nature of which a perfect or imperfect universe depended; yet the
atom was always seeking union with other

atoms, and those unions were the real reason for its own existence. The parallel between the atom and the individual appears, most clearly, in the Epicurean theory of free-will.[19] While the atoms obeyed the laws of Nature, whether in their downward fall or in their various combinations, they had, at some uncertain time and place, as Epicurus had arbitrarily [20] maintained, asserted an independence of law, and they had swerved ever so little from the course that Nature and her otherwise inexorable laws had decreed. This freedom, violently wrenched from the laws of Nature, Necessity, Fate — call it what you will — represented victory over the determinism of a mechanical and materialistic universe; it had secured individual human free-will, and it was the final guarantee of individual human virtue and happiness, alike. The elation of the passage calls to mind the sweeping movement of the 'Victory of Samothrace.' Lucretius dared to defy his own limited knowledge of the laws of Nature and he proclaimed the need of belief in a greater freedom for the atom. Science is confirming the validity of that ancient assumption. A deeper

[19] Lucr., II. 251–293.
[20] Cf., however, p. 76.

knowledge was what Lucretius sought, to enable man to live a life worthy of the gods — a life of wisdom, virtue, happiness, freedom — to perfect the *individual* and make him well-nigh divine.

Whatever we think of the steps in Lucretius' reasoning on problems of ethics, his final conclusions were of importance to the world. His own ethical ideal was set forth, clearly enough, for those who chose to read him carefully. The pity of it is that Lucretius did not treat the subject of ethics more clearly and fully in a single book, for the better guidance of the footsteps of the Roman world to which he addressed himself so earnestly. The dogmatic exponent of the atomic theory, the scientist and positivist, could have written an exposition and defense of Epicurean ethics that would have been a real challenge to Stoicism and to the Rome of his day. Unrelenting and merciless in his opposition to sin, Lucretius loved honesty and hated cant with all the strength of his passionate soul. As Epicurean, he was defender of the important Epicurean doctrine that 'pleasure' (better call it 'joy' or 'happiness') is a proper motive of conduct, that happiness cannot be permanent

without intelligence, and that intelligence secures happiness and virtue alike. Lucretius
failed to present his ethics, systematically. But
wisdom, virtue, and happiness are essentials
in this Epicurean's creed and he followed Epicurus, in these essentials. *Wisdom?* Plato had
preached this doctrine of salvation and Epicurus followed the Greek tradition, albeit his
interpretation of the world of nature was so
unlike Plato's. The Christian world early
placed its hope in Faith. Whether wisdom
can save or not, we are, to-day, or think we are,
scientific in our outlook, committed to education
of the masses, and we subscribe to the Englishman's agonized prayer: " More brains, O Lord,
more brains! " Let me quote the Lucretian
verse:

quid dubitas quin omni' sit haec rationi' potestas?

Virtue? Plato had written, in dithyrambic
style, of ἀρετή. Stoics came to believe themselves sole custodians and guardians of *virtus*.
An old antithesis between the Stoic and Epicurean schools beclouded men's minds, and
Christianity, for long, could hardly discover
what hedonistic Epicureanism had in common
with the virtues. The Renaissance had redis-

covered Lucretius, but it was the poet who charmed, and not the teacher of ethical probity, least of all the stern moralist and uncompromising satirist. Yet we know that Lucretius set his stern stone face against vice as truly as any Puritan, — a Savonarola in ancient Rome! and moral principles shine with splendor in his poem. *Happiness?* often misunderstood by critics of the Epicurean school and debased by professed "Epicureans." *Voluptas,* an Epicurean symbol, often signifying sensual enjoyment. *Voluptas,* a fluttering red rag to Cicero and the Stoics. Christian Fathers abhorred the hedonistic doctrine, which signified to them delight and weakness of the flesh; the triumph of the soul and of the spirit depended upon complete victory over all happiness, except that of virtue, duty, and adoration of God. Far more soberly, Lucretius had eloquently defended a broader freedom and happiness — controlled, to be sure, by high reason and intelligence — and held them aloft as torches in the procession of life. Hedonism has made its way slowly in European philosophy, since the close of the seventeenth century. Gradually it has entered into almost all thinking. The Declaration of Independence laid emphasis on

life, liberty, and happiness; social philosophy recognizes, I believe, that life without
happiness is a tragic mockery; and in education, the doctrine of 'interest' also represents
a resumption of an essentially Epicurean
dogma.

The world has never read Lucretius, primarily, for his ethics; he has not become an
ethical leader, but it were well to remember
that Lucretius was an ethical idealist with a
vision of a new world, perhaps beyond realization, in which Intelligence, Virtue, Happiness,
and Freedom might, perchance, prevail. Lucretius offered no philosophical solution of the
ethical problem, while declaring his unwavering
faith in these principles, as cardinal essentials
for right living. Solution has varied from age
to age, while the problem has remained per-
sistently perplexing. The history of sophistry
and the experience of the four leading Greek
philosophic schools, dogmatic, but in conflict
with one another, had, perhaps, taught Lucretius this lesson. He chose to dogmatize and
particularize in science. But to maintain belief in the principles was his privilege and his
duty. While Lucretius had an almost sublime
faith, theoretically, in the power of education

to lift mankind to the level of the gods,[21] while gradations of wisdom alone secured a firmer hold on virtue, happiness, and freedom, his own survey [22] of the evolution of human society left him, I fear, with small confidence in any ultimate or full realization of these ethical ideals. The miracle might or might not transpire. The result would be a miracle, — but within the laws of natural processes. Abandonment of a primitive, selfish, individualistic rule of might, development of language, agriculture, weaving, cultivation of family life, exercise of the humanizing forces of pity and of friendship, the rise of laws and customs, the influence of religious beliefs and of the arts had not been sufficient to curb the vices that spring from love of wealth and of power, from ambition, jealousy, and envy. *Intellectual development* presented difficulties that inspired pessimism:

Let men continue to be weary and sweat blood, all in vain, as they struggle along the narrow path of ambition; they seek wisdom from the lips of others and on hearsay, rather than from the evidence of their own senses; so it is now, and will be, as it has been from the beginning [23]

[21] III. 322; cf. V. 51 (Epicurus).
[22] V. 925–1457; *e.g.,* 1194–1197.
[23] V. 1131–1135.

Inherent *sin*, with all of social development and cultivation of many virtues and a glorious evolution of the arts, still left injustice and crime rampant in the world. Almost as a prophet, Lucretius said of war:

Thus sad discord has brought to light horror on horror for the nations in arms and has added constant increase to the terrors of war [24]

Happiness, too, had been an elusive wraith, because of insufficiency of intelligence to realize the limits of *vera voluptas*.[25] So this picture of man's ethical development unfolded itself to the mind of the moralist and idealist. Over against that picture, drawn at times with fullness of details and with ferocity, over against that gigantic panorama of human living, of the pride, stupidity, and folly of mankind, blinded and blurred by false frenzies — an ominous succession of days, touched with tragedy and despair, lighted by hope and illusion — Lucretius merely sketched his own Epicurean ideal of a life of equanimity, a *vita placida et pacata,* secure amidst its simplicities, and illuminated by what he regarded as the *vera ratio*. Wisdom, Virtue, Happiness, Freedom were magic

[24] V. 1305–1307.
[25] V. 1430 seq.

terms and ideas to conjure with. Lucretius believed in their power to ameliorate human conditions, to mould the *individual* life in courage,
honor, kindliness, justice, and peace, and,
thereby, end the old strife between the broad
claims of individualism and of society. Wisdom, virtue, true happiness, freedom plodded
along their weary way. None the less, as ardent missionary, Lucretius summoned Rome to
leave all and to follow him.[26] Brevity of human
life spurred him on, and thought of the world's
ultimate destruction did not dismay. If not
on Earth, at least in a Heaven of the gods
these ideals were realized, and man might observe their fulfillment in the perfection of deity:
wise, virtuous, happy, free, — calm and pas-
sionless, peaceful, tranquil and serene! There,
at least, immortality was an ally.[27]

[26] III. 1071.
[27] I have tried to present the ethical problem, as it appeared to Lucretius. The weaknesses of the Epicurean system have often been pointed out and ridiculed. But I do
not find in Lucretius the negation of the world and of
effort, the apathy, the flight from the world, the selfish
egoism that all critics associate with the ethics of Epicurus.

IX. LUCRETIUS AND THE ROMAN EMPIRE

A STUDY of the vicissitudes of Lucretius' fame, fortune, and influence during the early Roman Empire will next engage us. As proclaimed by Ovid and affirmed by Vitruvius and Velleius Paterculus, Rome believed that Lucretius' fame was secure in the keeping of the ages. Seneca entertained the same belief and Lucretius' reputation soared on high. Lucretius exerted a deep influence on the literary technique of Manilius. In the minds of the ' Virgilians,' however, as Quintilian was their spokesman, Lucretius hardly deserved such great glory and Quintilian sought to dim its brilliancy. We begin to meet cross-currents in the first century after Christ. Quintilian's strong preference for Virgil represents a movement hostile to appreciation of Lucretius' versification and hostile to a type of Latin poetry of a very definite kind, quite unlike the Virgilian. But Tacitus records for us the fact that there were those who went back to that earlier poetry and recognized its grand qualities. They were the ultra-conservatives, who were driven back upon the old by dissatisfaction with contemporary versification and with the new Latin stylistic composition. Meantime, Statius, showing a very catholic, even if not critical taste, unhesitatingly extolled Lucretius, marvelled at Virgil, and eulogized Lucan as their peer. Lucretius' fame lived on, but it is the poet every time, who figures so largely in these testimonies and discussions.

Although the Stoic, Manilius, was influenced by Lucretius, as poet, he wrote his *Astronomica,* in part at least, as answer to the false beliefs of the Epicureans. While Seneca responded with sympathy and, even, with enthusiasm, to the poet, he was, of course, as Stoic, unalterably opposed to the doctrines of Lucretius. Vitruvius, the architect, had recognized the scientist, but Quintilian scornfully, it appears to me, ignored Lucretius as philosopher. It would seem incredible that the ultra-conservatives of Tacitus' record who had approved of the poet Lucretius, approved of his thinking. That would be a paradox past belief. Pliny the Elder, the scientist, who lost his life in 79 A.D. through the eruption of Vesuvius, observed a silence in regard to Lucretius that suggests opposition. It might not be easy, from evidence of this kind, to determine the nature and extent of the influence of Lucretius, as an Epicurean; we know, however, that there were professed 'Epicureans' in Rome and elsewhere, during the first two centuries of the Empire; [1] to them, what Epicurus had written and the *De Rerum Natura* of Lucretius must have been the Alpha and Omega of all thinking. The rehabilitation of the school, in Athens, under the Antonines, placed Epicureanism on an equal official footing with the other schools of Plato, of Aristotle, and of the Stoic Zeno. Pliny the Elder was not an 'Epicurean'; he never cites Lucretius, by name, in his great work; in fact, he quite ignores him; but he has left us the clearest possible statement of belief in the soul's mortality. He had embraced this doctrine of Epicureanism which was quite as likely — as an expression of despair — to commend itself to thoughtful men and women, especially under cruel emperors, as was the Stoic or the Platonic

[1] Cf., *e.g.,* Zeller (see Bibl.), p. 416; to this list of names should be added that of Diogenes of Oenoanda. Nor should one forget Petronius, for example, the Bosco Reale cups, or Timgad. Apuleius' *Voluptas* will also come to mind and the graffiti of Pompeii that seem to quote part of the first verse of Lucretius.

belief in some form of immortality, of escape, and of reward. Tombstone inscriptions [2] of members of all classes of society evidence the same belief in nothingness after death:

Nil mali ubi nil est,

which is an epitome of feeling, of intense indignation against things as they were, here, and of resignation. These inscriptions also express the popular Epicurean conception of the brevity of life and the "eat, drink, and be merry" philosophy of the frivolous-minded.

Neither expulsion of philosophers [3] from Italy, nor suppression of free speech [4] could check Stoic or Epicurean speculation. Lucretius' *De Rerum Natura* was never, as far as we know, banned or burned. On the contrary, it was honored by being 'edited' by Probus, and 'Epicureans' must have used the edition wherever they were. With the second

[2] J. A. Tolman, Jr., *A Study of the Sepulchral Inscriptions* in Buecheler's "Carmina Epigraphica Latina," University of Chicago Press, 1910. (Many inscriptions in Buecheler seem to me to echo Lucretius very distinctly) ; Franz Cumont, *After Life in Roman Paganism*, Yale University Press, 1922; Samuel Dill, *Roman Society from Nero to Marcus Aurelius*, pp. 478 seq., London & New York, Macmillan and Co., 1904.

[3] I have Pliny's *Letters*, especially, in mind, and Tacitus' *Agricola*.

[4] Cf. the second chapter of the *Agricola*.

century, the *De Rerum Natura* found a great champion in Fronto. Literary appreciation of Lucretius' poem took on a new life, and Fronto's prestige for hundreds of years might have served Lucretius well, if paganism had prevailed. Of course all literary reputations may be transitory owing to changes in taste, and the reputations of Homer, even, and Virgil have suffered, at times. Fronto and Aulus Gellius could save the great poet, for a space, but they had not reckoned with Christianity.

Velleius Paterculus who, in the reign of Tiberius, wrote an abridgment of Roman history, recalls the names of eminent men of letters who by their talent had made Rome illustrious during the days of Cicero and of Augustus.[5] The catalogue, as the world knows, is a distinguished one. Velleius was fully aware [6] of the glories of Athens' hey-day in the arts, and Rome had no cause for shame in any comparison: Augustus overshadowed all men of all races by his greatness; Cicero was 'princeps' among the orators; Hortensius, Crassus, Brutus, Caesar, Pollio are not forgotten, nor yet, among historians, Sallust and Livy; the

[5] *Hist. Rom.*, II. 36; cf., also, II. 9; and especially II. 66 for the panegyric of Cicero.   [6] Cf. I. 16 and 17.

poets mentioned are Varro (Atacinus), Lucretius, and Catullus who ranked second to none in his chosen field of literature:

Auctoresque carminum Varronem ac Lucretium neque ullo in suscepti operis sui conamine minorem Catullum;

Virgil, Tibullus, and Ovid are regarded as foremost in poetry,

> perfectissimi in forma operis sui,

poets who had achieved perfection in their respective branches of literary form. Others' names, now somewhat dimmed by time, also appear.[7]

Velleius, the soldier, was no great stylist, nor great critic, but his interest in literature was very real; and that Velleius, the historian, should have recognized the importance of literature in his own history of Rome is notable. In a glamorous age, Lucretius had gained a fame that assured his inclusion in this brilliant galaxy of immortals. Lucretius' authority, his place, and his prestige are taken for granted — as known to all at the beginning of the Empire.[8]

---

[7] The omission of certain names, as of Horace and Plautus, is surprising, but speculation, here, were idle.

[8] Quis enim ignorat etc., II. 36. 2.

Velleius' belief we may take as a reflection of prevalent opinion.[9]

Manilius cannot be dismissed with a word. The reputed author of the *Astronomica* whose work was done in the days of Augustus and of Tiberius, deserves a place beside Lucretius because of his moral elevation and because of his enthusiasm as a student of the natural universe. In these respects, Manilius and Lucretius drew near to each other, although the Stoic and Epicurean approaches to Nature and interpretations of Nature were widely different. Each felt that his own intellectual victories raised him to a level with heaven. Although Lucretius' conclusions about God and providence and about the mortality of the soul were anathema to the Stoics, Manilius felt the dignity and the solemnity of Lucretius, whose verses [10] left an un-

---

[9] I take it for granted, for example, that Lucretius was known to Juvenal and others who do not mention him, as, to Plutarch; Persius (III. 83) may refer to L., and Petronius, too (cf. L., IV. 361, 966). Whatever the date of the *Aetna*, there is large Lucretian influence there.

[10] Cf., *e.g.*, Lucr., I. 8 seq. and Manilius, III. 653 seq.; L., I. 79 and M., I. 97–103 seq., and II. 452;

L., III. 28 seq.	and M., I. 35;
L., V. 416 seq.	and M., I. 118 seq.;
L., II. *init.*, et *passim*,	and M., IV. *init.*;
L., V. 958, 973, etc.	and M., I. 66 seq.

Edition of Manilius, A. E. Housman, London, Grant Richards, 1903 seq.

deniable mark on the *Astronomicon* of his successor. Manilius, thus, in subtle ways expressed his obligations to and his admiration of the literary power of his Epicurean predecessor, as Seneca, a little later, did more openly. It is at least interesting that the Italian humanist, Poggio, re-discovered Manilius and Lucretius and first made them known to Italy of the Renaissance.

In a very striking manner, Seneca, whose own name is synonymous with Stoicism, reveals to us that Lucretius' position in Roman thought and letters was clearly and sharply defined. Seneca is arguing about the meaning of genera and of species; man is a 'species,' as are horse and dog; 'animal' is the general term and defines the genus; but 'man' is also a generic term and man comprises several species, either, as differentiated by nations, Greeks, Romans, Parthians, by color, whether white, black, or yellow, or by individual characteristics, as Cato, Cicero, and Lucretius:

Tamquam homo genus est. Habet enim in se nationum species: Graecos, Romanos, Parthos; colorum: albos, nigros, flavos; habet singulos: Catonem, Ciceronem, Lucretium.[11]

[11] *Ep.*, 58. 12; this letter begins with what may well be

Just as Velleius, Seneca assumed that the
world knew ' Lucretius ' and what he stood for!
We wish that Seneca had developed his statement and in his own gorgeous rhetoric drawn
a pen picture of Cato, the man, Cicero, the individual, and of Lucretius' personality. What
a gift that had been to us!

Seneca's exposition of Stoicism inevitably
carried criticism, explicit or implicit, of Epicureanism, of Epicurean denial of divine providence and of immortality, of Epicurean defense
of pleasure, of Epicurean cosmology, and of
Epicurean theory of sense-perception, but nowhere do I find criticism of Lucretius, — which,
I take it, indicates admiration for him whom
Seneca must have regarded as his chief an-
tagonist in the history of Roman philosophy.
Nor was Seneca lacking in power of satire.
Epicurus he did not spare, the almost innumerable times he referred to him, by name,
and to his doctrine, with scorn and ridicule.[12]
Seneca [13] quotes Lucretius several times and the

---

a conscious reminiscence of Lucretius, I. 139, 832 or III. 260
(egestatem linguae, sermonis egestas).

[12] Seneca, however, is eminently fair to Epicurus in *De
Vita Beata*, 13. 1–2.

[13] *De Tranq. An.*, 2. 14 quotes Lucr., III. 1068. (Hoc se
quisque modo fugit) and shows knowledge of and repeats
the argument of L., III. 37–86.

[168]

citations are, always, of significant verses or passages. In extolling philosophy as speculative or contemplative, as well as practical, he has philosophy exclaim:

Totum . . . mundum scrutor . . . Magna me vocant supraque vos posita

I investigate the entire universe . . . great problems invite me and they are situate far above you.

And this reminds Seneca[14] of his Lucretius:

Nam tibi de summa caeli ratione deumque
Disserere incipiam et rerum primordia pandam,
Unde omnis natura creet res auctet alatque,
Quoque eadem rursus natura perempta, resolvat,
ut ait Lucretius

For I shall begin to discuss my theory of highest heaven and of the gods. And the atoms I shall ex-

Ep., 95. 10–11, L., I. 54–57 (Nam tibi de summa caeli ratione, etc.)

Ep., 106. 8, L., I. 304 (Tangere enim et tangi, nisi corpus, nulla potest res).

Ep., 110. 6, L., II. 55–56 or III. 87–88 or VI. 35–36 (Nam veluti pueri trepidant, etc.) critical of Lucretian interpretation, but very restrained.

N. Q., IV. 3. 3–4, L., I. 313 (quotations from Virgil and Ovid in the *N. Q.* are numerous); cf. John Clarke, *Physical Science in the Time of Nero,* London, Macmillan & Co., 1910 (for study of Sen. and Lucr. on 'natural questions').

Cf., also, Sen., *Dial.,* XI. 4. 3 = *Ad Polyb.,* for knowledge of Lucr., V. 226 (on the crying of babies at birth).

[14] *Ep.,* 95. 10–11 (Lucr., I. 54–57); this is an accurate quotation, except that *quove eadem rursum* are the Lucretian words of vs. 57.

[169]

plain, from which nature creates all, as she increases and nurtures all, and to which, in turn, she resolves all at the time of dissolution, as Lucretius says.

Thus Seneca pays this tacit tribute of high praise to the noble verses of a *poet* whose philosophy he spent his life in seeking to destroy. They are not the greatest verses, by any means, in the *De Rerum Natura,* but they are simple, direct, and sonorous. Although they express belief in an atomic doctrine to which Seneca did not subscribe, he quotes them. The admiration of Seneca, the poet, for the poet, Lucretius, is written in all of such passages and this seems to me real gallantry.

In the *Troades*[15] we have a remarkable testimony to the power and influence of that abhorrent philosophy of nihilism. At one point, the chorus speculates on the possibilities of a future life and concludes that there is no life after death. And no student of Lucretius can doubt that the hand of the dead master was controlling the pen (and, perhaps, for the moment, the mind) of Seneca at the time of composition.

> Verum est an timidos fabula decipit
> umbras corporibus vivere conditis,

[15] Sen., *Tr.,* vss. 371–408; cf. *Ep.,* 54. 3–4 (Mors est non esse. Id quale sit, iam scio. Hoc erit post me, quod ante me fuit).

cum coniunx oculis imposuit manum
supremusque dies solibus obstitit
et tristis cineres urna coercuit?
non prodest animam tradere funeri,
sed restat miseris vivere longius?
an toti morimur nullaque pars manet
nostri, cum profugo spiritus halitu
immixtus nebulis cessit in aera

. . .

. . . ut calidis fumus ab ignibus
vanescit, spatium per breve sordidus,

. . .

sic hic, quo regimur, spiritus effluet.
post mortem nihil est ipsaque mors nihil,
velocis spatii meta novissima;

. . .

quaeris quo iaceas post obitum loco?
quo non nata iacent.

*Is it true that our shades live on after the body's
burial or does some myth beguile our timidity,
when your wife has laid her hand upon your eyes
to close them and when your last day has met the
sun and the funeral urn holds your sad ashes? Does
it not avail to consign the soul to burial and does
naught of life remain beyond for wretched mortals?
Or do we die utterly and does naught of us remain,
when the spirit on fleeting breath has flown into the
air and mingled with the clouds? . . . As smoke
vanishes from heat and fire. . . . Thus this spirit
that controls us will float away. After death, noth-*

[171]

ing, and death itself is nothingness, the final goal of a swift race. . . . Death destroys soul and body. (Taenarus, Pluto, Cerberus are but idle tales and empty words, a myth that is like a troubled dream.) You ask, then, where you may lie, once you are dead? Where they lie who are not born.

Quintilian's attitude toward Lucretius was not so generous as was that of Seneca and the reasons, in part at least, lie beneath the surface. In his famous survey of Roman literature, Quintilian does not fail to mention Lucretius — that would have been unpardonable. Homer is his great admiration, while Virgil yields only to the divine and immortal Greek. All other Roman poets followed Virgil at a long distance. Quintilian was entitled to his opinion and Virgil was, clearly, his métier in poetry:

Ceteri omnes longe sequentur: Nam Macer et Lucretius legendi quidem, sed non ut phrasin, id est, corpus eloquentiae faciant, elegantes in sua quisque materia, sed alter humilis, alter difficilis.[16]

All our other poets follow Virgil, after a long distance. Macer and Lucretius ought to be read, to be sure, but not as patterns of eloquence nor that we should imitate their diction and style.[17] *Each*

[16] Quint., *Inst. Orat.*, X. 1. 87.
[17] *Ibid.*, VIII. 1. 1 (phrasin = elocutio, choice of words and combination of words).

[1 7 2]

*deals elegantly with his theme, but the former is
tame (commonplace) while the latter is difficult.*

We cannot judge of the propriety of bracketing
Lucretius' name with that of Macer. Macer,
we know, enjoyed high repute among competent
ancient critics. Quintilian's strictures, while
severe, are, in a sense, just. Lucretius had not
achieved the perfection of the Virgilian art
and, often, he is 'difficult.' But it is surprising
that Quintilian, with all of his prejudice in
favor of Virgil, does not recognize the greatness of Lucretius, as poet. A long gallery of
Roman writers is presented and we read acute
criticisms, neat verdicts, and judicious esti-
mates of many.[18] Despite his wide knowledge
of literature and despite his generally good
judgment, Quintilian failed to appreciate Lucretius' great gifts as a poet. The eloquence
and the passion of Lucretius, the place he occupied in the development of Roman poetry, the
victories over language and metre that were his,
the debt of his successors to him — these are

---

[18] *E.g.,* Varro of Atax, Ennius, Ovid, Cornelius Severus,
Serranus, Valerius Flaccus, Bassus, Lucan, Tibullus, Propertius, Gallus, Lucilius, Horace, Persius, Varro, Catullus, Accius and Pacuvius, Varius, Plautus and Terence; historians
and orators, and, later, philosophers; his praise of Domitian (91) and his feeble criticism of Catullus (96) illustrate
Quintilian's shortcomings.

not properly acknowledged by Quintilian, and the word 'elegantes,' applied to Macer and Lucretius, expressive of a graceful handling of material, is an entirely inadequate definition of the majestic work of the didactic, epic poet. But our disappointment is somewhat mitigated by a later statement that while Homer and Virgil were the supreme poets and while the genius of Demosthenes and of Cicero was unrivalled, yet, before the days of Virgil, in Rome, Lucretius was counted 'optimus.' This is a slight recognition, despite its brevity, of Lucretius' immense importance to the history of Roman literature:

Quin immo si hanc cogitationem homines habuissent, ut nemo se meliorem fore eo qui optimus fuisset, arbitraretur, ii ipsi, qui sunt optimi, non fuissent, neque post Lucretium ac Macrum Vergilius nec post Crassum et Hortensium Cicero . . .

Nay, if this belief had possessed men, that it was impossible to surpass the man who at the time had been (or, was regarded as) best, those who are (or, who are recognized as) the best would never have arisen; and a Virgil would never have followed Lucretius and Macer, nor a Cicero — Crassus and Hortensius.[19]

[19] *Ibid.*, XII. ii. 27 (the words that follow — sed nec illi, qui post eos fuerunt — are puzzling.)

[174]

All of this means that, to Quintilian's mind, Virgil was, relatively, the peerless poet, the finest flower of Roman poetic genius. Lucretius' ruggedness, Lucretius' pioneering, Lucretius' affinity with Ennius [20] left him far behind Virgil.

Quintilian advocated the reading of the poets and of prose authors in the schools (*i.e.*, of the *grammaticus*), and his tribute to the study of literature is as eloquent as any in Cicero:

necessaria pueris, iucunda senibus, dulcis secretorum comes, et quae vel sola in omni studiorum genere plus habeat operis quam ostentationis.[21]

Philosophy was not to be ignored, because of the numerous passages concerned with the subtleties of 'natural questions' that appeared in almost every kind of poetry:

'grammatical training' must not remain ignorant of philosophy, because of the numerous passages based on the inner subtleties of natural philosophy which you find in almost all poetry.

and, Quintilian continues,

because we have Empedocles, among the Greeks, and Varro and Lucretius among the Latin poets,

[20] Cf., **X.** 1. 88, comment on Ennius.
[21] I. 4. 5.

who have set forth their precepts of philosophy in verse.[22]

(grammatice) nec ignara philosophiae, cum propter plurimos in omnibus fere carminibus locos ex intima naturalium quaestionum subtilitate repetitos,

and

tum vel propter Empedoclea in Graecis, Varronem ac Lucretium in Latinis, qui praecepta sapientiae versibus tradiderunt.

Study of philosophy was distinctly reckoned as a handmaid to a study of literature, and the 'philosophy' that Quintilian had in mind for these schools was the philosophy of 'natural questions.' The association of the name of Empedocles makes this doubly clear and the honor of association of Lucretius' name with Empedocles' was very great. But to couple Varro's[23] name with that of Lucretius may or may not have been a compliment. We hardly know enough about Varro's *Cosmographia* to decide. Quintilian's mention of Lucretius seems to me to have been rather of necessity

[22] I. 4. 4.
[23] *I.e.,* Varro Atacinus, author of a *Cosmographia;* his *Argonautica* won praise; Quintilian did not think very highly of it (X. 1. 87) nor, apparently, of Varro's other work.

[176]

than of choice! I cannot believe that Quintilian, the schoolmaster, favored the use of an unexpurgated text of Lucretius in the schools; for a reading of even Lucretius' 'natural philosophy' could not but have shaken the religious belief of boys in the schools of the 'grammaticus.' However this may be, Quintilian did think of Lucretius as a scientist, wisely or unwisely associated him with Varro, and recommended him to the schools. This recommendation, however, was hardly likely to bring Vitruvius' prophecy to fulfillment.

Finally, Lucretius as an Epicurean philosopher:

Supersunt qui de philosophia scripserint, quo in genere paucissimos adhuc eloquentes litterae Romanae tulerunt.[24]

There remain the philosophic writers; Roman literature has, thus far, produced very few in this class, who are distinguished in style.

Cicero is regarded as a rival of Plato; Brutus, Cornelius Celsus, and the Stoic Plautus are mentioned; then,

In Epicureis levis quidem, sed non iniucundus tamen auctor est Catius.

[24] *Inst. Orat.,* X. 1. 123, 124.

[177]

Among the Epicureans, Catius, an author, light to be sure, but not displeasing.

Lucretius is not even mentioned! After this strange oversight, Quintilian discusses Seneca's work at some length, criticizing both the stylist and the philosopher. But no discussion, whatever, of the significance of Lucretius, as philosopher and thinker.[25]

Half-hearted the commendation of Lucretius that we find in Quintilian's history of Roman literature; no enthusiasm accompanies Quintilian's recommendation of Lucretius for reading in the schools; and where we expect to find a list of names of writers, who represented Epicurean philosophy in Rome, with Lucretius occupying the position of honor, the name of Catius,[26] alone, appears. This is astounding! [27]

[25] Quintilian's opposition to Epicurus and to Epicureanism is, doubtless, in part, at least, responsible for this slight; cf. *e.g.*, *Inst. Orat.*, II. 17. 15, V. 6. 3, VII. 3. 5, XII. 2. 24.

[26] Cic., *Ep.*, XV. 16. 1 (Catius, an Insubrian Gaul, and an Epicurean, is spoken of as though closely identified with the Epicurean theory of images; he had died shortly before 45 B.C.) ; *ibid.*, XV. 19. 2 (Catius and Amafinius are condemned as poor writers) ; Plin., *Ep.*, IV. 28. 1 (speaks of a Titus Catius, who may, however, be another Catius) ; Porphyr., on Hor., *Sat.*, II. 4. 1 (says that Catius, the Epicurean, wrote four books on the subjects of *De Rerum Natura et De Summo Bono*). This is all, I think, that we know of Catius, and there is much uncertainty in this information.

[27] Quintilian quotes from Lucretius, twice:

Quintilian was very distinctly opposed to Lucretius. As a 'Virgilian' and a 'Ciceronian,' he was as little inclined to appreciate the earlier poetry of Lucretius as he was to be fair to the prose style of Seneca. However in Tacitus' *Dialogus* we find a spirited discussion on the subject of the relative values of the new and the old in literature, especially of oratory, and discover that Lucretius had his admirers. The stage is set: Maternus, poet and dramatist, and Messalla, a Roman of high birth, are champions of the old and of the past; to their minds Demosthenes and Cicero represent the perfect flowering in oratory; [28] Aper and Julius Secundus, on the other hand, the one, an advocate, the other, a polished historian, both of Gallic origin, praise the new style in oratory and are eulogists, as they believe, of progress. The

---

III. I. 4 (Lucr., I. 936–938, IV. 11–13); regretting that the study of rhetoric might not be attractive because of arid rules involved, he desires to make his exposition more beguiling by a pleasant style and is reminded of Lucretius whose difficulties to wed philosophy to poetry were equally great and who had used the following simile, "*as was well-known*":
 .   Ac veluti pueris absinthia taetra medentes, etc.
(the quotation is not quite exact); and, again,
VIII. 6. 45 (Lucr., IV. 1 = I. 926)
             Avia Pieridum peragro loca,
quoted along with Horace and Virgil who appear very often.
 [28] Ch. 25.

LUCRETIUS AND HIS INFLUENCE

battle of the books was no mere academic issue
and feeling ran high. Outside of these immediate lists, Pliny the Younger, we know, preferred Ciceronian oratory and was bitterly opposed to his contemporary orator, Regulus.

Maternus says of Aper's speech:

Adgnoscitisne . . . vim et ardorem Apri nostri?
Quo torrente, quo impetu saeculum nostrum de-
fendit! Quam copiose ac varie vexavit antiquos! [29]

*You recognize, of course, the impetuosity and the
passion of our friend Aper. With what a torrent of
eloquence and with what violence he has defended
our own times. With what richness and variety of
language he has assailed the ancients!*

Aper is impatient with the irrational eulogists
of antiquity and of Messalla he says:

Non desinis, Messalla, vetera tantum et antiqua
mirari, nostrorum autem temporum studia inridere
atque contemnere.[30]

*You never cease, Messalla, admiring the old and the
ancient, ridiculing and scorning the culture of our
own times.*

One sentence, in particular, from this furious
combat concerns us here and there is a distilla-

[29] Ch. 24.
[30] Ch. 15.

tion of Aper's scorn in his words of condemnation of extravagant admirers of the older school:

Sed vobis utique versantur ante oculos illi, qui Lucilium pro Horatio, et Lucretium pro Vergilio legunt.[31]

Those who call themselves 'orators of the old school' hover before your minds; they read Lucilius in preference to Horace, and Lucretius to Virgil!

It was bad enough to go back to Virgil, in this stubborn opposition to anything new, but, incredible as it seemed, there were even those who chose Lucretius as their poet, in preference to Virgil. These were the conservative lovers of antiquity who, curiously, are always with us; and we have a statement of real significance to the student of Lucretius' position and influence. How numerous these admirers were we cannot tell; whether approval of his Epicurean philosophy accompanied admiration for his poetry also remains beyond our ken. But we can well imagine the fate of Lucretius, had decision rested with Aper and others of similar

[31] Ch. 23; Quint., X. 1. 93, said much the same thing: Lucilius quosdam ita deditos sibi adhuc habet amatores, ut eum non eiusdem modo operis (*i.e.*, cf. Satire) auctoribus (*e.g.*, Horace), sed omnibus poetis praeferre non dubitent.

taste who represented a new and radical school of literature. Meantime — curious paradox — the most conservative element favored the poet, Lucretius, who in such important aspects of thought was a radical and an iconoclast!

Whatever uncertainties the attitude of Quintilian and the discussion in Tacitus suggest regarding the future position of Lucretius, Statius, at least, boldly proclaimed the belief that the world would remember the great learning of the passionate poet. For Statius, Lucretius' star still blazed fiercely in the skies. Statius addressed his *Genethliacon Lucani,* an ode in honor of Lucan's birthday, to Lucan's widow, Polla. The extravagant praise he accords Lucan, as 'the high-priest of the Roman choir,' is, perhaps, to be attributed to the circumstances of the ode's composition; but Ennius, Lucretius, Varro Atacinus, Ovid, and Virgil are the great names with which Lucan is associated for his own greater honor:

> Cedet Musa rudis ferocis Enni
> et docti furor arduus Lucreti,
> et qui per freta duxit Argonautas,
> et qui corpora prima transfigurat.
> quid maius loquar? ipsa te Latinis
> Aeneis venerabitur canentem.

*The untutored Muse of Ennius, the bold, will yield
to you (i.e., Lucan), and the lofty frenzy of the
learned Lucretius; he too, who led the Argonauts
across the seas, and he who wrote of bodies' ancient transformations. What greater praise can I
give? Even the Aeneid will venerate you, as to the
Latins you sing.*[32]

The searching nature of Statius' brief but preg-
nant phrase is quite a perfect characterization
of Lucretius.

The two Plinies grant scant credit to Lucretius or to his work, and this fact may be
taken as an augury of the sharp decline that
followed, in the later centuries, of Lucretian
influence, whether literary or philosophical. In
an extremely graceful letter to Arrius Antoninus, as charming as it is graceful, Pliny the
Younger[33] laments the fact that the 'poverty'
of the Latin language had made it impossible
for him to do justice, in a translation, to the
Greek epigrams which Antoninus had written:

Accidit hoc primum imbecillitate ingenii mei, deinde
inopia ac potius, ut Lucretius ait, " egestate patrii
sermonis."

*This (unfortunate result) comes, first, from the
weakness of my (poetic) genius, in the second place,*

[32] Stat., *Silv.*, II. 7. 75–80; cf. vs. 23 (Lucan).
[33] *Ep.*, IV. 18. 1 (Lucr., III. 260; cf. I. 139, 832).

[183]

*from the insufficiency or, rather, as Lucretius says,
" from the extreme poverty of our native language."*

Pliny, who knew his poets well, Virgil, Silius
Italicus, Martial, probably quoted Lucretius
from memory; [34] the difficulties of translating
from the Greek were well known to Cicero
and to Seneca, and the words of Lucretius had,
perhaps, become almost proverbial. This is the
only time that the younger Pliny cites Lucretius and it is hardly a philosophically significant or poetically characteristic phrase. Pliny's
devotion to a notable group of Stoics during the
savage days of Domitian's persecution may indicate, sufficiently well, not only his inclination
to Stoic principles but also an aversion to Epicureanism as he understood it and saw it in
practice. His silence on the subject of Lucretius is, probably, not accidental and the
choice of this phrase may, perhaps, be illumi-
nating and suggestive of his feeling that the
poetry of Lucretius was imperfect. It is
equally true of Pliny the Elder that he does
not do justice to Lucretius, although he certainly had many opportunities to demonstrate

[34] That is, the words are not Lucretius' ' patrii sermonis egestas,' ' propter egestatem linguae '; Pliny's words
might be fitted with difficulty into the hexameter.

his knowledge of the Roman poet and to admit his obligations. The erudition of Pliny the Elder was vast and he was an omniverous reader. He makes a special point of acknowledging his sources. The name of Lucretius appears only once, *i.e.*, in the list of names of sources for his tenth book. In this book there are only two passages,[35] relatively of very slight importance, that might owe anything to Lucretius. Pliny's Books II and VII, that discuss the themes of the ' Mundus,' and of ' Man,' might have shown Lucretian influence. But in the second book Pliny writes, throughout, in the tradition of Platonists, Pythagoreans, and Stoics; he acknowledges indebtedness to Greek and Roman authors, but he does not recognize Lucretius,[36] at least, by name, in his physical speculations, not even honoring him with refutation. Similarly, in the seventh book, Lucretius, it would seem, is intentionally ignored.[37] It is in this book that we find a

[35] Pliny, *Nat. Hist.*, X. 23. 33. 69 and X. 72. 92. 197 and Lucr., IV. 640–641 (on certain poisonous plants that were regarded as good food for goats and for quails) ; Pliny, VII. 2. 2. 15 and Lucr., IV. 637–639 are similar.

[36] He might have had Lucr. in mind, at several points, II. 133, 134, 142, 227, 228, 233.

[37] We are certainly reminded of Lucr. at one point, VII. 1. 1. 2 (Lucr., V. 225 seq., about the infant crying at birth).

famous declaration of belief in the soul's mortality. The passage is pure Epicureanism.

What madness this is, of yours, to suppose that life is renewed in death, what repose are we, after birth, ever to experience, if souls in heaven, if shades in the lower world retain consciousness? This sweet delusion and (vain) credulity in very fact destroy nature's chief gift of death, our greatest blessing, and double the anxiety of the dying with fearful thought of his future. . . . How much easier and more certain it is for each one to put trust in himself and out of his pre-natal experience (*i.e.*, of nothingness) draw the pattern of his future freedom from care! [38]

From whatever source Pliny derived his knowledge of this Epicurean denial of life after death, he does not even mention the great Roman exponent who had most ardently preached the same doctrine, who had written in the same vein of indignation, and who, we suspect, inspired this very passage. Strange silence, indeed!

That Lucretius was 'edited' by Marcus Valerius Probus may be taken as a token that the poet was counted among the 'classics' during the Flavian period. Terence, Lucretius, Virgil, Horace, and Persius were the poets Pro-

[38] Plin., *N. H.*, VII. 55. 56. 190.

bus chose for his editorial labors. But, unhappily, the edition of Lucretius has not survived nor have we any citation from it in later grammarians. Probus was counted an illustrious critic and grammarian; of course his work on Lucretius was a labor of love, whatever the nature of his commentary, whether the latter was chiefly concerned with a study of words or of syntax or both.[39] An 'edition' of Lucretius in the first century of our era — forerunner of the Aldine and Juntine editions of the early Renaissance, of Lambinus, Munro, Giussani of later and distinguished fame!

In the second century it is, in particular, in the work of Fronto and of Aulus Gellius that we learn of the fate of Lucretius. The new Senecan style which Quintilian deplored, the Quintilian championship of the perfection of Cicero and of Virgil, indicate the sharp conflicts of opinion that were waging. "Silver" Latin enjoyed its day but Tacitus' *Dialogus* shows us the trend that was setting in, in favor of the pre-Virgilian modes. The ultra-conservatives were equally opposed to the artificialities of Silver Latin, with its false con-

[39] Cf. J. Aistermann, *De M. Valerio Probo*, Bonnae, Fr. Cohen, 1910.

[187]

ventions and its glittering epigrams, and to undue admiration of authors of the 'Golden' Age as well, and they found vitality in an earlier period. Fronto inherited this reactionary belief, and his commanding influence as a literary critic favored, for the time, a new appreciation of Lucretius. Fronto's net gathered in Ennius, Cato, and the Gracchi; in such writers, Rome was to find living material that might contribute to the creation of the "elocutio novella." Therefore, in the correspondence of Fronto with his friend and pupil, Marcus Aurelius, we find high praise of Lucretius, who again gains his place in the Sun.

Fronto exhorts Marcus Aurelius to be on his guard, constantly, in his choice of words and he gives a number of examples of correct and incorrect usage:

Quam ob rem rari admodum veterum scriptorum in eum laborem studiumque et periculum verba industriosius quaerendi sese commisere.

"Wherefore few indeed of our old writers have surrendered themselves to that toil, pursuit, and hazard of seeking out words with special diligence." [40]

[40] *Ep. ad M. Caes.*, IV. 3. 2, Domino meo Fronto (p. 4, vol. I., tr. of C. R. Haines, in the *L. C. L.*) ; Cato, Sallust, Plautus, Ennius, Naevius, Lucretius, etc. are mentioned.

[188]

The writers he mentions are all, except Cicero who is acknowledged to be

caput atque fons Romanae eloquentiae,

of the earlier stylistic period, and Lucretius was singled out with a few others as conspicuous in discrimination. This late appreciation recalls Lucretius' own testimony [41] to his fervid desire to create, beautifully and nobly.

In another letter [42] of the " Correspondence of Marcus Cornelius Fronto," one addressed to Fronto by Marcus Antoninus, *i.e.,* Pius, the Emperor, the latter asks for prose that is eloquent, as of Cato's, Cicero's, Sallust's, or of Gracchus', and poetry of a kind that may uplift him, extracts from Ennius or Lucretius, 'sonorous' lines and such as 'may give the impress of character.' The writer wished to be exalted and he knew that the poet-philosopher had written many passages of real grandeur. I wish that the letter specified particular passages. The estimate is very like that of Fronto's, in which he says of Ennius, Accius, and Lucretius:

[41] I. 136–145; 921–950.
[42] *Ep. ad Ant. Imp.,* II. 1, magistro meo, 161 A.D. (p. 300, vol. I., Haines) ; εὔφωνα is his word.

ampliore iam mugitu personantes [43]

ringing, now, with deeper, fuller roar.

In keeping with this expression, is the use of the adjective *sublimis* which is applied to Lucretius, elsewhere, in this correspondence, in a letter of Fronto's [44] that manifests the same enthusiasm for Lucretius that Ovid had betrayed in an earlier day! [45]

Whether the archaizing tendencies of the school of Fronto were wise or not, whether this methodology could serve a real purpose or not, the fact remains that this zealous champion of certain canons of style, for a time, at least, re-established the position of Lucretius which had been seriously challenged by another powerful judge of literary standards, viz. Quintilian. Of course, this championship in no way

[43] *Ep. ad Ant. Aug., De Eloquentia*, 3. 2, Fronto (p. 74, vol. II., Haines).

[44] *Ep. ad Verum (?) Imp.*, I. 1. 2 (p. 48, vol. II., Haines); this estimate of Lucretius is taken for granted: In poetis autem quis ignorat ut gracilis sit Lucilius . . . sublimis Lucretius . . . etc. (the phrase, quis ignorat, recalls Velleius Paterculus). Fronto reviews a large number of artists and writers; his use of *sublimis* is no accident!

[45] Other possible references to L.: Fronto to Marcus, *De Fer. Als.*, 3. 1 (p. 5, vol. II., Haines); *ibid.* 8 (p. 15, Haines) employs words of Lucr., VI. 141; Fronto to Ant. Aug., *De El.*, 2. 1, employs words of Lucr., I. 925 (p. 71, vol. II., Haines); I am not sure that these are 'echoes' of Lucretius, as some editors believe.

[190]

carried with it approval of Lucretius' philosophy; Fronto was no philosopher and Marcus Aurelius was, perhaps, the most saintly of the Stoics.

Fronto's appeal to Lucretius, as well as to other early writers of power, could not, perhaps — certainly did not — vitalize the creative spirit and did not result in a new bloom of literature. The tranquillity of the age of the Antonines was accompanied, rather, by a literary decadence, and Aulus Gellius' admiration for the older literature, pleasing but pedantic interest in the miscellanies of learning, language, literature, and customs, all gathered together in his *Attic Nights,* lacked the necessary breath of life. Admiration for Lucretius [46] we find, knowledge of rare usages in the *De Rerum Natura,* familiarity with at least four books of Lucretius, and fine praise: Lucretius is compared with Cicero and Virgil for paying heed to

[46] Aul. Gell., *N. A.,* X. 26. 6–10 (Lucr., IV. 528–9, quoted exactly) on the use of *gradiens;*

A. G., XII. 10. 6–8 (Lucr., VI. 1275) on the use of the words *aeditumi* and *aedituentes;*

A. G., XIII. 21. 21 (Lucr., II. 1153–4, quoted exactly) on the use of the phrase *aurea funis;* Lucr., *elegans;*

A. G., XVI. 5. 6–7 (Lucr., I. 326) on the use of the phrase *vesco sale* and etymology of *vestibulum;*

A. G., V. 15. 1–9 (Lucr., I. 304) whether 'voice' is corporeal or not; Lucr. has *tangere enim et* (not *aut*) etc.

[191]

the sound of words, to the music of his verse, and this finer sense lifted Lucretius, in the opinion of Aulus Gellius, into the ranks of *scriptores elegantissimi.* It is a wonder that Gellius does not cite some memorable verses of splendor. He quotes the opinion of his literary friend, Favorinus, that Lucretius was a poet of 'genius and eloquence.' [47] But it is very obvious that Gellius did not appreciate the philosopher so much; his discussion of Lucretian words leads to no comment on the 'films' or idols, on the plague, on the Lucretian theory that all life springs from this earth and has not been let down from the sky by a golden cord, nor to any discussion of the atoms. He quotes the verse:

Tangere enim aut tangi, nisi corpus, nulla potest res,

For naught but body (i.e., *matter*) *can touch or be touched.*

Seneca [48] also quoted this important verse. It is an essential part of Lucretius' stern and dogmatic discussion about matter that *is,* though

[47] *N. A.,* I. 21. 5 (Virgil had not scorned to follow the authority of Lucretius: auctoritatem poetae ingenio et facundia praecellentis) ; on the word *amaror* (Lucr., IV. 224, quoted exactly).

[48] See n. 13, p. 169 (cf., also, Tertullian and Nonius).

it remains invisible. It is an essential of the Epicurean theory of matter, for which Lucretius argues with vehemence; to touch and to be touched, to act and to be acted upon were properties of matter to which Lucretius attached utmost importance. But Aulus Gellius cared little whether voice was corporeal or not; he cared little what Stoics, Democritus, or Epicurus thought; and Lucretius, as philosopher, did not hold him. He agreed with Ennius' Neoptolemus, who had said:

Philosophandum est paucis; nam omnino haut placet.

Philosophize — a few they must; for all, assuredly, do not find it pleasing.

Aulus Gellius is, ordinarily, quite fair to Epicurus whenever he refers to him and his doctrines, as he does, a number of times. But at one point,[49] he reveals his hostility clearly enough, when he says:

Taurus autem noster, quotiens facta mentio Epicuri erat, in ore atque in lingua habebat verba haec Hieroclis Stoici, viri sancti et gravis, ἡδονὴ τέλος, πόρνης δόγμα· οὐκ ἔστιν πρόνοια, οὐδὲ πόρνης δόγμα.

Whenever mention was made of Epicurus, our friend Taurus always had on his lips and his tongue

[49] *N. A.,* IX. 5. 8.

*the following words of Hierocles, the Stoic, a man
righteous and stern: " Pleasure an end, is a harlot's
doctrine; there is no Providence, not even a harlot
could accept that creed."*

Anyone who could pen such slurring comment,
had not comprehended Lucretius' ethics and
certainly had not accepted, and, probably, had
not understood, Lucretius' earnest and vehement protestations on true religion.

A real, genuine interest in earlier poetry was
largely responsible for a continuance, in the
second century, of Lucretian influence in letters. It is one of those ironies of history that
we are not informed, more fully, of Lucretius'
influence among the ' Epicureans ' of the period.
The Emperor, Marcus Aurelius, as I have said
before, re-established the four leading schools
at Athens; and Epicureanism had its followers,
whose testimony to the empire of Lucretius'
speculation over their minds we should rejoice
to possess. As for example, that group of ' Epicureans ' who dared defy Alexander, the false
prophet of Abonoteichus. Lucian [50] does not
fail to praise Epicurus, and that praise of Epicurus, as saintly and divine, as a liberator of
mankind reminds us of the eulogies of Lu-

[50] *Alexander,* 25, 38, 47, 61.

[194]

cretius. These ' Epicureans ' are represented as exposing the trickeries of Alexander and they are grouped with Christians as the chief enemies of Alexander's religious impostures: " Out with the Christians," " Out with the Epicureans " was Alexander's command, and he publicly burned the Κύριαι Δόξαι, those golden maxims of Epicurus. The Epicurean Celsus, to whom Lucian's essay is addressed, is praised as gentle, reasonable, peaceful, and courteous, which recalls the fine tributes bestowed upon distinguished Epicureans in Rome, in the first century before Christ. But not a word do we hear of Lucretius — whose book was, perhaps, not read in far-away Paphlagonia. It was in remote Oenoanda, in Lycia, that a faithful disciple of Epicurus, Diogenes, built his monument (a portico), to which were affixed the marble slabs bearing his famous Greek Epicurean inscription for all to read who passed that way. Here the ' golden maxims ' of Epicurus were repeated; the temptation is strong to interpret the words that appear in the inscription, τοῦ θαυμασίου Κάρου , as referring to the ' marvellous ' Titus Lucretius Carus.[51]

[51] Cf. R. Heberdey and E. Kalinka, " L'Inscription Philosophique D'Oenoanda," in *Bull. de Corr. Hell.*, XXI.

Such is the story that can be told of Lucretius' place in the early Roman empire. His fame as a poet was exceedingly great, although he had his detractors. Epicureanism assuredly did not lack its followers, and it was, in particular, the doctrines of no Providence, of mortality, and of pleasure that either repelled men or intrigued them and made them converts. Unfortunately, we do not possess the testimony of the Epicureans themselves and, therefore, we do not know how influential Lucretius' definitions of Epicurean ethics and religion were. Stoicism, in a certain sense, in the person of Marcus Aurelius, became the official philosophical creed of the State in the second century and, thereby, Lucretius' influence must have suffered. The two centuries were not favorable, either, to the study of science,[52] and

345–443 (1897); A. Körte, " T. Lucr. Carus bei Diogenes von Oinoanda? ", in *Rh. Mus.*, LIII. 160–165 (1898).

[52] One of the most significant later citations from Lucretius, suggestive of real influence, is that which appears in the medical poem, *De Medicina*, of Serenus Sammonicus. The author, whether the famous physician and polymath who died in A.D. 212, or his son, knew Lucretius' dissertations on child-birth, his protests against the futility of prayer to gods for the blessing of children, his satire against evil practices. About two hundred and fifty years after Lucretius' death, we find this astonishing echo and late tribute to the scientific mind of the " great " Roman.
Cf. Vss. 603 seq.,
Inrita coniugii sterilis si munera languent

in the rush and turmoil of military life, in the conflicts of society, Lucretius must have seemed a personality apart from everyday existence. Virgil's *Aeneid* might command the more immediate attention of dreamers and idealists, the satire of Juvenal and of Tacitus might express, more directly, the sentiments of the realists, and Suetonius gained every ear. Titus Lucretius Carus remained the more remote witness and judge, whose verse continued to charm while his science still seemed a thing somewhat alien to Rome and her world.

nec sobolis spes est, multos iam vana per annos,
femineo fiat vitio res, necne silebo:
hoc poterit magni quartus monstrare Lucreti;
(cf. L., IV. 1233 seq.)   Ser. Sam., *De Med.*, in Baehrens, *Poetae Latini Minores*.   I know of no reference to L. in Celsus; Galen may have known L. (cf. Munro, n., IV. 641).

X. LUCRETIUS AND THE MIDDLE AGES

THE PEACEFUL age of the Antonines and the days of Fronto's great influence were destined to be followed by events, in every way inimical to Lucretius and to all that he stood for. Between the days of Tertullian (A.D. 155–222) and those of Augustine (A.D. 354–430), the world beheld the decline and the fall of the prodigious structure of the Roman Empire and the rise of the Church. Among the 'Fathers of the Church,' Arnobius (fl. A.D. 300) still felt the power of Lucretius' mind, and Epicurean speculation appears in the texture of his Christianity. Lactantius, his pupil, however, pilloried Lucretius, and his merciless attack was intended to be Lucretius' crucifixion, was meant to bring about Lucretius' end. Lactantius would hardly have singled out Lucretius for such conspicuous and frequent assault and refutation unless he had thought that Lucretius was the high priest of Epicureanism for Latin-speaking peoples. Lac-

tantius' condemnation[1] of the Epicurean system was all the more intense because he
believed that its adaptability to different tem-
peraments and its misleading gospel of 'pleasure' had been the secret of its easy success in
the past, was in the present, and might continue
to be in the future. The Church marched on,
and Augustine's *City of God* (publ. A.D. 413–
426) is conclusive testimony to the triumph of
the Church. Epicurean influence had, of
course, continued beyond Lactantius, but Augustine believed that, in his day, Epicureanism
had died.[2] And the voice of Lucretius was
still.[3] The world, at the time, could hardly
appreciate the drama that had been enacted
nor understand the tragedy of his silence. But
when men's faces were turned to Heaven, when
belief in Providence was all that saved from
despair, when hope in Immortality was all that
lighted this world's gloom, when Virtue crowned

[1] Lact., *Div. Inst.*, III. 17.
[2] *Epist.*, II. 118 c. (II. 20, 21; Migne, 2. 442): Quos
iam certe nostra aetate sic obmutuisse conspicimus, ut vix
iam in scholis rhetorum commemoretur tantum quae fuerint
illorum sententiae. As far as I know Augustine refers to
Lucretius and mentions his name, only once, in all of his
vast work [*De Util. Cred.*, 4. 10].
[3] Augustine, possibly, was over-confident. Claudianus
Mamertus still found it necessary to argue against Epicurus
and Lucretius; cf., too, n. 7, p. 12.

the saint, and the monk sought the desert, there was little regard for Nature and her laws, for the appeal, even the beautiful appeal, of the senses and of 'pleasure.' I hardly need to speak of secular events that transpired after the second century A.D.: of plagues, of wars, persecution of Christians, of the transfer of government to Constantinople, of edicts announcing the official end of pagan cults, of Alaric's sack of Rome in 410 A.D.; this panorama of history leads us into the fifth century of bewilderment and paralysis, in which the *City of God* shone as the only sun, moon, or star in the sky. What do we hear of Lucretius in this century that has been called the door to the Middle Ages? Apollinaris Sidonius' sweeping rejection of pagan gods, and his equally sweeping banishment of Greek and Latin authors,[4] including Lucretius; and Jerome's famous dictum that Lucretius had died a madman and a suicide! while Epicurus appears at Martianus Capella's *Nuptials of Mercury and Philology,* bearing roses and violets and all the enticements of pleasure.[5]

[4] *Carm.,* IX. 265, non Lucilius hic Lucretiusque est. (Sidonius was born at Lyons, *ca.* A.D. 431 and died, as Bishop, at Clermont, *ca.* A.D. 489).

[5] II. 213, Epicurus vero mixtas violis rosas et totas

Such was the fifth century Christian world's opinion of Epicurus, and Christianity was no less hostile to his Roman interpreter.[6] Boethius (*ca.* 480–524), admirer of Plato and Aristotle, and Cassiodorus (*ca.* 490–*ca.* 585), historian, statesman, and, perhaps, monk of the Benedictine order, carry this tradition of hostility forward in the fifth and sixth centuries. Boethius scorned the Epicurean doctrine of pleasure and, no less, the atomic theory. 'Epicurus errat' expresses his polemic sentiment briefly, but accurately. He cites Lucretius, apparently, only once;[7] and the purpose is to refute Lucretius and maintain that the universe is created of four 'elements.' Scant attention this, to Lucretius! and when we recall the immense prestige of the *De Consolatione Philosophiae,* throughout the Middle Ages, the fact that it was translated into Anglo-Saxon, into English by

---

apportabat inlecebras voluptatum. Martianus refers to Lucretius, twice — once, on the spelling of a word; once, on a declension.

[6] Of course, there are occasional (real or alleged) imitations of or, even, quotations from Lucretius in the Christian and the secular literature of the third, fourth and fifth centuries that have not escaped scholars: *e.g.,* in Ausonius, Claudian, Commodianus, Juvencus, Prudentius.

[7] *De Inst. Arith.,* II. 1 (Lucr., I. 715); Lucr. is not named.

Chaucer, into German, French, Italian, Spanish before the end of the fifteenth century, we realize what a poor recommendation Lucretius had through Boethius. Cassiodorus, friend of Boethius, was no more friend of Lucretius than was Boethius and he, too, seems to cite Lucretius only a single time, on an unimportant point, and he may be borrowing from Martianus Capella, at that! [8]

Little did these 'Fathers' and the Christian world, at large, comprehend the truth of Lucretius' philosophy of religion. The denial of providence, the idea of 'do-nothing' gods had completely obscured the deeper significance of Lucretius' message. Denial of divine providence had barred Lucretius from any favor that was his due. We have learned that to Lucretius and to Philodemus knowledge of God and communion with God was the supreme 'voluptas.' But neither Christians nor Neo-Platonists, who equally found true happiness in God alone, could grant that Lucretius even had 'religio.'

If space permitted, I should like to follow Lucretius, through the pages of the 'Fathers,' here, but I shall limit myself to a brief presenta-

[8] *De art.*, c. 1. *de nom.*

tion of his ' case' as it appeared to Arnobius and to Lactantius.[9]

ARNOBIUS

It was at Sicca, in Numidia, not far away from Carthage, under Diocletian, that Arnobius [10] wrote his seven volumes *Against the Heathen, ca.* A.D. 295; this work was at once a violent polemic against the heathen, a renunciation of pagan beliefs, and an apologia for his own late conversion to Christianity. Did Arnobius know Lucretius? It has not only been maintained [11] that he knew Lucretius,

[9] Lack of space forbids anything like a full discussion of the ' Fathers' and their references to Epicureanism and Lucretius. Arnobius and Lactantius appear to me particularly interesting, while Augustine's later testimony is, for us, extremely important. Tertullian (*ca.* A.D. 155–222) quotes Lucretius and refutes his soul theory; Jerome (*ca.* A.D. 345–420) and Ambrose (*ca.* 340–397) were violently opposed to the Epicurean theory of *voluptas;* the former raises a question about ' de natura rerum ' and says that he might cite Lucretius, Epicurus, Aristotle, Plato, Zeno, but he prefers to consult the Scriptures, *ubi norma est veritatis* [Hieron., *Adv. Ruf.,* III. 29]; Minucius Felix, St. Hilary, and many others might be cited to illustrate knowledge of and opposition to Lucretius and Epicureanism.

[10] I have followed the text of Aug. Reifferscheid, *Arnobii Adversus Nationes,* Vindobonae, apud C. Geroldi Filium, 1875, in the *Corpus Scriptorum Ecclesiasticorum Latinorum,* vol. IV. I might add that I have read Arnobius, through; but only a small portion of the evidence for my conclusions can be presented here.

[11] J. Jessen, *Ueber Lucrez und sein Verhältniss zu Catull*

thoroughly, but even argued[12] that Arnobius
had been an Epicurean and that it was his
studies in Lucretius, the iconoclast, in particular, that were responsible for his own rebellion
against paganism and his conversion to Christianity. If the truth of the latter claim could
be established, we should have Lucretius appearing in an extraordinarily interesting rôle.
But even if this extravagant claim is not true,
Lucretius' relation toward Arnobius remains
highly significant. Lucretius appears to have
been Arnobius' chief informant on the subject
of Epicurean philosophy, and in so far as Arnobius drew some strands from Epicurean speculation on the nature of God and on the nature
of the soul, and wove them into the web of his
own Christian beliefs, Lucretius was exerting
a very real influence upon the gradual shaping
of Christian dogma. Arnobius does not admit
his obligations frankly, and the truth of the
hypothesis emerges only from a careful reading of a text that is often full of contradictions.
The challenge, however, meets us at many a

---

und Späteren, Kiel, Schmidt und Klaunig, 1872; A. Röhricht,
Die Seelenlehre des Arnobius, Hamburg, Rauhen, 1893.

[12] E. Klussmann, "Arnobius und Lucrez, oder sein
Durch-gang durch den Epikuräismus zum Christenthum,"
in *Philologus,* XXVI. 362–366 (1867).

turn and the ghost of Lucretius appears very
often, in the pages of Arnobius' work, expressing thoughts and speaking a language that is
entirely familiar to the student of the *De Rerum Natura.*

Arnobius mentions Epicurus, by name, twice,
but on neither occasion does he express any
preference or admiration for Epicurus. The
contradictions of all Greek philosophers are
stressed as well as their insufficiency in comparison with Faith in Christ. Arnobius manifests little patience with Epicureans and their
atomic theories. If he ever had been a follower
of Epicurus, he certainly does not admit it.

He actually mentions Lucretius' name [13] only
once. The Christian rebelled against the pagan
conception of gods in human form; he violently
resented associations of sex and sensuality with
divinity:

Yet the pagan mind longed to see, in the great
palaces of the sky, gods and goddesses uncovered
and bare, the full-breasted Ceres of whom Lucretius
has told us . . .

But Arnobius does Lucretius a great injustice;
the verse he has in mind is very far from repre-

[13] III. 10 (p. 118. 18 R.); Lucr., IV. 1168 (Cererem
mammosam).

[205]

senting Lucretius' notions about divinity; a careless reader might easily have been misled. The verse comes in the midst of Lucretius' satire on the blindness of lovers. The Arnobius passage does not indicate the slightest appreciation of the religious thought of the Roman poet.

Did Arnobius understand the Epicurean-Lucretian theory of religion? Of course he knew of the Epicurean denial of Providence:

Thus some deny that there are gods; others say that they are in doubt as to their existence anywhere; *others believe that the gods exist, but that they do not watch over human affairs;* while still others maintain that gods do take part in the affairs of mortals and guide earthly calculations.[14]

Arnobius vigorously opposed the orthodox pagan notion of anthropomorphic gods and he poured all manner of ridicule and contempt upon this ancient belief; sex, generation, passions, human form, mythologies, limitation of any kind, images — such ideas could not be associated with divinity. Arnobius' wonder at God approached mysticism:

If you wish to hear the truth, either God has no form, or, if he is embodied in any form, assuredly

[14] II. 56 (p. 92. 28 R.).

[206]

we do not know what it is. For we do not regard it a disgrace not to know what we have never seen.[15]

One thing alone is certain — that god has been from everlasting to everlasting; he knows no birth nor death, and incorporeality is a possibility of his condition. The true gods are exempt from anger, because this emotion would at once relate them with mortality.[16]

Arnobius' speculation, at first, hardly seems to me to owe much to Epicurean-Lucretian thinking. Arnobius subscribed to the doctrine of divine creation; Lucretius and the Epicureans did not; Arnobius believed in Providence, but ridiculed the minute providential regard of the pagan gods; [17] in the latter form of criticism, he was at one with the Epicureans; Arnobius was unalterably opposed to the pagan anthropomorphic conception of divinity; Lucretius was not; Arnobius hesitated to define the form or appearance of god; Lucretius and the Epicureans did not; Arnobius thought that the gods might be incorporeal; Lucretius believed them to be atomic, although the fineness of those atoms might seem, to some, to lead

[15] III. 17 (p. 123. 20 R.).
[16] VII. 5 (p. 241. 15 R.); cf. III. 11; VII. 23 (p. 256. 1 R.), etc.   [17] III. 20–28.

[207]

away from corporeality; Arnobius despised the mythologies; the Epicureans and Lucretius, also, rejected them as unworthy of divinity; of course others before Epicurus had done so, likewise; Arnobius denied divine anger,[18] and, in this denial, he was in accord with positive Epicurean-Lucretian dogma. His argument and phraseology of denial are remarkably similar to those of Lucretius. Lactantius, on the other hand, re-affirmed the strongest belief in the anger of god and the necessity of such belief.[19] Arnobius may have known and understood the Epicurean-Lucretian theory of god and of religion, but, if he did, he does not admit the fact or any obligation to the school. His utter rejection of the pagan gods [20] and his search for the true god did not result in acknowledgment, at any rate, of indebtedness to Epicurean-Lucretian iconoclastic philosophy. The finest religious outburst of all, an effort to define the divine,[21] carries no suggestion of the Epicurean gods. Arnobius, for all we know, arrived at most of his conclusions in-

[18] VII. 5, 23.
[19] Lact., *Div. Inst.*, III. 17. 35–41 (with refutation of Lucr.).
[20] III. 28 (p. 130. 27 R.).
[21] I. 31 (God, as creator, invisible and incomprehensible, illimitable, not of bodily shape, immortal, perfect, supreme).

dependently of Lucretius. In the absence of acknowledged indebtedness to Epicurus or to Lucretius as his guide in religious speculation, we have no right to draw the conclusion that Lucretius actually led this pagan rebel to his new faith — a service Lucretius could well have rendered him — but we do not know that he did. However, influence of Epicureanism is clearly manifest in important points, and Arnobius certainly knew his Lucretius.

Arnobius was, undoubtedly, we shall see, familiar with the text of Lucretius and it is more than likely that the splendid lines

nec pietas ullast velatum saepe videri
vertier ad lapidem atque omnis accedere ad aras [22]

fell under his eye. His pupil Lactantius quotes the lines. But, even if Arnobius never saw them, his own thinking and other reading could have carried him into his violent tirades against statues, against sacrifice of victims, and the burning of incense. In fact, Epicurean worship was not opposed to the use of images in cult, and Arnobius specifically cites Varro as his pagan witness that sacrifices are worse than futile.[23]

[22] Lucr., V. 1198 seq.
[23] Arnob., VII. 1 (p. 238. 1 R.).

In his discussion of the soul [24] and its origin, Arnobius shows that he has knowledge of the Epicurean doctrine, though he is far from subscribing to it, and his lines occasionally suggest acquaintance with the verses of Lucretius. Learned men, Arnobius says, have been divided in their opinions: some maintain that the soul is subject to death, while others claim that it is divine and immortal.[25] Neither of these conclusions commended itself to Arnobius, because belief in the soul's mortality as well as its immortality did not guarantee ethical standards. Arnobius' cynical conclusion that belief in the soul's mortality justified unrestricted sensual license hardly represents Lucretius' view, and, if Arnobius had ever been a follower of Epicurus, he had certainly rejected both Lucretius' belief in the mortality of all, and, also, the ethical implications of that belief. Although Arnobius felt that, *per se,* the soul was not necessarily either mortal or immortal, yet he believed that the soul might receive life everlasting by the will of the Lord, while savage death might mean the extinction of those souls not received by God.[26] This conclusion clearly

[24] II. 13 seq.   [25] II. 31; cf. ch. 57.
[26] II. 36; cf. 62 (servare animas alius nisi deus omnipotens non potest, etc.) ; *et passim.*

[2 1 0]

steers a middle course between Epicurean theory of nihilism, and, on the other hand, Platonic theories and Christian beliefs in immortality! As for the origin of the soul, Arnobius indignantly and vehemently denies that souls are the children of the Supreme Ruler and that God sent them into this world.[27] A long, bitter tirade[28] on the evils of the human soul and of the world refutes that notion, but gives no suggestion that Arnobius subscribed to the Epicurean-Lucretian theory of the genesis of 'souls.' On the contrary, we have the flat statement:

item confitemur nos istud ignorare, nescire, etc.[29]

If Arnobius ever had been an out-and-out Epicurean, if he ever had genuinely held to the Epicurean views on the origin and fate of the soul, the fact is sufficiently veiled in his second book. There are, however, indications that, at one time, the Epicurean views may have held him. He knew those views and they affected his final conclusions, profoundly. That there are many verbal and other reminiscences of

[27] II. 36 and 43–45.
[28] II. 37–47.
[29] II. 47 (p. 85. 10 R.); cf., however, I. 38, II. 61, for contradictory statements.

[2 1 1]

Lucretius' third book becomes doubly interesting.[30]

There is a very large number of words[31] that students of Lucretius and Arnobius have come to believe were taken from the former by the latter to add piquancy to his style. It is very easy for the subjective element to enter into such studies. But as some, at least, of these very striking words can be shown to be 'Lucretian,' as they appear in Lucretius and then re-appear, for the first time, after hundreds of years, in Arnobius, we have a relatively safe objective criterion and can, without hesitation, believe in the theory of conscious borrowing.[32] This constitutes a rather remarkable

[30] *E.g.,* the use of the word *repetentia* and the argument that goes with it in Arnob., II. 26 and 28 (cf. 18, 19, 28), is accepted by almost all editors [Munro, Merrill, Giussani, Heinze, Ernout, Rouse, Bailey] as Lucretian (III. 670–78, 851); disease, a sign of soul-mortality (Arnob., II. 14, 27; Lucret., III., *passim*); cf., also, Arnob., II. 26 (p. 70. 3 R.) and Lucr., III. 971 (vitaque mancipio nulli datur, omnibus usu); Arnob., II. 30 (p. 73. 17 R.), II. 27, II. 65, II. 2 and Lucr. use of phrase *ianua leti,* V. 373, I. 1111–1112, III. 66–67, VI. 762.

[31] Cf., especially, Röhricht and Diels.

[32] *E.g., circumcaesura* (Lucr., III. 219, IV. 647; Arnob., III. 13 = p. 120. 15 R.): editors agree on this borrowing, which was known, years ago, to Wakefield; *differitas* (Lucr., IV. 636; Arnob., II. 16, etc.); also in Non.; *pestilitas* (Lucr., VI. 1098, 1125, 1132; Arnob., VII. 43 = p. 276. 16 R.); cf., also, Non.; *maximitas* (Lucr., II. 498; Arnob., VI. 18 = p. 230. 20 R.); also in Non.; *aversabilis* (Lucr., VI.

linkage between the two writers and suggests
many interesting conclusions to the detective
mind. Lucretius used the word *pestilitas* in his
gruesome account of the horrors of the plague
at Athens; Arnobius employed it in an un-
merciful condemnation of the Jupiter-concept,
as a cruel, ruthless, irrational god, — which recalls the bitterness of the Lucretian irony.[33]
The two thinkers were in complete agreement
on this score; Arnobius doubtless knew this
Lucretian diatribe against Jupiter and thrusts
this Lucretian word for *pestilentia* into his own
pen-picture of the cruel god. I hardly need to
dwell upon the importance of Arnobius' knowledge of this bold, reckless Lucretian attack
upon Jupiter. Even if Arnobius did not follow
Lucretius in all of his religious speculation,
even if he did not comprehend its significance,
fully, in this passage, at least, he found a pagan religious rebel after his own heart. Lucretius had used the strange, new word *aversabilis* (meaning 'abominable') in the course
of his second fierce condemnation of the pagan
concept of Jupiter, and Arnobius lifts it from

390; Arnob., VII. 45 = p. 279. 12 R.); *repetentia,* see
n. 30, above.
   [33] II. 1090 seq.

this passage and uses the rare word in his ridicule of another pagan god. And it is in Lucretius and Arnobius, alone, that words of this kind are known to appear.[34]

While we have, unquestionably, echoes of Lucretius in Arnobius, while there are significant traces of Lucretian-Epicurean philosophy in Arnobius' theorizing about God and the soul, it is Plato whom Arnobius calls *sublimis*

Plato ille sublimis apex philosophorum et columen,[35]

and it is Cicero to whom he pays a handsome tribute, as the most eloquent of the Roman race who did not fear charges of impiety but who bravely expressed his opinion about God and gods — pietate cum maiore.[36] Such praise is not given Lucretius. Arnobius' famous panegyric[37] on Christ has seemed to many a reflection, undoubtedly, of Lucretius' eulogy of Epicurus; but granted the truth of this, we can hardly claim that Arnobius came under the

[34] Whether all of the words and phrases for which Röhricht argues were actually borrowed from Lucretius by Arnobius is certainly debatable, but a residue remains on which all, I think, can agree.

[35] Arnob., I. 8 (p. 9. 17 R.); cf. II. 36.

[36] III. 6 (p. 116. 1 R.); cf. III. 7 (p. 116. 15 R.); III. 16 (p. 123. 9 R.); V. 38 (p. 208. 13 R.).

[37] I. 38 (p. 25. 1 R.) shows no attachment to Epicurean school; Lucr., V. 1–54; cf. Arnob., I. 39–42 (no mention of Epicurus); II. 60–61 (contradicts I. 38).

spell of Epicurus and Lucretius, or that Lucretius was Arnobius' real spiritual leader. There were too many items in Lucretius' philosophy of religion, to which Arnobius could not subscribe, notably that of sweeping denial of divine providence, for Arnobius to realize the full significance of Lucretius' criticism of and reconstruction of the old pagan beliefs as a two-edged sword, to use against the old religion and in defense of Christianity. Arnobius knew his Lucretius and, I take it, knew him well, and Lucretius, we believe, was his chief literary source of information about the Epicurean doctrines. Christian dogma was in the making and the influence of Lucretius upon Arnobius was potent. The concessions Arnobius, as Christian, made to Lucretian thinking are notable and must not be overlooked. Presently, Arnobius' pupil, Lactantius, and, a little later, Augustine, show us the irreconcilable antithesis between the doctrines of pleasure, soul-mortality, and no Providence — and the new Faith. When that time comes, Lucretius' days are numbered.

LACTANTIUS

While we discover compromises in Arnobius, not so in Lactantius, his pupil. Born a pagan, Lactantius was professor of eloquence in Nicomedia, *ca.* A.D. 290; and, not without good reason, did he come to be known as the 'Christian Cicero' from the style of his *Institutiones Divinae* which was dedicated to Constantine and which remains one of the great doctrinal treatises of the Catholic Church. All of his eloquence was employed in exposition of his own views, and his attitude toward Lucretius and Epicureanism is written very clearly in his works:[38] 'The Divine Institutes,' 'The Work of God,' and 'The Wrath of God.' We see two powerful minds in conflict and the spectacle is no less exciting than was that of gladiators in the Coliseum. As a Christian, Lactantius was entirely out of sympathy with Epicurean denial of divine creation and divine providence; as a

[38] I have used the text of the Vienna *Corpus Scriptorum Ecclesiasticorum Latinorum:* vol. XIX, L. Caeli Firmiani Lactanti Opera Omnia, ed. by S. Brandt and G. von Laubmann, Pars I., *Divinae Institutiones,* libri VII, 1890; vol. XXVII, same editors, Pars II, *De Opificio Dei liber* and *De Ira Dei liber,* etc., 1893, Lipsiae, G. Freytag. I am actually citing only a small proportion of evidence I have collected in full.

Christian, he was equally and unqualifiedly opposed to Epicurean denial of immortality; the Epicurean hedonistic ethical doctrines similarly provoked his opposition. On these three grounds, then, Lactantius argued, fiercely, against the well-known Epicurean doctrines, and to his mind Lucretius was utterly and hopelessly in error. Nor could Lactantius see any values in the atomic theory. So that, had final decision rested with Lactantius, Lucretius would have been banished, forever and ever, from the minds of the thoughtful and the pious.

Lactantius' knowledge of Greek and Latin literature was very large, and for Platonists, Cicero, and Stoics, despite their paganism and the limitations of all pagan knowledge, Lactantius often has highest praise. His conversion to Christianity, which came not long after A.D. 290, carried with it a re-interpretation of pagan literature, to which he had, before, been indebted for his intellectual training. He cites and quotes, very frequently, from a wide range of Greek and Latin authors. Ciceronian and Virgilian citations are particularly numerous, and references to Lucretius follow, next, in frequency. Lactantius was familiar with all six books of the *De Rerum Natura;* he often

[2 1 7]

refers to Lucretius by name; he comments on passages, great and small; he quotes from his Lucretius and quotes with remarkable accuracy. Lucretius owed his importance to Lactantius because of views that seemed false and dangerous to the Christian apologist. Lactantius leaves us in no doubt about his own opinions; dogmatism of Lucretius is met with equal positivism on the part of Lactantius, certitude conflicts with certitude, and reconciliation between the two was out of the question.

The following passage, perhaps as well as any other single passage, shows Lactantius' complete and absolute rejection of Epicureanism and its two leading literary exponents:

Non possum hoc loco teneri quominus Epicuri stultitiam rursum coarguam; illius enim sunt omnia quae delirat Lucretius.

I cannot refrain, at this point, from refuting, a second time, the folly of Epicurus: for his are all of those arguments which Lucretius employs as he raves.[39]

Lucretius' admiration for Epicurus and, especially, his praise of him as divine, evoke particular scorn: [40]

[39] *De Op. Dei*, 6. 1.
[40] *Div. Inst.*, III. 17. 28–29 (Lucr., III. 1043 seq., quoted

He (i.e., Epicurus) *is the man,*
W*ho surpassed the human race in genius, and his*
light
T*he light of all extinguished, even as the etherial*
sun quenches the stars.
I *can, indeed, never read these verses without*
laughter.

Such praise Lactantius felt might have been bestowed, with some justification, upon Socrates
or Plato, but not upon Epicurus, while Lucretius is called: poeta inanissimus.

Lactantius believed, deeply and sincerely, in
divine creation of man and of the world and in
divine providence; to such a mind, Lucretius'
contrary arguments were abhorrent. The tele-
ologist placed the law, the will, the purpose
of God before all else, and natural law was
but an expression of divine intention. The
marvellous construction of the universe, the
amazing adaptation of means to ends in animal
and human organisms were, to the mind of
Lactantius,[41] convincing demonstration of the
divine plan and of divine creation. Epicurus,
that 'homo divinus,' as he is ironically called

---

correctly); cf. *ibid.*, III. 14. 1–4 (Lucr., V. 6 seq. and 50
seq., also correctly quoted).
[41] *Div. Inst.*, III. 17. 16–23; cf. *De Op. Dei*, 6. 8 seq.;
10. 1–13; *De Ira Dei*, 14. 1 seq.

with recollection of Lucretian phrases, had foolishly taken refuge in observation of imperfections in nature, as Lucretius did after him,

tanta stat praedita culpa,

in order to prove that the universe was not divine. Lactantius [42] felt a call to proclaim the truth of the ' *sacramentum mundi et hominis,*' and Epicurus' ignorance and Lucretius' audacity are held up to scorn. Lactantius was familiar with and quoted from the magnificent Lucretian denial of divine creation, in order to combat the Epicurean view. God had made the world and had made man, and this was *veritas:*

deus igitur rerum omnium machinator fecit hominem.[43]

Even Cicero had seen this; Platonists and Stoics knew this truth, and, in the pagan world, Epicureans were conspicuous for their isolation. God is our ' pater noster,' our ' dominus ' who

---

[42] *Div. Inst.,* VII. 3. 13 (Lucr., V. 156–234 quoted correctly) ; *De Op. Dei,* 3. 2 seq. (Lucr., V. 227 is quoted accurately).

[43] *Div. Inst.,* II. 11. 14 (§ 1. this passage is accompanied with ridicule of Lucretius' exposition of the origin of life, V. 771 seq.) ; cf. *Div. Inst.,* VII. 27. 5 and *De Ira,* 10. 16 (cites L.).

created heaven and earth *e nihilo* (a flat contradiction of Epicurean science), and his providence was secure.

Lactantius failed, completely, to apprehend the importance of atomism.[44] Epicurean science was in conflict with his own theory of providence and, therefore, received only scornful treatment from him. But neither Epicurus nor Lucretius believed that their science was in conflict with religion — which Lactantius supposed was the case. Desire for release from fear of false gods did involve abandonment of the principle of providence, but, at the same time, it prepared the way for understanding of and worship of the true god — neither Arnobius nor Lactantius ever discovered this from their reading of Lucretius.

It was inevitable, perhaps, that Lactantius should feel that denial of divine providence was incompatible with worship, prayer, cult — in short, all religious belief and devotion. Earlier critics, Cicero among the rest, and many since Lactantius' day have similarly belabored Epicurean argument and misunderstood Lucretius. Lactantius, indeed, goes so far as to maintain

[44] Cf., *e.g., De Ira,* 10. 3 seq. (ridicule of atomism, without reservation; Lucr. is in his mind, constantly); *Div. Inst.,* III. 17. 23.

that Lucretius had regarded all cult as vain and had said so: [45]

That philosopher and poet sternly accuses those men as humble and abject, who, contrary to the design of their nature, prostrate themselves before and worship images of clay; for he says:

*they abase their souls for dread of gods
and to the earth they crush their depressed spirits.*

Lucretius is criticizing neither idolatry nor worship but only cowardly, debasing fear of gods. And Lactantius quotes the great lines on *pietas* to prove that Lucretius regarded all religious ceremonies and worship of God as an idle service:

for piety does not consist in appearing veiled and turning toward a stone, approaching every altar, falling prostrate on the ground, in spreading palms before the shrines of gods, and sprinkling the altars with the blood of many victims, nor yet in linking vow to vow.

Lucretius, however, did not advocate abolition of worship, because of his denial of providence; and Lactantius failed to quote the concluding verse which defined true *pietas:*

[45] *Div. Inst.*, II. 3. 10–11 (Lucr., VI. 52 seq. and V. 1198–2002; quotations are essentially correct); cf. *Epit.*, 20 (25). 4.

sed mage pacata posse omnia mente tueri,

piety consists in cherishing [46] *these rites, while we keep our minds at peace and free from fear.*

Lactantius could not, apparently, understand the Lucretian definition. Lucretius, who denied providence, and Lactantius, who defended it, locked horns. The latter believed that religion rested on this basic principle, the former championed a new Heaven and a new Earth, without Providence.

Lactantius rejoiced to find critics of the old religion among the pagans.[47] And he [48] pounced upon Lucretius' stinging rebuke of the practice of human sacrifice; in so doing, he gives Lucretius credit for his horror at the hideous idea of human immolation; he closes his chapter with another citation [49] that should have given him some idea of Lucretius' ethical idealism but did not do so. Lactantius [50] availed him-

---

[46] ' observing ' (in a double sense) would seem to me a perfect translation of *tueri*.

[47] *Div. Inst.*, II. 3. 12.

[48] *Ibid.*, I. 21. 14 (Lucr., I. 101, is quoted correctly; a second line, L., I. 83, is treated somewhat freely).

[49] *Div. Inst.*, I. 21. 48 (quotes Lucr., II. 14–16, which, however, has no bearing on the religious practices of which Lactantius is speaking; the quotation is nearly exact).

[50] *Div. Inst.*, III. 17. 10 (Lucr., II. 1101–1104, quotation very nearly exact).

self, too, of the Lucretian criticism of the Jupiter-concept, known to him and, as we have seen, to Arnobius as well. But he failed to give Lucretius credit for his courage or praise for his poetry and, apparently, failed to see that the iconoclast was breaking the old mould and, so far, preparing the world for ultimate acceptance of a new religion.

Although Lactantius[51] suggested a Lucretian definition of the word 'religio' as the force that binds us to God, although he applauded[52] Lucretius' intent to release men's minds from superstition, he could see no values in the Epicurean-Lucretian conception of heaven and gods, and Lucretius' magnificent lines never suggest adoration to this devout Christian. All of the Lucretian enthusiasm for gods, as he envisaged them, was lost on Lactantius. On the contrary, religion would be destroyed by belief in gods, as Epicurus described them and as Lucretius ecstatically hymned them.[53] Religion is overthrown, if

---

[51] *Div. Inst.*, IV. 28. 12–13, *religio* and *religare* (Lucr., I. 932): eo melius ergo id nomen Lucretius interpretatus est, qui ait ' religionum se nodos solvere.'

[52] *Div. Inst.*, I. 16. 3.

[53] *De Ira*, 8. 1 seq. (Lucr., II. 646–651, correctly quoted).

we believe Epicurus. Cicero had said the same thing and his label of 'nihil agentes' the 'do-nothing' gods, to describe the gods of the Epicurean school, did them, I fear, irreparable damage — though the phrase, so easily bandied from mouth to mouth, is far from true. Lactantius has only ridicule for these gods and he summons Cicero as witness to the folly of worshipping gods who do not care; he concludes that intellectual and moral confusion will follow upon abandonment of the idea of providence:

haec dum sentit Epicurus, religionem funditus delet: qua sublata, confusio ac perturbatio vitae sequetur.

in entertaining such thoughts, Epicurus utterly destroys religion: take it (i.e., Providentia) away, and confusion and disorder will overtake life.[54]

Such was not Lucretius' belief, but Lactantius either could not rise to the idealism of the Roman poet or could not comprehend the subtleties of the Epicurean argument. Without providence and the old idea of reciprocal relations of give and take between man and

[54] *Ibid.*, 6 (in one sentence only does Lactantius hint at Lucretius' idealism, § 3).

god, religion was at an end. So Lactantius thought; at least he did not accuse Lucretius of atheism.[55]

Lactantius, his face turned toward God, held to the conviction that from God alone came wisdom and knowledge of good behavior. Pagan ethics were on a lower plane than the Christian: Socrates, Plato, Seneca caught glimpses of the truth, but even the most enlightened of the pagans saw but the shadow of virtue. God alone could honor virtue, the greatest reward of which was immortality:

est enim deus qui solus potest honorare virtutem, cuius merces immortalitas sola est.[56]

Epicurean defense of ' voluptas ' was anathema and Epicurus was merely a *voluptarius!* [57] As the denial of providence, so the denial of immortality, and the advocacy of pleasure meant absolute destruction of all private and public morals. Lactantius could hardly approve of the Lucretian denial of immortality:

---

[55] *De Ira*, 22. 2 (an attack on the Ep. idea of gods without anger; Arnobius had conceded this point).

[56] *Div. Inst.*, III. 27. 13.

[57] *Div. Inst.*, III. 27. 5; criticism of *voluptas* appears repeatedly; cf., especially, *ibid.*, III. 17. 1 seq.

Nunc argumenta eorum qui contra disserunt re-
fellamus: quae Lucretius tertio libro executus est.[58]

And he was blind to Lucretius' interpretation
of ethics. The former position we readily understand, but the latter, ignoring Lucretius as
moralist, ignoring Lucretius as satirist, was the
product of bigotry, of unyielding opposition to
voluptas. *Virtue* was enthroned and she had
no commerce with her enemy, pleasure which
meant death.[59]

The Roman follower of Epicurus fell under
Lactantius' stern disapproval, although this did
not prevent Lactantius from quoting a noble
passage of Lucretius, a eulogy of Epicurus, and
applying the words to the Son of God!

Him let us follow, let us all heed Him, and obey
Him with utmost devotion, because He, alone, as
Lucretius says,
purged men's hearts with words of truth,
and set a limit to desire and to fear,
explained the ' summum bonum ' for which all strive,

[58] *Div. Inst.,* VII. 12. 1 seq. (the chapter is full of
echoes of Lucr.).
[59] *Div. Inst.,* VI. 20–23. Cf. " The Pleasures of the
Senses," in English translation of F. A. Wright, *Fathers of
the Church,* pp. 160 seq., London, G. Routledge and Sons,
1928.

and pointed out the road, the narrow way,
by which we may struggle on, straight to our goal.[60]

Yet no appreciation of the ethical significance of these lines, of their lofty aspiration, accompanies the quotation! [61]

THE GRAMMARIANS

A long line of lexicographers, commentators, grammarians, and etymologists continued to quote Lucretius; and appearance of Lucretian verses in their work is not only evidence of an uninterrupted interest of a sort in the *De Rerum Natura,* from the time of Augustus to the ninth century, but also a guarantee that Lucretius was not wholly forgotten. By the fifth century, Augustine thought that the Epicurean poet's verse was hushed, and, perhaps, his influence was ended. The service the lexicographer and grammarian could render him was, at most, to prevent extinction of his name and his fame in the world. The lexicographer is interested in the use of words, the grammarian, in syntactical constructions, the

[60] *Div. Inst.,* VII. 27. 6 (Lucr., VI. 24 seq., correctly quoted, except for *hominum* of vs. 24 and *limite* of vs. 27).
[61] *Div. Inst.,* VI. 10. 7, praises Lucretius but the praise rests on a false interpretation of L., II. 991–992.

etymologist, in origins of words, but their combined work could save neither the radiant poet nor the buoyant thinker. Scholarship of this kind does not necessarily reveal the thought or the philosophy of the author who is quoted, whose words and grammatical constructions are subjected to study. Marcus Verrius Flaccus, or ' Pauli-Festus,' may be accurate in quotation but the *De Verborum Significatu* tells not one tittle about Lucretius' philosophy. Nonius Marcellus (fourth century) quotes the poet, with but few errors, but the grand lines he cites in his *De Conpendiosa Doctrina* leave the reader in complete ignorance about Lucretius' speculation. Priscian (fl. *ca.* 500) was of importance, as was Nonius, in transmission of the text; he exhibits accuracy in quotation; but Lucretius' existence in all of this work was but a pale reflection of his one-time logical vitality and poetic splendor. At least there was no animus in these writers, such as possessed Isidore; the Christian quoted Lucretius for his own purposes, but appears to suppress the Epicurean, with a conscious intent and hostility; Lucretius' stature has shrunk to insignificance. If the text of Lucretius had been lost, irrevocably, our lexicographers and grammarians would provide us with small material to reconstruct the *De Rerum Natura;* [62] those fragments, torn from the flesh and blood of their context, might suggest a poet of power, a poet to whom the word was a symbol of exact thought or of great beauty, a poet whose mind had touched on almost every theme of human interest, but they could not tell us that Lucretius had put into Latin verse an amazing exposition of Epicurean philosophy. Lucretius' name is carried on, in this tradition of the lexicographer and the grammarian, but his fame could be, at most, that of a gifted versifier, a lover of archaic language, and an artist with magic skill who had made a great name when Latin poetry was first coming into its own. [63]

[62] Too much, I think, has been made of the fact that the 'grammarians' transmitted Lucretius to the Middle Ages, as though that transmission carried with it real knowledge of the poet! I have examined all the relevant passages in Keil.

[63] I have, in the following pages, considered, more fully, a few of the 'grammarians.' But their testimony is typical. Lucretius was known to many others of the same period; we might surmise that, à priori. *E.g.*, Donatus (fourth century), teacher of Jerome, reproaches Lucretius violently for his immorality and refers, with scorn, to Lucretius' dissertation on love. Servius' (second half of fourth century) respect for Lucretius, as scientist, was genuine. Servius was not in sympathy with Lucretian denial of immortality; he fails to praise Lucretius, as poet, although he recognizes Lucretius' great influence upon Virgil. Even Macrobius' (fl. 395–423) numerous citations from Lucretius (about

The Varronian [64] interest in antiquarian lore on the part of Marcus Verrius Flaccus, the learned freedman and the preceptor of Augustus' grandsons, was manifested in his lexicon, *De Verborum Significatu*. The abridgment of Pompeius Festus, probably in the second century A.D., and the subsequent epitome made by Paulus Diaconus, contemporary of Charlemagne (742/3–814), indicate the importance of this dictionary for many hundred years. Lucretius appears sixteen times in this lexicon; sixteen times, words from Lucretius are discussed because of their antiquarian interest to the lexicographer; sixteen times, opportunity to dwell on Lucretius, as poet or philosopher, was neglected; but such was not the purpose of this student of words and their usage in Latin literature; sixteen times, we have testimony to Verrius' knowledge of the *De Rerum Natura* and its author. We see him pouring over words that seemed to him important, either because

---

forty in number) prove only that Macrobius knew all six books of the *De Rerum Natura* and that the *poet* was admired.

[64] Varro does not, to my knowledge, cite Lucretius in his *De Lingua Latina,* unless, perhaps, *Frag.* 91 (see Goetz & Schoell ed., 1910). This does not, of course, mean that he did not know Lucretius; he could not, possibly, have remained in ignorance of him.

they were archaic, unusual, obscure in meaning, strictly poetic, or used by Lucretius with new significance. We are rather surprised that *sagax* should call for citation from Lucretius or that *nectar*[65] should remind Verrius of the poet of the atomic theory. We are interested to learn that Verrius Flaccus quotes his Lucretius, correctly, in the main; indeed, we owe him the correct reading of one line; Verrius counted Lucretius among the "ancients," because of his vocabulary; we are amused by his errors and his curious selection of words.[66]

Nonius Marcellus[67] cites Lucretius one hundred and seven times, and verses from all six books of the *De Rerum Natura* appear in his huge lexical work that consisted of twenty books. These verses are quoted to illustrate the meaning of words, and Lucretius, the poet, was obviously well-known to Nonius, in the

[65] *Nectar* Graece significat deorum potionem. Unde Vergilius ait (*A.*, I. 433) . . . item Lucretius lib. II (847): et nardi florem, nectar qui naribus halet. (Lucr., II. 848, Fest. fr., p. 160. 20 L.) I have used the Teubner text, edited by W. M. Lindsay, 1913.

[66] *E.g.*, quamde, petulantes, tuditans, momen, suboles, etc.

[67] Nonius Marcellus wrote his lexical work, *De Conpendiosa Doctrina* libri XX, in all probability at the beginning of the fourth century. He was a native of Numidia. I have used the Teubner text, edited by W. M. Lindsay, 1903, 3 vols.

fourth century. He quotes these verses with remarkable accuracy and, if he was familiar with the context of the lines, he was acquainted with practically all of the great ideas of Lucretius. At least he knew that Lucretius had written many brilliant, many sonorous verses; his readers would also learn, from him, that the poet was more akin to the older writers who had preceded Lucretius, than he was to the poets of the Augustan age. As a student of words, Nonius was conscious of many striking qualities of the Lucretian vocabulary: Lucretius' use of newly coined words, his free use of old words with new meanings, and his fondness for archaisms; his reader would readily gather the impression that Lucretius was a poet of remarkable originality and boldness in the use of the Latin tongue.[68] But all of these quotations, assembled together, could not guarantee the life of a single doctrine in which Lucretius was so intensely interested. Nor are these doctrines revealed with any clarity by verses that are torn from their context:

humana ante oculos foede cum vita iaceret
in terris, obpressa gravi sub relligione [69]

[68] Some of these words appear in Arnobius.
[69] L., I. 62 seq. (Non., 314. 30, 327. 1, 379. 10); cf.

nec bene promeritis capitur neque tangitur ira [70]

ac veluti pueris absinthia taetra medentes
cum dare conantur [71]

No reader could possibly tell from Nonius' citations or from his commentary what the true
significance of these lines was — that we have,
here, high eulogy of Epicurus, definition of the
nature of divinity, and a famous statement of
Lucretius' scientific-poetic procedure.

To quote

tangere enim et tangi, nisi corpus, nulla potest res [72]

in order to illustrate the meaning of *tangere*
hardly proclaims Lucretius the materialist even
to the intelligent reader. And other citations
do not show us Lucretius, either as atomist or
as Epicurean. They leave us utterly in the
dark about the true nature of the Lucretian
philosophy and give us a pathetic presentation
of Lucretius' thought.

Vagor may be used for *Vagitus;* well and

Teubner text of Lindsay, 1903; Lucr. quoted under words
grave, iacet, religiosos.

[70] L., II. 651 (Non., 252. 38, 408. 23; Non. thought that
this verse came in Bk. I); Lucr. quoted under the words
capere, tangere.

[71] L., IV. 11 seq. = I. 936 (Non., 413. 17, 190. 25 *ac*
is not correct); Lucr. quoted under the words *taetrum,
absinthium.*

[72] L., I. 304 (Non., 408. 25).

good, and important enough as a lexical fact, but to quote

et superantur item; miscetur funere vagor [73]

without further comment, fails to indicate the important message of the original passage. From a reading of the lines quoted from the third book, anyone could infer that Lucretius had written about the soul, about disease and death, and about human conduct; but what Lucretius had actually thought about the soul, its nature, its mortality or its immortality, or about ethics does not appear from the quoted verses.[74] Likewise, the verses quoted from the fifth book are almost all meaningless, out of their setting; creation, evolution, the ultimate destruction of the universe — the great themes of the fifth book — vanish from our view.[75] And the context of the sixth book, too, must have remained almost a mystery to the reader of Nonius Marcellus.

For the transmission of the Lucretian text, Nonius was of real importance. Superb writing

[73] L., II. 576 (Non., 184. 20); Lucr. quoted under the word *vagor*.
[74] Non., 124. 10 will illustrate this. Cf., *e.g.*, e terra magnum alterius spectare laborem, L., II. 2 (Non., 402. 14).
[75] Non., 415. 31 gives one an inkling, but that is all.

there had been. But these verses are tantalizing fragments, that required restoration to their original setting to determine their real meaning. Winged words, to be sure, but a later age would be sadly put to it to gather their real import, and, could Lucretius have lived to see this collection of verses, it must have filled his soul with dismay that his doctrine was so obscured.

Twenty-six passages from Lucretius are quoted by Priscian and the reasons of the grammarian for quoting these are various: to illustrate the -*um* genitive plural ending for -*arum*, to call attention to peculiarities in the conjugation of verbs, to point to the -*ai* genitive ending of first declension nouns, to exhibit archaisms. This represents the kind of study of Lucretius that interested Priscian and the kind of references that we find to Lucretius, in his enormous work, *Institutiones Grammaticae*. The invocation to Venus provides Priscian with the word 'Aeneadum' for study; [76] the eulogy of Epicurus near the beginning of the first book arrests him because of the verb 'cupiret'; [77]

[76] L., I. 1; Pr., vol. I., p. 292. 18 H.
[77] Lucr., I. 70 seq.; Priscian, vol. I., p. 499. 8 H. (references are to Keil's *Grammatici Latini*, Teubner, 1855 and 1859, Ed. by Hertz).

the rationalization of the Tartarus myth calls for comment on 'Acherunte'; [78] a description of the behavior of atoms is quoted to discuss compounds of 'facio'! [79] Passages, great and small, are cited but absolutely without comment on their significance. Priscian quotes correctly in most cases, while his reading [80]

ex insensilibus ne credas sensile *nasci*

becomes the center of dispute regarding Honorius of Autun's knowledge of Lucretius.

Of Priscian's knowledge of the text of Lucretius there is, certainly, no doubt, and his knowledge was apparently extensive. His citations from the whole body of ancient literature plainly indicate the wide knowledge of Greek and Latin authors, still prevalent in the fifth century. Priscian was a native of Caesarea, in Mauretania, although he wrote his work in Constantinople, *ca.* 491–518. The fact that his work was widely read in the Middle Ages and after, secured the name, at least, of Lucretius from complete oblivion. But the fifth century in the West was no time for a proper

[78] L., III. 978; Pr., vol. I., p. 27. 2 H.
[79] L., II. 155 seq.; Pr., vol. I., p. 401. 12 H.
[80] Lucr., II. 888; Pr., vol. I., p. 132. 21 H. (Pr. reading *nasci,* incorrect).

study of Lucretius, and Lucretius' own words become prophetic:

nam neque nos agere hoc patriai tempore iniquo possumus aequo animo.[81]

Real knowledge of Lucretius was obliged to wait on happier days.

While Lucretius' position in the history of literary or philosophical culture, as revealed by Priscian, was insecure, by the time of Isidore, Bishop of Seville, *ca.* 602–636, the poet had fallen into greater obscurity, if we take Isidore's *Etymologiae* as evidence. Priscian, the grammarian, had at least been a careful student of texts and words; in Isidore's *Etymologiae* we find fewer citations, less accuracy in the transmission of the texts, and passages of lesser consequence cited.

In no sense does Isidore present Lucretius as a significant figure. In the *Etymologiae,*[82] Lucretius is cited fourteen times, but not a single citation proves him either a great poet or thinker, least of all as an Epicurean. Not

[81] I. 41 seq.
[82] Isidori Hispalensis Episcopi *Etymologiarum Sive Originum* libri XX, Ed., W. M. Lindsay, Oxonii, E Typographeo Clarendoniano, 2 vols., 1910. H. Dressel, *De Isidori Originum Fontibus,* Augustae Taurinorum, Vincentius Bona, 1874, includes Lucretius among the ' sources ' of Isidore.

[238]

the slightest trace of this appears in the Span-
iard's etymological work! Howsoever insufficient Isidore ranks as an etymologist, he cites
verses from Lucretius, it would appear, absolutely at random, and, in most cases, other
authors might very well have better been cited
to illustrate the meaning and the use of the
word under discussion.[83] From the Lucretian
citations, one might have concluded that Lucretius had written on a considerable variety of
subjects, as superstition, agriculture, Empedoclean philosophy, weather, city-streets, winds,
horticulture, mythology, animal life, metal-
lurgy — or almost any theme that these casual
words suggest. Lucretius, the poet of energy
and confidence, has become a mere shadow,
and if his place in the *Etymologiae* faithfully
reproduces the estimate of him, held by the
seventh century, Lucretius' influence, his fame,
his significance were well-nigh at an end, and
his name, only one of many, a mere name over
which cobwebs of forgetfulness were gathering.

The *Etymologiae* are encyclopaedic in character and many ancient authors are cited. In
such a comprehensive work, Lucretius would,

[83] Perhaps an exception should be made of the quotation from Lucr., V. 1275.

undoubtedly, have played a larger rôle, if Lucretius and his science, his theory of God and of the soul had occupied a place of importance in the mind of Isidore. Book VIII includes a chapter entitled "De Philosophis Gentium"; Lucretius is not honored with mention. Epicurus is roundly condemned as the lover of *voluptas,* who had denied divine providence, who had explained the world on the basis of behavior of atoms and chance, who had said that the soul was corporeal.[84] This passage shows, clearly enough, a deep prejudice against the doctrines of the Epicurean school. Book XIII is on the subject of the universe, 'elements,' atoms; five passages from Lucretius appear in this book, but not a sign of Lucretian science is betrayed or knowledge of it. Even granting that, as etymologist, Isidore was under no constraint to reveal the truth about Lucretius, it is difficult to imagine a more complete concealment of knowledge, if knowledge he had. Lucretius emerges scarcely as important or even as enlightened. I cannot believe that Isidore recognized the high rank of the Roman poet of science; or, perhaps, he did not wish to. When we remember that the *Etymologiae*

[84] *Etym.,* VIII. 6. 15-16.

gather together so much of all of Isidore's work
and that it fairly represents the intellectual
culture of the early Middle Ages, that in spite
of its blunders and shallow thinking it exerted
a great and wide influence for long, we discover the prison in which Lucretius was con-
fined.

Isidore quotes a verse from Lucretius in a
manner that is entirely misleading.[85]   Under
the word *imber,* he says:

Ex his enim cuncta creantur, unde et Lucretius,
E*x igni, terra atque anima nascuntur et imbri* —

which is Empedoclean and not Epicurean philosophy. He may properly illustrate the meaning of a word by a citation from Lucretius; [86]
or even quote a verse, quite aptly: [87]

Vulturnus, quod alte tonat, De quo Lucretius
Altitonans Vulturnus et Auster fulmine pollens.

There are no citations from the third book
of the *De Rerum Natura,* and the largest number of verses, six in number, is quoted from

---

[85] *Etym.,* XIII. 10. 4; Lucr., I. 715, not quoted exactly.
[86] On *caelum,* used for *aer; Etym.,* XIII. 4. 3; Lucr.,
IV. 132, not quoted exactly.
[87] *Etym.,* XIII. 11. 5; Lucr., V. 745 (one of the few
distinguished lines quoted).

[241]

book V. Isidore was not in sympathy with the Epicurean denial of immortality or with the Epicurean theory of natural creation and evolution. The six passages that are cited from the fifth book are, as quoted, quite harmless,[88] and, similarly, in Isidore's *De Natura Rerum*,[89] there is no suggestion of Lucretius' bold iconoclasm.[90] I can hardly conclude that Lucretius loomed large to the mind or to the imagination of Isidore, and, if we take the Bishop of Seville as an index of his age, Lucretius did not figure, greatly, in the thought of the seventh century. Almost complete neglect, in fact, has overtaken the Roman poet, and the great vogue of Isidore's *De Natura Rerum* through the Middle Ages is in ironical contrast to the oblivion that was enshrouding the earlier, the mighty *De Rerum Natura*.

[88] His comment on Lucr., V. 1275 seq. is sufficiently ample to suggest that Isidore may have been familiar with the great Lucretian discussion of the evolution of human society; *Etymol.*, XVI. 20. 1.

[89] Edition of Migne, *Patrologiae Cursus Completus,* i.e. *Patrologiae Latinae,* Tomus LXXXIII, 1862. The date of the *De Natura Rerum* is fixed by its dedication to King Sisebutus (612–620). Isidore cites Lucretius, at least twice, and there are a few ' echoes ' of Lucretius besides.

[90] Isidore's *De Natura Rerum* covers a wide variety of themes and made direct or indirect use of many earlier authors. His *Praefatio*, while professing real scientific independence, acknowledges the authority, in particular, of ' catholicorum virorum.'

Conclusion

The Church had frowned on Epicureanism, and, as early as the fifth century, as far as the Church was concerned, 'Epicureanism' was no more. 'Grammarians' concerned themselves with Lucretius and we have seen the kind of existence that was his, in their work, as late as the eighth century of Charlemagne. Cramped at the best, that existence became of less and less importance, until Lucretius distinctly appears of minor consequence in the pages of Isidore. After Boethius' death, his *De Consolatione Philosophiae* reigned for hundreds of years. The Christian movement, taking advantage of affiliations in thought with Platonism, swept all before it; and, if Lucretius was known at all, at first hand, for hundreds of years after the ninth century, it was only sporadically and accidentally that he was known and it becomes an increasingly difficult task to determine the fact. It is commonly held [91] that the poet and philosopher passed into an eclipse that was virtually complete and, as far as real influence is concerned, that is

[91] *E.g.*, Munro, Sandys, Teuffel, etc. *vs.* Manitius, Jessen, Philippe.

[243]

practically true. Perhaps not an extraordinary phenomenon, — considering the contemporary profound belief of the Middle Ages in God and in providence, the certain conviction that the soul is immortal and that virtue is an essential for admission to Heaven. During these centuries, Epicureanism was an unwelcome philosophy and Lucretius was an alien. His ostracism from the lives and thoughts of men is all but complete and is comparable to the phenomenon, even more astonishing, of his physical, personal disappearance from the human scene in the first century before Christ.

Known, somewhat, to the Venerable Bede (672/3–735),[92] through the medium of the grammarians, which indicates a slight knowledge, at least, of Lucretius in England, Lucretius was also known to Rabanus [93] Maurus (ca. 784–856); but here, too, we cannot establish with any certainty that Rabanus knew Lu-

[92] Cf. Bede's *De Arte Metrica* for two slight references to Lucretius by name, and *De Nat. Rer.*, c. 40, which seems to show knowledge of Lucr., VI. 608 (cf., also, L., VI. 868 and Bede).

[93] *E.g., De Laudibus Sanctae Crucis,* (prol.) on 'synaloepha' and Lucretius. 'Synaloepha,' which is mentioned both by Bede and Rabanus, is discussed in Isidore (*Etym.,* I. 35. 5). Philippe makes, I think, too much of L.'s influence on Bede and on Rabanus. We must remember the large extent of their total work.

cretius in any real sense; some incidental quotations may be derived from Priscian and Isidore, while it is just possible that Rabanus had access to the MS of Lucretius that lay in the library of St. Martin's church at Mainz, Rabanus' see. This MS is one of the two famous MSS of Lucretius, now in Leyden. But we have the suggestion, in this incident, that some slight knowledge of Lucretius in Germany was a possibility. Wilhelm of Hirschau, abbot of the famous Benedictine monastery in Hirschau, in Württemberg, from 1069–1091, seems to quote a verse of Lucretius, that also appears in a work ascribed to Honorius of Autun (fl. *ca.* 1120); but we are not certain of the proper ascription of the works in question, to Wilhelm or to Honorius, and, in any case, the verse is quoted inaccurately and seems, quite certainly, to be derived from Priscian's inaccurate citation: [94]

ex insensilibus ne credas sensile *nasci.*

Marbod, bishop of Rennes, who died in 1123, is known to have opposed 'Epicureanism' in his day; [95] he appears, somehow, to have had

[94] Priscian, see n. 80.
[95] Likewise Villani, in Florence, later.

some acquaintance with Lucretius.[96]   But all
of these stray references, waifs that appear,
here and there, in a large literature of centuries, and a few more that might be cited[97]
truly sound like echoes from a grave and they
are in marked contrast to the fuller knowledge
of and admiration for Cicero and Virgil.   The
few extant Lucretian MSS of which we have
knowledge exerted, apparently, a minimum of
influence: the one at Mainz, of the ninth century, now at Leyden, and called "A"; the
other, also, now, in Leyden, and called "B,"
of the tenth (or, perhaps, of the ninth century),
which reposed in the abbey of St. Bertin which
is near St. Omer and Corbie; MSS are known

[96] The 'echo' of Lucr. [omnia cum vita tollentur com-
moda vitae] is said to be based on L., III. 2 and 898 seq.
This does not seem convincing to me.

[97] Cf., J. E. Sandys, *A History of Classical Scholarship*,
vol. I, pp. 608 seq. (The case of Richard of Bury is
especially interesting; he may have known of Lucretius
only through Aulus Gellius and Macrobius; I cannot guess
how Ermenrich of Ellwagen [*ca.* 850] happened to know
L., I. 150–156) and Manitius, Munro, Philippe. I should
like to add the name of Sicco Polenton to this brief list
of later writers who knew something of Lucretius. Sicco
was born in 1375/1376 and his references indicate that he
knew about Lucretius through Quintilian, Donatus and
Jerome; Sicco wrote that L. might have been a *summus
poeta*, if not insane (cf., B. L. Ullman, *Sicconis Polentoni*,
etc., Papers and Monographs of the Am. Ac. in Rome,
vol. VI., 1928). Jean de Meung (d. 1305) may also have
had some knowledge of L.

[246]

to have been at Corbie (near Amiens) *ca.* 1200, at Murbach in the upper Vosges, and at Bobbio. They lay neglected and all but unknown, and their small number is also witness to the long disappearance of Lucretius from the world of thought and of letters — from the European mind for five or six hundred years!

Lucretius' name had not perished, his work was slightly known, here and there, but darkness and complete oblivion might have enveloped him if the other-worldliness [98] of the Middle Ages had not yielded to the spirit of the Renaissance.

[98] No one would claim that Dante († 1321) knew Lucretius in any other way but at second-hand. Dante's unfavorable opinion of Epicurus is well-known. Dante may have known Statius' fine eulogy of L. There are a number of striking passages in D. that sound 'Lucretian.' If they are real echoes of L., they were derived from current quotations from L. The connecting link may be difficult to determine but I hope, some day, to make the relation clear.

XI. LUCRETIUS AND THE
RENAISSANCE

PETRARCH (1304–1374) knew Lucretius only at second-hand, and his chief informant, Macrobius, could, at best, acquaint him with single lines or with groups of verses that proclaimed Lucretius akin to Ennius, in style; as, occasionally, a poet of the grand manner who had influenced Virgil; but neither as scientist nor as iconoclast. Petrarch could not possibly have had any real or full knowledge of Lucretius who is so largely obscured by these fragments of poetry and of thought that happen to lie buried in Macrobius' *Saturnalia*. Petrarch was enraptured with the style of Cicero and of Virgil, his acquaintance with Latin literature was wide, he had a passion for discovering and transcribing new MSS, but his "Letters to Dead Authors"[1] include no address to Lucretius, whom Italy did not know sufficiently well in the fourteenth

[1] To Cicero, Virgil, Horace, Livy, Seneca, Quintilian, Homer.

[248]

century. Boccaccio (1313–1375) was equally, perhaps even more remotely, familiar with the *De Rerum Natura*. Had the author of the *Decameron* known Lucretius' masterpiece, we can well imagine the enthusiasm with which he would have acclaimed it. Boccaccio, as humanist and scholar, was intensely interested in the ancient civilization, in general; in Livy and Tacitus, in particular; and in acquiring a knowledge of Greek. Lucretius was all but outside his ken. Italy of the fourteenth century had almost forgotten one of her greatest poets. The day of his re-discovery, however, was near at hand; what with air, tingling with the excitement of the Renaissance, Petrarch, Boccaccio, and Salutati eagerly discovering new MSS, and Chrysoloras (*ca.* 1350–1415), called 'litterarum Graecarum restitutor,' arousing enthusiasm for the study of Greek, the dazzling light of Lucretius that had been all but extinguished, was soon to shine again. Chrysoloras died in Constance, and among the mourners at his funeral was Poggio Bracciolini.

It was the latter, the distinguished Italian humanist, Poggio (1380–1459), who restored Lucretius to fifteenth-century Italy. He was in attendance upon the Council of Constance (1414– May of 1418), as apostolic secretary for the Pope, and it was during those years, between May of 1415 and November of 1417, that Poggio engaged in expeditions that set out from Constance, and conducted enthusiastic explorations for precious Latin MSS that lay neglected and forgotten in monasteries. These expeditions were four in number and were conducted in the summer of 1415, again in 1416, early in 1417, and in the summer of 1417; the first of these was to Cluni and it was richly rewarded; the second, to St. Gall, and the spoils were even richer; the third, amid wintry snows, to St. Gall and other monasteries, and, again, the discoveries were brilliant; and the fourth, probably to Langres on the Marne, and to unnamed monasteries of France and Germany. Among his prizes Poggio counted Ciceronian orations, Quintilian, Vitruvius, Manilius — and Lucretius! In a letter, written between January and May of 1418, and addressed to Francesco Barbaro in Venice, Poggio writes, from Constance, of some of his great discoveries; in this letter we find the first reference to what was the greatest find of all, the text of Lucretius:

Lucretius mihi nondum redditus est, cum sit scriptus; locus est satis longinquus, neque unde aliqui veniant, itaque exspectabo quoad aliqui accedant qui illum deferant; sin autem nulli venient, non praeponam publica privatis.[2]

Lucretius has not yet been returned to me, although the copy has been made; the place is sufficiently far away; it is not a place from which any people come, here; therefore I shall wait until some people may go there to bring me the book; but if no one comes, I shall not place public duties before my personal affairs.

The text can only mean that at some place, at an inconvenient distance from Constance, the startling discovery of an ancient Lucretian manuscript had been made, some time in 1417, that this manuscript had been transcribed, and that Poggio was impatiently awaiting receipt of either the original MS or of that transcription.[3] Poggio did not mean to wait much longer; he was prepared to let official duties yield to his own, urgent, personal interests. Some details of this episode remain obscure:

[2] Cf., *e.g.*, "The Literary Discoveries of Poggio," by A. C. Clark, in *The Cl. Rev.*, XIII. 119–130 (1899).

[3] Hosius thinks that Poggio did *not* get the original! Lehnerdt believes that Niccoli's transcript was made from a copy of the original codex. From a reading of the Poggio *Letters*, I believe it to be true that as late as 1427 Poggio still hoped to gain that original; cf. *Ep.*, III. 12.

where was this ancient manuscript found? We are not informed by the correspondence of Poggio. If the library of St. Martin's church in Mainz, the abbey at St. Bertin, near St. Omer, Corbie and Bobbio — four places where MSS of Lucretius are known to have been reposing, at the time and before — are excluded, as being all too far from Constance; if the monasteries of St. Gall and Cluni are not counted as possibilities because we have no knowledge of the existence of any Lucretian MS, there, the monastic library at Murbach in Elsass — a mediaeval catalogue of Murbach lists a Lucretius — remains a possibility, and Poggio may well have visited this library on his way to or from Langres. This relatively obscure monastery in Germany seems to have given Lucretius to the world, again.

The 'Lucretius' was sent, probably in 1418, to Poggio's friend, the Florentine scholar and patron of classical studies, Niccolò de' Niccoli, who clung to it jealously, but unjustly. In 1425, Poggio wrote solicitously:

Si mittes mihi Lucretium, facies rem gratissimam multis.[4]

[4] Poggii, *Ep.*, II. 26 (June 14). Poggio promised to return the MS in a month!

As late as 1429, Niccoli still held that manuscript. It might have been possible, perhaps, for Poggio to secure it by process of law; feelings of friendship, responsible for the considerate behavior of Poggio, were treated, strangely and lightly, by Niccoli. In 1429, Poggio wrote:

Cura ut habeam Lucretium, si fieri potest; non enim adhuc potui universum librum legere, cum semper fuerit peregrinus.[5]

Let me have my Lucretius, if possible; for I have not been able to read him through, as yet, since he has, all this time, been away from home.

The tone of impatience was more than justified. No copies had as yet been distributed; that seems quite clear; and thus dissemination of knowledge of Lucretius was delayed. Poggio claims that Niccoli held the book "twelve" years; a little later, he says "fourteen," asking whether Niccoli wished to keep the treasure "another ten." In 1434, Poggio probably saw his Lucretius again; in that year he accompanied Pope Eugene IV on a journey to Florence and he may even have recovered his invaluable document. Full information, however, is lacking, and Poggio may not have re-

[5] Poggii, *Ep.*, IV. 2 (Dec. 13).

gained possession of his beloved Lucretius at all. Poggio must, it seems to me, have mentioned Lucretius by name and have quoted him, later, if he had really come to know him; he displays no intimate knowledge of the author whom he had rescued.[6] Niccoli, meantime, before his death in 1437, prepared his own beautifully written transcript, which is now in the Laurentian library (no. XXXV. 30). At the end of book VI, we find:

T· LUCRETI· CARI· DE· RERV̄
NATURA· LIBER· VI·
EXPLICIT· LEGE·
FELICITER·
·AMEN·

While Poggio's own 'Lucretius' has been lost — how, when, or where — no one knows — Niccoli's transcript has survived; and either the Niccoli transcript, which Niccoli wrote with his own hand, or the lost Poggio, or both MSS became the parents, as far as we know, directly or indirectly, of all copies made during the fifteenth century. For some time, therefore, the fate of Lucretius hung upon a slender thread. The number of MS copies of Lu-

[6] The *De Miseria Conditionis Humanae may* have an echo of Lucr., V. 221 seq. (cf. p. 93, *Opera,* Basiliae).

cretius gradually grew and they guaranteed the preservation of the poet. A letter of 1436, written by Filelfo to Antonio Beccadelli, clearly refers to one of these MSS of Lucretius, owned in Siena; Filelfo hoped to be able to borrow this volume, but the owner was not disposed to allow his valuable possession to pass out of his hands. Copies of Lucretius multiplied in due time; no one knows, to-day, how many manuscripts of Lucretius were available before the close of the fifteenth century;[7] some were, of course, written before the publication of the *editio princeps* of 1473, the majority, probably; but some, indeed, followed. Of these fifteenth-century manuscripts, now extant, eight (including Niccoli's transcript) are in the Florentine Laurentian library,[8] eight are in the Vati-

[7] Lehnerdt gives, as far as I know, the most complete statement of all less well-known Lucretian MSS of which we have any knowledge. They have not all been sufficiently studied; cf. the able article by Carl Hosius, in the *Rh. M.*, LXIX. 109–122 (1914). In addition to the Laurentian and Vatican MSS, which I have studied with care, I have examined the one in the Vittorio Emanuele library in Rome; it is of less consequence than the others in Italy.

[8] The Laurentian Lucretian MSS are numbered XXXV. 25, 26, 27, 28, 29, 30, 31, 32. No. 30 is the Niccoli copy, as has been explained; No. 29 is the Politian owned MS, with his own glosses, notes, and various kinds of marginalia; it is written in a very clear hand; No. 32 also has notes and corrections, and Politian is cited; 25, 26, 27, 28, 31 are more ornate, with much fine, colored lettering.

can; [9] a number are in England,[10] and one, the codex 'Victorianus,' is in Munich. Of all of these fifteenth-century manuscripts, the Niccoli transcript is certainly the oldest copy of Poggio's Lucretius, and, for many reasons, invaluable. One MS in the Vatican is dated 1442 and another, 1483. Gradually fifteenth-century Italy had the opportunity to become familiar with her poet, after *ca.* 1434, or after 1437, and editions of the poet, after 1473, greatly enhanced that knowledge.

Even before Dante's day, Epicureanism was popularly understood as a system of hedonistic ethics that advocated a life of pleasure, as a philosophy that opposed the ideas of divine providence and of immortality; it was, therefore, conceived of, as an enemy of the Church. Some of the foremost Italian humanists and scholars of the fifteenth century, the century of Lucretius' resurrection, either show no sign

[9] The eight Vatican MSS are catalogued as follows: Vat. lat. 1569 (bears date of 1483), 3275, 3276 (date, 1442); Ottob. lat. 1136, 1954 (bears date of 1466); Urb. lat. 640 (ends with a *Deo Gratias* of the scribe); Reg. lat. 1706; Barb. lat. 154. Some of these MSS are very handsome, *e.g.*, 1569, 3276, 1954, 640, 1706, 154 (with fine letters and colors).

[10] In the British Museum, at Oxford, and in Cambridge (some of these may be of the sixteenth century). Munro rated the Cambridge MS very high.

of Lucretian influence, as Francesco Filelfo (1398–1481), or knew Lucretius only at second-hand, as Lorenzo Valla (1407–1457).[11] The latter's dramatic dialogue, called *De Voluptate*, which was written in 1431, shows not only a knowledge of but even an undue interest in Epicureanism, and Valla was obliged to defend himself against reproaches and suspicions, because of his arguments for sense-pleasures. Ironical, indeed, that Valla who knew Lucretius' bitter condemnation of the Jupiter concept and who quoted the fine line,

ipsaque deducit dux vitae dia voluptas,[12]

did not see the text of Lucretius, that was so near and yet so far from him. Marsilio Ficino (1433–1499), however, was the first philosopher of the fifteenth century who undoubtedly knew Lucretius' *De Rerum Natura*. As a youth, he wrote a commentary on Lucretius which, however, he is said to have destroyed in the fire. But presently, lover of Plato, translator of Plato and of Plotinus, one of the founders of the Florentine (Platonic) 'Acad-

[11] Valla knew Gellius, Nonius, Donatus, Servius, Lactantius, Isidore, and Priscian, — all of whom told him, more or less, about Lucretius.

[12] L., II. 172.

[2 5 7]

emy ' in 1469, which revered the memory of
Plato, Ficino spent much of his life in trying
to reconcile Platonism with Christianity, and
thus he appears as an opponent of the materialism of the Epicureans whom he calls ' Lucre-
tiani '! Ficino wrote a polemic against Lucretius' denial of divine creation and his denial
of immortality. These were Lucretian conclusions that inevitably stirred the wrath of the
faithful followers of Christian doctrine and, as
had happened so frequently before, Epicurus
and Lucretius were condemned as impious
' atheists.' So poorly was the Epicurean philosophy of religion understood. No wonder that
Ficino subscribed to the old tradition that Lucretius was insane and that he had committed
suicide.[13]

But admirers of Lucretius, as poet, rapidly
grew in number, and conspicuous among these
were Pontanus, Marullus, and Politian. Lucretius' influence on philosophic thought was,
at first, negligible, as was to be expected. It
was the poetry of Lucretius that impressed the
early Renaissance in Italy, and, as had hap-

[13] Ficino's illustrious friend and contemporary, Giovanni
Pico della Mirandola, admitted the charm of Lucretius'
style, but he preferred the philosophy of an orthodox
thinker, Ioannes, although the latter had written *insulse* and
ruditer.

pened in Rome in the first century before Christ
and in the first centuries after Christ, the
power and the brilliant inspiration of the poet
counted for vastly more than the conclusions
of the philosopher; the nature and behavior of
the atom, the atomic creation of the universe,
its limitlessness, mortality of the soul, and denial of divine providence were as little popular
now as they had been in the days of Augustus
or of the Plinies. A popular conception of
Epicurean ethics enjoyed a vogue, but Lucretius appealed to his readers because of the majesty of his verse. After a thousand years of
obscurity, from *ca.* 500 to *ca.* 1500 A.D., the
judgments of Ovid and of Statius were re-affirmed and the 'sublime' *poet* was, once more,
coming into his own.

Pontanus and Marullus deserve chief credit
for this renaissance of Lucretius. Giovanni
Pontano (1426–1503) was a most ardent admirer and a capable student of Lucretius. In
his *Amores* it is: sacri . . . *sublimis* Musa
Lucreti; Ovid's enthusiasm is kindled, anew,
in the heart of this later Italian who was, himself, distinguished for the elegance of his Latin
verses. In his great didactic poem, *Urania Sive
De Stellis,* we find a song on the origin of super-

stition, of truly Lucretian power, a description of the origin and evolution of man that follows Lucretius, and, even, an exposition of the origins of religion which is portrayed as the product of man's fear of gods who do not care. Yet Pontanus does not follow Lucretius, the philosopher, with any consistency: the world is god-made, and, in his ethics, Pontanus is influenced by Aristotle. Numerous echoes of Lucretius appear in the *Amores* and in the *Urania*. But Pontanus remains Christian, even while he acknowledges Lucretius' extraordinary power to bewitch and almost to persuade,[14] and Lucretius is placed on a level with Virgil. But it is not only as poet but also as scholar that Pontanus proved his deep admiration for Lucretius. As is well-known, he devoted more than twenty years to a study of the text; the fruits of his labors appear, in part at least, in the Juntine edition of Candidus of 1512. As late as the summer of 1502, he was engaged with his able friend and pupil, Girolamo Borgia, in work

[14] Cf. Pontanus' words of praise in his *Actius:* Christe optime, quid copiae, quid ornatus, quantus e clarissimis luminibus eius emicat in altero (*i.e.,* Lucretio) splendor! rapit quo vult lectorem, probat ad quod intendit summa cum subtilitate et artificio, hortatur, deterret, incitat, retrahit, etc. (Lucretius and Manilius are compared.)

upon his text-emendations and other marginalia, which appear in the volume of the printed
Lucretius which he owned; [15] this book is a
1495 Venice edition of Lucretius, and the British Museum is the fortunate possessor of this
invaluable volume.[16] Pontanus, therefore, was
establishing the fame of Lucretius in Naples,
and other members [17] of the Neapolitan Academy fell under the spell of the ancient Roman.

No less was the poet and scholar Marullus
inseparably associated with this revival of enthusiastic interest in the *De Rerum Natura*.
Michael Tarchaniota Marullus Constantino-
politanus (?–1500) made Florence his home
and here, also, we have a center of radiant Lucretian admiration. The 1497 edition of Marullus' poetry gives unmistakable evidence of
his intense love for Lucretius, whose influence
upon his own verse was profound: the language
of the famous pessimistic Lucretian passage on
the child's cry at birth

[15] The preface, in the handwriting of Borgius, makes it
quite clear that Borgius wrote these emendations and marginalia in his own hand.

[16] Another copy of the 1495 Venice edition is in Munich,
with Pontanus' corrections, written in by the hand of Victorius.

[17] *E.g.,* Sannazaro, Christian and Virgilian though he
was, slightly.

tum porro puer, ut saevis proiectus ab undis
navita, nudus humi iacet, infans, indigus omni
vitali auxilio, cum primum in luminis oras
nixibus ex alvo matris natura profudit,
vagituque locum lugubri complet

is caught up by Marullus in his 'Hymns to
Earth,' and, while Marullus had great admiration for other Latin poets, as Horace, Catullus,
Tibullus, Terence, it was his expressed belief
that Lucretius and Virgil ought to be committed
to memory. But it was the poet, not the philosopher, who captivated Marullus, who found
the atomic swerve-theory, sheer madness; he
was essentially a Neo-Platonist in thought, although circumstances of his own life led him to
accept as true the doctrine of annihilation. Such
were the contradictions in his own thinking, well-illustrated by his preference for two
poets so widely different as were Virgil and
Lucretius.

Higher tribute could hardly be paid to Marullus, as textual critic, than was voiced by
Munro, who regarded him "as an amender of
Lucretius immediately after Lambinus and
Lachmann, if not indeed in the same front
rank." Though Marullus did not publish his
studies of the text, they were not lost. We

have these emendations in a copy of the 1495 Venice edition of Lucretius, where they appear, written in by the hand of Victorius. This book is in Munich. We have them, also, or many of them, in the Juntine edition of Candidus of 1512, of which a word will follow, presently. In his preface, Candidus [18] refers, feelingly, to Marullus' death, which occurred on the tenth of April 1500 in the waters of the Cecina river, near Volterra. Marullus had with him, at the time of his tragic death, a copy of his treasured Roman poet.

The edition of Candidus had placed the text of Lucretius on a comparatively safe basis so that it was possible to read him, with some confidence. Pontanus and Marullus had definitely proclaimed his greatness to Renaissance Italy. Second only to them in knowledge of and admiration for Lucretius was their contemporary, the illustrious Politian. Angelo Poliziano (1454–1494) was a great poet and scholar, professor of Greek and Latin at Florence, textual critic, Platonist, and he has been called

---

[18] Cf., also, Lucretianae adeo veneris per omnem aetatem (a slight exaggeration) studiosus (*i.e.*, Marullus) fuit, ut nuspiam fere non eo comite itaret, numquam cubitum . . . nisi perlectis aliquot exploratisque Cari carminibus sese reciperet.

[263]

" the ideal Italian humanist." He owned one of the fifteenth-century manuscripts of Lucretius, derived from Niccoli's famous document, and it rests, to-day, in the Laurentian library (XXXV. 29), bearing the marginalia written in his own hand.[19] Politian quotes his Lucretius in defense of his own art of poetic borrowings; he made Lucretius his own, and many echoes of Lucretius appear in his own poetry. His *Rusticus* undoubtedly shows Virgilian influence, but a description of a procession of the Seasons may well owe much to Lucretius' justly famous word-picture of that continual march of Spring, Summer, Autumn, Winter, with their companions Venus and Cupid, Flora and Zephyrus, Ceres, and the various winds. Through Politian, it is claimed, the famous Florentine painter, Botticelli (1444–1510), caught his inspiration for his immortal masterpiece, *Primavera,* in part at least, from Lucretius. This problem has been much dis-

[19] This manuscript is written in an extremely neat hand. On the page opposite the first page of the Lucretian text, Politian assembled some ancient *testimonia,* quoting Eusebius, Ovid's words (carmina sublimis etc.), Statius; citing Cicero's Epistle and Cornelius Nepos; referring to Lactantius, and to Virgil's heavy debt to Lucretius. So early did admirers of Lucretius gather together this kind of information about their author. (Note ref. to ' Eusebius ' and Cic., ' Ep ad *Att.*')

cussed. Vasari believed that the subject was probably suggested by Lucretius. Perhaps this is claiming too much. The painting owes something to Politian's *Stanze* on Spring, in which Flora and Zephyrus appear; it shows the influence, too, of Lorenzo's *Selve d' Amore,* in which Flora is captured by Zephyrus. It may owe something to Horace (*Car.,* I. 30), who associates Venus with the Graces and Mercury. Botticelli's canvas presents a lovely Venus in the center, with Cupid above her head; the Graces and Mercury at the left; and Spring, scattering flowers, Flora and Zephyrus at the right. Politian's devotion to Lucretius may have brought the Roman poet's verses to the attention of his friend and contemporary, Botticelli, and, if this be true, we have, here, a remarkable illustration of transmission of inspiration from one genius to another: an inspiration held in the sensuous language of Lucretian poetry and reproduced in the glowing medium of the painter. While the passage in the fifth book of the *De Rerum Natura* [20] is always cited in discussions of this intensely interesting problem:

[20] Lucr., V. 737-747.

it ver et Venus, et Veneris praenuntius ante
pennatus graditur, Zephyri vestigia propter
Flora quibus mater praespargens ante viai
cuncta coloribus egregiis et odoribus opplet,

words of the Lucretian invocation, also, provide a partial parallel to the painting:

> *alma Venus....................*
> *.............................*
> *.........tibi suavis daedala tellus*
> *summittit flores.*

If Lucretius was in Botticelli's mind, both passages may have contributed to the exquisite
charm of this scene of love, life, beauty, happiness — Epicurean themes, Lucretian motives —
treated with utmost delicacy by the Italian of
the fifteenth century.

Pontanus, Marullus, and Politian assured
Lucretian influence in European poetry, and
his influence as philosopher was contingent
thereupon. Virgil, Catullus, Horace, and Ovid
were, at the time, far better known; no translation of Lucretius had, as yet, appeared. But
the Italian editions of Lucretius were in circulation and it was, no doubt, in Florence, Venice,
and Naples, that he was, at first, known best,

although Bologna and Verona did not remain far behind.[21] Of course the Renaissance meant a prodigious swing from the limitations of the Middle Ages toward a greater fullness of life. In a certain sense 'Epicurean,' pleasure-loving Florence had welcomed Lucretius, as one more exponent of that beauty of living, as one more lover of nature, as one more emancipator from the dullness and greyness of the Middle Ages. But this Florentine renaissance was full of contradictions: Lorenzo the Magnificent, the ascetic Savonarola, the apostle of secular despotism, Machiavelli, all played their rôles here; Italian painting [22] emphasized the birth of the new freedom and the new passion for color; but the Church presided triumphant, and Lucretius' welcome could not be complete; it was accompanied by large reservations. And what was true of Florence was largely true of the rest

[21] Rome remains behind and the reasons are not far to seek. Previous editions of certain other Latin Classics in Italy hardly predisposed readers to any sympathy for Lucretius, as, for example, the edition of Lactantius that appeared in Subiaco in 1465, or of Augustine's *City of God;* the Rome edition of Gellius (1469) might have whetted readers' appetites, likewise the 1470 Venice edition of Priscian, or the 1470 Rome edition of Quintilian, or the 1472 Venice edition of Macrobius.

[22] Raphael's 'School of Athens' shows a head, garland-crowned, which may be that of Epicurus.

of Europe during the two centuries, the fifteenth and sixteenth.

The story of the early editions [23] of Lucretius is well-known to Lucretian scholars and it is full of problems that hardly demand recital, here. The appearance of these editions made Italy more and more acquainted with the character of her great Latin poet. It is obvious that the earliest editions would, necessarily,

	Date	*Place of Publication*	*Editor*
[23] *ca.*	1473	Brescia	
	1486	Verona	
	1495	Venice	
	1500	Venice, the first Aldine; Avancius	
	1511	Bologna — (with huge commentary) J. B. Pius	
		(reprinted in Paris, 1514)	
	1512	Florence, the first Juntine; Candidus	
	1515	Venice, the second Aldine; Navagero	

(the patrician humanist of Venice, Navagero [or Naugerius], followed the Juntine edition, closely, although the first Aldine also served as a model)

	1531	Basle	
	1534, 1540	Lyons — (also, 1546, 1548, and 1576)	
	1563/64	Paris	Lambinus

(second ed., 1565; third, 1570)

| | 1566 | Antwerp | Gifanius |

(Gifanius, the unscrupulous Lambinus-plagiarist; 1595, new ed., Leyden)

Thus Lucretius appeared in Italy, France, Switzerland, Belgium, and Holland before the close of the sixteenth century. (The 1515 Aldine edition was reprinted in Paris in 1539; Lucretius was published in Paris in 1543 and in 1567, and the Lambinus text-edition appeared in Lyons, in 1576.) This is *not* a *complete* list.

have to rest, primarily, upon such manuscript copies of the Niccoli text as were in existence at the time. The *editio princeps* of 1473 is, now, one of the rarest of books. The first Venice Aldine of 1500, edited by Avancius of Verona, represented a more serious effort to establish the text: the editor made use of some earlier grammarians who had quoted Lucretius and he, also, had before him the invaluable notes of Marullus; Avancius is said to have known his poet by heart. In a dedication, Aldus apologizes for the publication of a Lucretius, who had written so much that was un-Christian and untrue.[24] But the 1512 edition of Candidus, published by the Juntine press in Florence, was of first importance. Although Candidus used the first Aldine, he introduced many brilliant corrections, he collated all the Florentine manuscripts, and, besides, quite fully recognized the immense value of the Lucretian studies of Pontanus and Marullus, upon whose revisions his own text was mainly grounded. Lucretius soon crossed the Alps; and the editions of Lambinus, that appeared in Paris between 1563/64 and 1570, rank among the greatest

[24] L., a great poet and philosopher, but full of errors, — in both Aldine editions, 1500 and 1515.

[269]

editions of the Classics of all time. Before
his publication, editions of Lucretius had appeared in Italy, France, and Switzerland; but,
despite the importance of the Juntine edition
of Candidus, Lambinus' work marked a new
epoch in the history of Lucretian study.
Dionysius Lambinus (1520–1572), or Denys
Lambin as he was called in his own language,
was illustrious in sixteenth century France;
his masterly edition of Lucretius rested on an
independent collation of manuscripts, including
one of greatest importance that had not been
used before. In the monastery of St. Bertin,
near Saint-Omer, there lay a MS now called the
Leyden " B " or " Q " MS, the quarto, that
ranks with the other Leyden MS " A " or " O "
(oblongus) as, together, being the most valuable, because they are the most ancient, complete MSS of Lucretius in existence at the present time.[25] Lambinus had this manuscript,
called by him the codex Bertinianus, sent to
him to Paris and it was collated for him by
Turnebus. What with his perfect command of
Latin and of Latin literature, his thorough
knowledge of Lucretius, and deep admiration
of the poet, Lambinus produced his annotated

[25] Cf. p. 353.

edition that remained for almost three hundred years, to the days of Lachmann and Munro, the commanding edition of Lucretius in the world. Lambinus' dedication of his work 'Karolo Nono, Regi Christianissimo, S.D.' expresses unbounded enthusiasm for Lucretius, the poet, and there is a veritable riot of color in his language of praise; the Latin language supplied Lambinus with many terms of eulogy which he used unhesitatingly of Lucretius, with greater profusion than any student of Lucretius before or after his time. But all of this praise was accompanied by the sincerest declaration that this publication was not a defense of Epicurean-Lucretian doctrine: the atomic theory, the doctrine of innumerable worlds, denial of immortality, denial of divine providence, elevation of 'pleasure' to the rank of the 'summum bonum' were as abhorrent to him as to other Christians, contemporary or earlier; refutation was, indeed, wholly unnecessary; all pagan literature was un-Christian and, thereby, in error; but the literature was read for its aesthetic and historical values, and Lucretius, from whom even Virgil borrowed, was the peer of all:

Equidem hoc tibi, Karole, non dubitanter affirmabo, nullum in tota lingua Latina scriptorem Lucretio Latine melius esse locutum.

No one had gone farther than this in praise of Lucretius, no one, at the time, could claim more. At least Lambinus restored Lucretius to the world's literature, permanently, and to accomplish this was Lambinus' main purpose.[26]

Lucretius' safe position in the minds of the French who were promoting the literary culture of France of the sixteenth century, is clearly revealed by the numerous citations from the *De Rerum Natura* that appear in Montaigne's *Essays*. Not only is their frequency testimony to Montaigne's acquaintance with the poem, but the manner of citation places Lucretius in the category of the well-known poets of the past, whether Catullus, Ovid, Virgil, or Horace, to mention a few who are quoted frequently and without further, unnecessary identification. Of Montaigne (1533–1592) it has been said

[26] Torquato Tasso (1544–1595) could not help knowing something about Lucretius. It is at least interesting that he was in Paris, in 1570. The Virgilian and romanticist could have had little sympathy with the philosophy of the *De Rerum Natura,* but the indebtedness of *La Gerusalemme Liberata* (Bk. 1, Str. 3) to Lucr., I. 926 seq., is, I think, acknowledged by all students of Tasso.

that through him French personality emerges and secures self-expression. He had studied Epicureanism in Lucretius, and Stoicism, mainly in Seneca. He blended his readings in philosophy and enriched his life from many sources, from Plutarch (in translation), notably, and from Italian literature. Lucretius, as scientist, was of less importance to him than as poet; the dogmatism of Lucretius and his intense earnestness and moral fervor counted for less than his splendid poetry. After a fashion, Montaigne was an ' Epicurean' because of his recognition of happiness as a universal, human aim; Nature and natural appetites were not our foes; soul and body, alike, were recognized as gifts of God. It was an urbane Epicureanism that this professed Catholic cultivated, as he skeptically mused on life's vanities and pleasures. Lucretian verses are quoted — verses of indignation or of sadness, of exhortation and of poetic charm — to illustrate an argument or to illuminate a page. Of course Lucretius does not become Montaigne's guide. At one point [27] Montaigne exclaims: Voylà des paroles tres magnifiques et belles. At another,

[27] Bk. II, *Es.* 12 (said of Lucr. praise of Epicurus, *De Rerum N.,* V. *init.*)

he raises the old question whether Lucretius or Virgil were the greater poet,[28] but he avoids an uncomfortable decision. Members of the memorable *La Pléiade,* Joachim Du Bellay and Pierre de Ronsard in particular, had evidently settled that problem with their famous dictum that if Virgil and Cicero had been content simply to imitate earlier authors, Latin literature might have stopped with Ennius and Lucretius! Ronsard was friend of Lambinus, who had called him ' Poetarum Gallicorum Princeps.' The two friends were not quite agreed on this important literary problem, but Lucretius' great distinction is recognized, anew, by the controversy.[29]

Poggio had resurrected Lucretius from his all-but-forgotten grave in Germany. Lambinus crowned him in Paris. Lucretius was widely hailed as poet, in Italy and in France; and the century of Lambinus witnessed his influence in England, as well. The winged words of the Lucretian invocation flew into the mind of Edmund Spenser (*ca.* 1552–1599), who incorporated them in his *Faerie Queene.* As so often before, this adoption of the language of the

[28] Bk. II, *Es.* 10.
[29] Cf. Quint. and Tac., chapter IX; Pontanus, Marullus, Lambinus (this chapter).

Roman poet implies no acceptance of his philosophy, for Spenser, although alive to the wider scope and adequacy of life, as represented by the classic literature, was in no real sense an intellectual disciple of Lucretius. But he had, very apparently, read Lucretius, and his hymn [30] to the goddess of Love owes a manifest debt to the Roman poet's splendid lines:

xliv. *Great Venus: Queene of beautie and of grace,*
The joy of Gods and men, that under skie
Doest fayrest shine, and most adorne thy
place;
That with thy smyling looke doest pacifie
The raging seas and makst the stormes to
flie;
Thee, goddesse, thee the winds, the clouds
doe feare . . .
And heavens laugh, and all the world shews
joyous cheare.

xlv. *Then doth the daedale earth throw forth to*
thee
Out of her fruitfull lap aboundant
flowres; . . .

xlvii. *So all the world by thee at first was made,*
And dayly yet thou doest the same re-
payre; . . .

[30] *F. Q.,* Bk. IV, Canto X, §§ 44–47; cf. Bk. III, for other (possible) Lucretian reminiscences, and Edwin Greenlaw, " Spenser and Lucretius," in *University of North Carolina Studies in Philology,* XVII. 439–464 (1920).

Earthly Love assuredly is not antagonistic to
Heavenly Love; and sensuous love is not condemned in consequence of Biblical or Platonic
teaching. Perhaps in this there is a deep communion of spirit between Spenser and Lucretius,
both of whom, also, were haunted by the
thought of the mutability of things earthly and
the brevity of human life. While Spenser borrowed the language of Lucretius, freely, for
his anthem, his description of the Court of
Venus is voluptuous to a degree that some
might have regarded as 'Epicurean'; in this
respect it is not in the least Lucretian. The
same is true of his Garden of Adonis,[31] in which
Cupid and Psyche and their child, *Voluptas*,
appear. With his Puritan hatred of Rome,
Spenser might have taken a leaf from Lucretius, the religious iconoclast of false form
and the moralist, but Lucretius, I fear, was not
well enough understood, at the time, for that.
Spenser employed his ancient sources, freely;
and, strange as it may appear, matter and
phrase from the Bible, strands from Plato,
Aristotle, Boethius, as well as from Lucretius

[31] *F. Q.*, Bk. III, Canto VI; cf. J. W. Bennett, " Spenser's Garden of Adonis," in *Publ. of the Mod. Lang. Ass.
of America*, XLVII. 46–80 (1932).

were all woven together in his own rich tapestry.[32]

However, fifteenth- and sixteenth-century Europe was far from accepting Lucretius, as thinker, however widely he was read and admired as a poet. As we have seen, Ficino, Pontanus, Marullus, Aldus, Lambinus — one and all — rejected the essentials of Lucretius' philosophizing.

To be sure, Cosma Raimondi had, in the fifteenth century, written his defense of Epicurean ethics, based on Cicero; Valla, as we have seen, wrote his *De Voluptate,* which brought him under suspicion. Francesco Colonna had composed his allegorical romance, a glorification of Epicurean ethics, in which the importance of the five senses for the discovery of truth is fully acknowledged and in which Amor, Venus, and Gloria Mundi are portrayed in glowing colors. But formal philosophy followed the lead of Ficino whose hostility to Epicurean doctrines and to Lucretius represented a renewal of the old, implacable hatred of Lactantius, long before. In the nature of the

---

[32] It is said that no other trace of Lucretius appears in the Elizabethan age. Shakespeare may have known something about Lucretius, from Montaigne (in translation); parallels between S. and L., of course, abound (cf. p. 106).

case, Catholicism was a bitter foe of Epicureanism; nor did this philosophy fare any better
in the camp of the Protestants. A priori, Calvin, Luther, and Knox were Lucretius' foes, —
with or without knowing him. In the fifteenth
century and in the sixteenth, too, Lucretius,
the arrogant dogmatist, could expect to find few
friends in things of the mind; and, while the
manner of his writing won great applause, the
substance of his thought was out of harmony
with the prevailing intellectual spirit of the age.
Never was he more lonely, in spite of the fact
that his prestige as poet was immense. Entomb-
ment, in the Middle Ages, was almost prefer-
able to this kind of existence. Free religious
thought was pursued with utmost danger in
Italy, France, England, Spain. Not one of these
countries provided the proper soil for the
growth of his Epicurean seed. Religious wars
and intolerance, Saint-Bartholomew's Day,
political despotism were equally opposed to the
Lucretian gospel of intellectual religious freedom and the Epicurean doctrine of individualism. As for any philosophy of hedonism for the
common man — Charles V of Spain, Francis I,
Henry VIII and Queen Elizabeth cared little
enough for that! And atomism was all but for-

gotten. A spirit of rationalism was finally born out of a long, ferocious struggle of the two great members of the Christian Church. It is hardly necessary to mention the names of Desperiers, Rabelais, Charron, of Thomas More, Marlowe,[33] Raleigh, Francis Bacon, Pomponazzi, in order to realize the significance of those tempestuous days of bitter struggle. In Germany there was little intellectual light; in Spain, the tyranny of the Church and of the Crown, the terror of the Inquisition closed the door to free speech and even to free thought. Under all these circumstances, there could be but slight understanding and even less appreciation of Lucretius' intellectual honesty and of Lucretius' bold iconoclasm.[34] The tragedy of Giordano Bruno illustrates this fantastically and dramatically.

The first startling illustration of Lucretius'

[33] Whether the classically-trained Marlowe ever read the third book of Lucretius or not, we may not know; but the Faust legend gave the free-thinker opportunity to express daring thoughts, Lucretian in character, as when Mephisto says: " Hell hath no limits . . . for where we are is Hell," and Faustus: " Come, I think Hell's a fable " (*Doctor Faustus,* Act II, Scene I). And in Robert Greene's *Selimus* (vss. 351 seq.) we find a denial of future life, that even more reminds one of Lucretius.

[34] Advance in medical science, in the arts, *etc.,* does not affect the truth of this statement.

influence, as a thinker, appears in the works of Giordano Bruno (*ca.* 1548–1600). Bruno had eagerly accepted the discoveries of Copernicus and his praise of Copernicus sounds strangely like Lucretius' eulogies of Epicurus. Copernicus' (1473–1543) heliocentric theory was proclaimed in his epoch-making *De Revolutionibus Orbium Coelestium,* in 1543. Bruno proceeded to even bolder conclusions, and his revolutionary doctrines of the infinity of the universe and of innumerable worlds was fully stated and defended in his *De Immenso et Innumerabilibus seu De Universo et Mundis,* a didactic poem of length, which appeared in 1586. A sensational doctrine, at the time, it was none the less old, because such beliefs had been part of Epicurean physical thinking; but the contemporary Graeco-Roman world had paid little heed to these views, whether expounded by Epicurus or, more brilliantly, by Lucretius. The ancient world had an habitual preference for limitation; Aristotle and the Ptolemaic astronomy had established the commonly-accepted Graeco-Roman views of the universe, as bounded definitely and comfortably. The Copernican system challenged the old geo-centric theory that represented the sun as revolving about the

[280]

earth; it opened up a revelation of infinity and of many suns; it began the process of breaking down the old prison walls; it represented the earth as revolving upon its own axis and whirling about the sun! Bruno carried these speculations further and, widely read in Greek philosophy, he certainly received support, in his own independent studies of nature, from Epicurean philosophy, and he quoted Lucretius [35] in defense of his own belief that the universe has no bounds.

For Lucretius, this view represented a flight of the imagination, supported, to be sure, by argument — no bounds, no center, no bottom, space so vast that the lightning, racing through the sky, could never reach an end — a flight that meant release of the human spirit from cramping confines. For Giordano Bruno, no less, this imaginative leap to unverifiable conclusions was accompanied by an enthusiasm that carries suggestions of the frenzy, as well as clearest echoes of the language of Lucretius. Bruno touches Lucretius at this one flaming point and he drew strength from the Roman's poetry.

A terrifying idea, because of its awesome

[35] *E.g., De l'infinito universo et mondi* (1584).

vastness, which figures of "light-years" but feebly define; an idea that almost defies comprehension and from which, even now, many a mind might shrink, as Alfred Noyes[36] has recognized. An unorthodox view, that threatened the old distinction between Heaven and Earth and jeopardized Christian legend. And for Bruno such notions were heresy. The Church had accepted the Aristotelian doctrine, and to challenge Aristotle was to challenge the infallibility of the Church. Aristotle's proud pinnacle in the Middle Ages had been recognized by Dante, in the thirteenth century, in an immortal phrase; his eminence in Christian thought was secured by Saint Thomas Aquinas (*ca.* 1227–1274). Aristotle reigned at Oxford and ruled in Paris in the sixteenth century of Bruno. Yet Bruno dared rebel against authority and tradition with an intensity of feeling, near to hate. The earth moves[37] and space is limitless; these were formulae of the new science and of the new reason; they were expressive of intellectual freedom, cherished by men at their peril. Bruno died for his views; Lucretius remained unmolested; neither now nor

[36] *Earth-Bound.*

[37] Of course the theory was as old as Aristarchus, who was accused of 'impiety' for his beliefs.

[282]

later was his book placed on the *Index* of for-
bidden volumes. His written words remained,
either haughtily ignored or an unrecognized
challenge, to inspire others, later, as they did
Voltaire. Bruno died, though his creed before
the Inquisition included belief in God, as im-
manent and final cause, belief in the immortality of the human soul, belief in a universal
providence — ideas to which Lucretius was far
from subscribing.

An infinite universe, infinite space, endless
finite worlds — a natural view to be held by
some in Rome in the first century before Christ,
with the expansion of Empire; a view almost
inevitable, again, in the sixteenth century of
Sir Francis Drake, a century that had been
preceded by voyagings across the Atlantic; a
century of extended physical horizons and,
slowly, of enlarged intellectual vistas. Lucretius has his place very clearly in this history of human thought, and for Lucretius, as
for Giordano Bruno, the idea was a fundamental conviction and of tremendously vital significance.

XII

A — The Seventeenth Century

THUS began the seventeenth century for Lucretius, with rejection of this principle and, thereby, by implication, with rejection of much of his science and philosophy. Lambinus had spoken truly for his century in expressing admiration for the Roman poet but in rejecting, even without argument, the claims of the 'impious' thinker. In Bruno there burned the ardor of the prophet, united with the eloquence of poetry; Bruno and Lucretius were akin. The degradation of the human mind was complete in the act that included rejection of Lucretius and imposition of the death-sentence upon Bruno. Bruno met his death with Socratic calm, and, had Lucretius witnessed the event, he must have heaped upon the jurors the scorn that was part of his nature or met the inevitable with tolerance born of his own intellectual conviction that ideas and right win to victory, slowly, in this world. But

a reaction against the tyranny of orthodox beliefs began to set in with the growing spirit of
rationalism, and the seventeenth century witnessed some of the results. In spite of this, the
seventeenth century bristled with hostilities
against Lucretius.

The new science of astronomy made its
marvellous way slowly and painfully enough,
by experiment and demonstration, and Galileo
(1564–1642) and Kepler (1571–1630) did not
live in vain. Tragedies marked the progress,
and Galileo's life of triumph was turned into
one of humiliation. Joshua and Scripture,
theologians and the rabid Aristotelians yielded
stubbornly; but the boundaries of the visible
physical universe were vastly extended by the
telescope, and denial of Lucretius' infinite universe and unfathomable abysses became, in
time, an impertinence and a futility.

Atomism, too, gradually and at last, gained
a proper hearing, and, as is well known, Francis Bacon (1560/61–1626), Pierre Gassendi
(1592–1655), Sir Isaac Newton (1642/43–
1727) championed the cause of the atom; and
the monadology of Leibnitz (1646–1716) was
another version of the atomic doctrine of the
universe. Robert Boyle (1627–1691) was, of

[285]

course, a conspicuous torch-bearer in the same procession. Under such circumstances, there could be a better understanding of Lucretius, the atomist, and a warmer appreciation of his pioneering in the science of atomism, on the part of those, few enough in number, competent to grasp his argument. Not that Lucretius was the only schoolmaster of this age, in atomism; far from it. Bacon learned from Democritus and Epicurus; Gassendi, from Epicurus, primarily; but Lucretius figured in all of this speculation, as the well-known Roman exponent of these views; Gassendi and Newton[1] were deeply beholden to him. Thought veered from Aristotle toward Democritus and Epicurus; in consequence, Lucretius' heroic defense of atomism was fully vindicated, although the atom was variously defined and its relation to divine power, differently expounded. Lucretius had fought with the courage of a brave soldier and with indomitable spirit; his own generation cared little for the atom; the fifteenth- and sixteenth-century eulogists of Lucretius, the poet, had, likewise, scant patience with his atomic physics. But Lucretius shared in the glory of

[1] *E.g., in re,* the nature of the atom and the corpuscular theory of light.

the new victories of ideas in seventeenth-century England, France, and Germany. The atom, so long despised, came, eventually, to be recognized as the well-nigh most important entity in the physical universe. From this time forward, the magnificent lines of the first book, with their electric vitality, could be admired not only as poetry but as rational argument for the existence of the atom; the ancient argument by analogy was, necessarily, the first step in the long process of thought to final demonstration. And, despite Lucretius' denial of divine power, his honorable place in the history of atomic studies was assured; no history of atomism can ignore him, however great the advances of chemistry. Lucretius' grasp on atomism was firm, and all that he could do was to pass the theory on to the judgment of posterity.

But the seventeenth century could not and did not follow Lucretius, the atomist, in his denial of divine creation and of providence. Bacon, though perhaps with difficulty, retained his belief in God as a creator. Gassendi, as we shall see, subscribed to this belief. Newton believed that the law of gravity was imposed by divine decree. René Descartes (1596–

1650), called " the great reformer and liberator of the European intellect," was a religious conformist. Leibnitz' God was the efficient cause and final harmony among the monads which were the constituent elements of all things. But, unlike Lucretius' atoms, the monads owed their character to aboriginal communication with God; they thus became percipient, self-active beings; like Lucretius' atoms, their individuality was as fundamental as their activity; like Lucretius' atoms, these monads made a dynamic universe. To the mind of Boyle, God appeared as the first originator of motion among the atoms. Lucretius, on the other hand, had resolutely refused to grant any rôle of causation, within the natural universe, to God or gods. The fall of the atom, the swerve of the atom, combinations of atoms, creation, too, of the atoms must be explained, somehow, by discovery of nature's laws, alone,

opera sine divom.

Along this trail, which he had blazed in the West, Lucretius continued to wander solitary. His passionate separation of scientific thinking from current theological orthodoxy set him apart, very definitely, for another two hundred

[288]

years and more, as long as Christian theology
remained in conflict with an advancing science. Lucretius' attempted reconciliation of
science and religion, his firm belief that his science alone could teach the truth about God, his
vehement rejection of false orthodox views
about divine creation and providence remained
all but incomprehensible to the mind of Europe
to the eighteenth century and beyond — to
such an extent that, far from grasping Lucretius'
belief in and adoration of gods, Lucretius was,
for long, condemned as ' atheist.' [2] Knowledge
of natural law, Lucretius had maintained,
would redeem and bless mankind — and such
knowledge led to worship of that perfection in the natural universe which we call
divinity!

The English deists of the seventeenth and
eighteenth centuries represent a rationalistic
movement of great magnitude, and the deistic
movement absorbed the intellectual energy of
many minds whose literary output was very

[2] Hardly any words in the English language have been
used more loosely than ' atheist ' and ' infidel.' The Stoics
had anciently called the Epicureans ἄθεοι — a charge that
was immediately denied. The early Christians and the
pagans called each other ' atheists.' The Christians and
Epicureans were called ' infidels ' by Alexander (see Ch. IX).

large. Opposed to the doctrine of divine revelation, the champions of this movement were in
bitter conflict with orthodoxy and its unbend-
ing defenders. Deists, touched by scientific
progress, were in rebellion against an unques-
tioning acceptance of Scripture, of theology,
and of Faith. The conflict was, inevitably, one
of extreme violence and of numerous misunder-
standings. Criticism, even scholarly criticism
of inconsistencies in the Old Testament and in
the New, criticism of the doctrines of the
Logos and of the Trinity, of miracles, of
biblical geology and astronomy, and of super-
naturalism was heresy, and the orthodox recklessly branded the deist as 'infidel' and laid
upon him the dread and ugly charge of 'atheist.' Severe punishments and persecution
constantly threatened human reason for its
defiance of church authority and of creed.
That the deist was actually a sincere searcher
for God and an earnest inquirer into the
true nature of divinity could, hardly, be
recognized, much less acknowledged, by his
bigoted opponent. The deist invoked the authority of Plato and of Cicero; the teleological
argument from design and the ontological or
subjective argument, *i.e.*, that our idea of God

must rest upon a psychological basis, did not help the deists with the orthodox, even though it did, at once, range them, as Platonists, in religious thinking, against the Epicureans, as the latter were understood. The Epicureans had denied divine creation and providence, and to orthodox church-men and to deists, alike, they were the pronounced ' atheists ' of antiquity. The deist Charles Blount (1679) expressed the formula perfectly: to deny God a continual personal and providential control of human affairs was to hold to atheism.[3]   In England, therefore, as long as this controversy raged, — to both parties to the controversy, the orthodox-minded and the deists, Epicurean philosophy of religion was a blinded, perverse, peculiarly pagan misunderstanding of the nature of God, if not an outright denial of God. Had the deists read their Cicero more carefully, they might have found in the *De Natura Deorum* an ascription to the Epicureans of a doctrine of a universal recognition and need of God. Had the deists read their Lucretius, with clearer under-

---

[3] I owe this reference to J. M. Robertson, *A Short History of Free Thought, Ancient and Modern,* London, Watts & Co., 1906,[2] vol. II, p. 129; cf., also, *ibid.,* p. 102, on Meric Casaubon (1668) *vs.* Epicurus and Gassendi, and on Nathaniel Ingelo, of Queen's College (1682), *vs.* Epicurus, etc.

standing, they might have found in the *De Rerum Natura* a powerful weapon for their own arguments in behalf of reason as against faith. But this was not to be, and Lucretius must have seemed to many the prince of ' atheists,' who said " No God," as Mrs. Browning put it even at a later date. In his pompous *The True Intellectual System of the Universe* (1678), Ralph Cudworth (1617–1688), who often compromised his deistic position by obscure thinking, expresses the current feeling freely and fully. Epicurus is rated as " the absolute atheist " and Lucretius, as " the atheistick poet." The Epicurean conception of gods and philosophy of religion are ridiculed without mercy, and many passages from Lucretius are cited, as evidence of his false beliefs. Cudworth, the Christian Platonist, was familiar with large parts of the *De Rerum Natura* and Cudworth even recognized the " elegant " poetry, although his prejudice against " all corporealists, as atheists " and " all atheists, as corporealists " was intense. He was no less certain of the absolute good in the mind of God, far above the flux of sense-impressions. Although scientific England was espousing atomism, England did not approve of Lucretius' denial of providence. Bacon [4] — with the bitter strife between church and dissenters in mind, and the horrors of wars of religion in France — had noted that the spectacle would have made Lucretius " seven times more Epicure and atheist than he was." By such judgments, Lucretius was ruled out of the company of the righteous and the holy, howsoever great his gifts as poet or astonishing his early recognition of the significance of the atom.

The fanatical Mrs. Lucy Hutchinson may not deserve a high place in the history of thought or of letters but her opinion of Lucretius becomes important for us as it shows, so very clearly, what the pious, orthodox Christian in England, in the seventeenth century, inevitably thought of the Roman. The highly interesting letter of dedication to the Earle of Anglesey,[5] that precedes her verse translation of Lucretius, reveals an intensity of feeling against Lucretius, a large measure of misunderstanding, and a positive horror that the Roman had so many admirers. " Atheisme "

[4] *Of Unity in Religion,* in *Essays, Civil and Moral,* III. Bacon, of course, knew his Lucretius and quotes him on occasion.
[5] Presented in 1675 to the Earle of Anglesey, the entire MS is, now, in the British Museum.

[293]

and "impietie" are charged against Lucretius, whose doctrine is branded as "pernitious" and "execrable"; the lady's complete belief in "supernaturall illumination" and in revelation leaves no room for admiration of Lucretian science or of a "foppish" and "Casuall, Ir-rationall Dance of Attomes," no respect for the Epicurean's religion or ethics; her indignation finds relief in the use of such denunciations as "this Dog" and "this Lunatick," who, along with other pagans, "debauched" the learned world. Mrs. Hutchinson says that she "learnt to abhorre" "this crabbed poet," and her translation was to serve as a warning to others to avoid him whom, as we have seen, Lactan-tius, long before, and whom Ficino, later, had also singled out for particularly savage criti-cism. The verse translation has slight merit; as, at the author's request, it remained unpub-lished, it exerted little influence; but Mrs. Hutchinson's confessions, those of a Puritan, are of real value to us.

Pierre Bayle praised the 1695 Oxford edition of Thomas Creech for its "belles notes" and this praise was quite deserved. But the Eng-lish edition is not comparable, in scholarship, to the edition of Lambinus from which Creech very largely drew his notes. The relative merits of these two editions reveal the vastly higher standard of Lucretian scholarship in France about a hundred years before — at least as far as published work is concerned. However, the clearness and brevity of the notes in the English edition and its excellent paraphrases recommended it to its readers and it enjoyed a long vogue.[6] The verse translation of Creech (1682) had also been welcome. What his readers in England thought of Lucretius is another question: the tumult of the deistic controversy in England was intense and obscured many an issue; we have seen, however, how it throws light upon our present problem. Creech, Evelyn, Dryden, and Milton further answer this question.

Creech thought the denial of providence " impious " and without justification; a dedication and a preface that precede the translation carried the usual criticisms [7] of Epicureanism

[6] To my knowledge, Creech was again printed in 1717, 1754, in London; in 1749 and in 1759, in Glasgow; in 1770, in Basle; in 1812, in Edinburgh; in 1818, in Oxford again (this time with Bentley's notes); in 1831 (Augustae Taurinorum). I have not seen the reputed 1776 Leipzig nor the 1785 Venice publications of this text.

[7] Creech, in fact, states it as his purpose to expose Epicurean hypotheses, to overthrow the evil unethical, irreligious, impious, atheistic doctrines.

and absolved Creech, who was a Fellow of All Souls' College, from any dangers of misunderstanding. The translation [8] is, perhaps, no better nor worse than that of Evelyn and it is in the same metre (and in rhymed heroic couplets). It owes its importance to the fact that it is the first translation into English of the six books of the *De Rerum Natura*.

Meantime, John Evelyn (1620–1706) had published his translation of the first book of the *De Rerum Natura* in 1656.[9] John Evelyn Esq. was careful to refute the " irreligion " of the *poet* whom he admired and, in his book, he published letters from friends who praised his own work, highly. It is obvious that an English translation of Lucretius was regarded as an important event. We may judge of its merit by the following, typical specimen:

> *For whilst our Country thus afflicted lies,*
> *With what content can we philosophize!*
> *Nor may brave Memmius then, wanting be*
> *To th' Publike peace in such perplexitie.*

[8] The translation passed through many editions, for almost one hundred years.

[9] *An Essay on the First Book of Titus Lucretius Carus* . . . Interpreted and made English Verse, by John Evelyn Esq., London, Gabriel Bedle and Thomas Collins, 1656.

In this tripping fashion, the stern Lucretius passed into English verse. His espousal of atomism had, by now, become well-known, but, in truly seventeenth-century spirit, Evelyn thought of Lucretius as "no great friend to Gods or Godesses" and he himself had no doubt about God's control of the atomic system.

Dryden (1631–1700), also, had translated passages from Lucretius, and his opinion of the Roman philosopher and poet is clearly expressed in his own Preface to his *Translations from Theocritus, Lucretius, and Horace.* Lucretius' subject-matter was hardly proper material for poetry but the poet had "adorned it with poetical descriptions and precepts of morality." Lucretius' aim to instruct is not regarded as the poet's proper function and, worse than that, the materialist was teaching Memmius to defy the invisible power of God. "In short, he was so much an atheist, that he forgot, sometimes, to be a poet." Of course Lucretius seemed to Dryden to be "often in the wrong" and the Roman's belief in mortality was "absurd." The doctrine of immortality seemed to the Englishman absolutely essential for human virtues. Yet Dryden admired the "sublime and daring genius," who had prepared the way for Virgil, he admired his " lofty expressions," and commented on the " torrent of his verse." Dryden's estimate is quite what we should expect and we may accept it as the view, too, of other men of letters of his time. Virgil excelled all other poets in his own language. *Lucretius dazzled but he was dangerous.* Dryden was naïvely pleased with his own translations,[10] which are in iambic pentameter and in rhymed couplets. These couplets impose great limitations upon his translation as they keep inspiration at bay; the continual break in rhythm is wholly unlike the relentless march of the Latin poetry. There is, often, fine, free rhetoric in Dryden but his verses are rarely an adequate rendering of the sombre splendor of the original.

Milton's *Tractate on Education* (1642) carries students forward through less difficult authors to those " poets which are now counted most hard," and he includes Lucretius in the list of the more difficult — which recalls Quintilian's dictum. Lucretius was read, to be sure,

---

[10] Lucr., I, Invocation; II, *initium,* vss. 1–61; III, ' Against Fear of Death,' vss. 830–*fin.*; IV, On Love, vss. 1037 seq.; V, 222–234, On the Child's Cry at Birth.

but the reservations of his readers, as we have seen, were numerous. That there are, possibly, many imitations [11] of Lucretius in *Paradise Lost* is known to prying scholarship; but these are trifling in the midst of Milton's sublime setting of Hebraic mythology, Puritan theology, and an antiquated science which he employed for his story of Adam, of Creation, of punishment and of Hades, and of the final triumph of God. The Lucretian denial of divine providence and insistence on natural law were absolutely alien to Milton's mind and temperament, — and he must have viewed them with deep prejudice; Epicurus and Epicureanism represented atheism and voluptuousness to the author of the *Areopagitica*. But Milton's positive passion for liberty countenanced free expression of thought and the *De Rerum Natura* was not foolishly banned. Stylistically, Lucretius and Milton deserve to be set side by side; both have been called ' sublime,' and ' Miltonic ' may not be a poor epithet to describe the grandeur of the Lucretian poetry. However, Addison's (1672–

[11] *E.g.*, L., I. 73 and V. 457–70 and *P. L.*, III. 712–721; L., V. 1256 and *P. L.*, XI. 565 seq., etc.; there are many parallels and I take

> The mind is its own place, and in itself
> Can make a Heaven of Hell, a Hell of Heaven

(*P. L.*, I. 254–255) to be one of these.

1719) preference for Homer and Virgil, Pope's (1688–1744) love of Homer and Horace, and Milton's veneration for the Mantuan indicate where real affection and intellectual approval lay. 'Epicureanism,' as it was misunderstood, was taboo among the great majority.

Many have lamented Bentley's failure to carry out his plan of editing Lucretius. Had Richard Bentley (1662–1742) acquired the Vossian MSS of Lucretius for the Bodleian in 1689 or 1690, the text of Lucretius might have had an editor in England, worthy of the task of restoration; endowed with extraordinary classical scholarship, this friend of Newton's was, moreover, possessed of great knowledge of Epicurus and Lucretius.[12] He might have surpassed Lambinus, and England's knowledge of the text of Lucretius and a proper appreciation of Lucretius might have been advanced by a hundred years or more. Emphatically, Bentley was not in sympathy with the Lucretian phi-

[12] Cf. the *Boyle Lectures* (1692), eight Sermons, well described by a general title " The Folly and Unreasonableness of Atheism, demonstrated from the Advantage and Pleasure of a Religious Life, The Faculties of Human Souls, The Structure of Animate Bodies, and the Origin and Frame of the World." Bentley's notes on Lucretius appear in the 1813 (Glasgow) Wakefield edition and in the 1818 Creech edition.

losophy of religion and of the soul; no one wrote more vehemently than he not only against these Epicurean doctrines but against deists, as well, who were condemned as ' infidels ' by his orthodox mind. The Epicurean gods are unmercifully ridiculed; atheism and immorality were Epicurean principles. Bentley was caught in the whirl of antipathy against Epicureanism and Lucretius suffered from such prejudices. But, in spite of all this misunderstanding, a Bentley edition of Lucretius would have been as the heavens above to the mundane, uninspired, timid editions of Creech. Lucretius could hardly come into his own, in England, as yet, although the philosophy of Thomas Hobbes (1588–1679) could not fail, in time, to break down some of the intense prejudice we have found existing against him.

In a world that was still, theoretically, ruled by the magisterial influence of Plato and his absolute Good and by the definitive prescriptions of the tablets of Sinai, Hobbes' revolutionary theory became the " starting-point for an independent, individualistic ethical philosophy in England." The old mold was not shattered at once; perhaps it never will be; but the old code of a transcendental, eternal, immutable objective morality was challenged and an ancient strife renewed in the world. The cardinal doctrine of Hobbes' moral philosophy that "man's appetites and desires are directed toward the preservation of life and to a heightening of it, through pleasure," is pure Epicureanism. Even unselfish-appearing emotions, as of pity and benevolence, were described as "phases of self-regard." Society and the state come into existence, not because of an Aristotelian principle that man is by nature a political animal nor because of divine dictates, but because fear and reason prescribe the law for the preservation of individual interests and the common security. This, too, is a renewal of an old problem. The Epicureans had maintained that society developed on the basis of the principle of self-interest; [13] Manilius and the Stoics saw altruism at work, there. Hobbes' rationalistic ethics became a fundamental dilemma for Christendom; and relativity of good and evil might spring from such premises.

Sense was regarded as a "prime factor in his account of subjective experience." Psycho-

[13] Cf. chapter VIII on Lucretius' re-interpretation of Epicurus' individualism.

physical phenomena were the result of material processes. The 'real' is *body* and the universe is corporeal. Epicurus and Lucretius are reasserting their beliefs, although Hobbes does not mention them by name nor accept the principle of atomism. But his was a thorough-going materialistic sensationalism and in the tradition of his master, Francis Bacon, who was disciple of Epicurus and reader of Lucretius. Locke, as the world knows, developed the thesis of an empirical psychology. Hobbes did not carry his beliefs forward, logically, to any denial of the soul's immortality, as Lucretius had done.

But the most astonishing of all was Hobbes' statement of the theory that religion was sprung from superstition and terror. A conscious revival of an Epicurean-Lucretian dogma? His words do not make this clear although Lucretius would seem to be indicated by " some of the old Poets " who had said " that the Gods were at first created by humane Feare." This was a bold annunciation that might jeopardize belief in revelation, in spite of Hobbes' explanation, that immediately follows, to the effect that acknowledgment of " one God Eternall, Infinite, and Omnipotent " might result, less from fear, more from a search for the " First and Eternall Cause " of all things. The divine origin of religion questioned? a germinal idea was at least released which became responsible for subsequent scientific studies in the history of religions.

Hobbes was not, of course, a thorough-going disciple of Epicurus; in no real sense was he a champion of Epicurus' views; but, none the less, through Hobbes Epicureanism began to filter into English philosophy. His opposition to theology and to established orthodoxy recalls Lucretius; his return to Faith was unlike the Lucretian appeal to reason; his argument that the nature of God was beyond human comprehension was unlike the Roman's belief that the mystery of God was a legitimate part of scientific inquiry; his absolutist theory of government that gave the state control over religion (*i.e.*, worship) and even the right of persecution was wholly un-Lucretian. But it is not my purpose to contrast the total of paradoxes and contradictions in Hobbes' philosophy with any other, but rather to call attention to some Epicurean arguments that lie embedded there. The *Leviathan* (1651) is a monument

to the author's courage, but the heavy price
Hobbes paid, in his late years, for his untimely
'heresies' incidentally and indirectly reveals
England's deep suspicion of Lucretius and his
creeds.

If there were any doubt about the existing hostility against 'Epicureanism,' Walter
Charleton's frank statement that "odium and
infamy," "envy and malice" were being heaped
upon Epicurus through the ignorance of those
who did not understand him should remove that
doubt. "The world was incensed" (is the
way he puts it) at "three capital crimes" of
Epicurus: his argument for soul-mortality, his
denial of Providence, his justification of suicide.
Without subscribing to these doctrines, Walter
Charleton pleads for fair play and truth; the
pathos and eloquence of this *Apologie for Epicurus* are, to-day, very touching. The Essay
on *Epicurus's Morals* that follows the *Apologie*
deserves to rank with Gassendi's work because
of the discovery of many virtues in the Epicurean ethical system. The distinguished
Charleton, friend of Hobbes, was acquainted
with much of the ancient literature on Epicureanism, such as the fragments of Epicurus,
Cicero, Seneca, Plutarch, Diogenes Laertius,

[305]

— and, of course, Lucretius, who can be detected with ease in these English pages.[14]

Robert Burton (1576/7–1640) echoes the prevalent feelings against Epicureanism and expresses the orthodox contempt for those contemporary professed ' Epicureans ' whose ethics signified love of luxury and ease, whose atheism and denial of immortality were an abomination. No reader of *The Anatomy of Melancholy* (1620) can doubt the existence of followers of Epicurean philosophy in England at the time; and Mrs. Hutchinson and Creech also bore testimony to the deplorable fact. The very considerable number of editions of Lucretius that were issued in the seventeenth century clearly reveals the demand for the Latin author in England and on the Continent. And Burton's *Anatomy* makes it very clear that Lucretius' text was a familiar one to all educated readers. The easy manner and frequency of citation from Lucretius place him on a par with the many other Greek and Latin authors from whom Burton quotes with an astonishing knowledge of the classical literature: a veritable Ro-

---

[14] *Epicurus's Morals* (1656); reprinted from the second edition and published by Peter Davies, London, 1926, with a charming introduction by Frederic Manning.

man and Greek anthology is spread before us by this artist in quotation whose mind ranged with utmost facility from Plautus to Petronius, from Homer to Lucian — with a delightful facility that was not, however, always accurate. But no explanations of Lucretius, as in any way a strange figure, were called for; everyone knew or thought that they knew what he stood for, and verses from at least five books [15] are quoted by Burton with the skill of a Montaigne. The *De Rerum Natura* had plainly become part of the learning of the educated Englishman.

It was not only a defense of atomism and an atomic universe that Gassendi [16] (1592–1655) promoted but a defense and revival of notable other aspects of Epicurean philosophy. And Lucretius played an important part in Gassendi's speculations. His rehabilitation of Epicurus completed the growing opposition to Aristotelianism and aided in the inauguration of the philosophy of materialism. [17] Atomism

[15] I have found actual quotations from Books I, II, III, IV, V, with many other references to Lucretius by name only. The edition of F. Dell and Paul Jordan-Smith, London, Routledge and Sons, 1930, gives an all-English text.

[16] We should also remember Daniel Sennert, of the University of Breslau, and Erycius Puteanus, of Louvain, as exponents of the atomism of Democritus and Epicurus, as precursors of Gassendi.

[17] F. A. Lange, *History of Materialism* (transl., E. C.

had been lifted from its humble place in antiquity and started on its career of lasting usefulness. In his doctrine of the atom and void, Gassendi followed Epicurus closely, and rejection of the Ptolemaic universe was accompanied by praises of the Copernican system. Materialism, however, had an ugly sound to many minds: it connoted atheism to many and sensual ethics to others. A philosophic defense of materialism was of utmost significance and an intellectual justification of some of its implications, epochal. Gassendi could not accept all of the Epicurean-Lucretian conclusions, however, — least of all the negation of Providence and denial of the soul's immortality. Gassendi, the priest, expressed his allegiance to church-doctrine in the word: *sequor;* and in these two principles he followed neither Epicurus nor Lucretius. He met the current suspicion that materialism signified atheism with his own firm belief in God, as creator of earth and sea, of plants and animals, in God who had, originally, bestowed motion upon the atoms. While Gassendi undertook a defense of the Epicurean explanation of sensation and of our sensible

Thomas), 3 vols., London, Kegan Paul, Trench, Trubner & Co., N. Y., Harcourt, Brace & Co., 1925,[3] remains invaluable.

qualities, as the product of atoms and space, the difficulties appeared to him as very great. He put Lucretius' explanations in the best possible light, but he could not follow Lucretius' ultimate conclusions; on the contrary, he regarded the soul as incorporeal and immortal spirit. This was, to be sure, quite out of harmony with his system; but Church doctrine or personal feeling or both led him to maintain and, sincerely, to proclaim his conviction that the soul cannot die. The contrary view of Epicurus seemed to him *impietas*.

While we know that neither Epicurus nor Lucretius was 'atheist,' in the true sense of the word, the seventeenth century felt differently. Epicurus' participation in established ritual and performance of sacrifice puzzled even his admirers and required explanation. Gassendi resorted to the subterfuge of the time, in maintaining that Epicurus was free to think, though not free to act. More than one thinker of the seventeenth and eighteenth centuries found himself in just such a conflict between church-authority and science. Hobbes stated a similar conclusion: that the state should, properly, control worship, though man's mind must be free! The outcome of such a situation was beyond the ken of philosopher or of prophet. Gassendi's explanation of Epicurean participation in established worship was, historically, inaccurate, but it represents an application of his own seventeenth-century psychology to that of the ancient Greeks and Romans. Every student of Epicureanism knows, to-day, that the sincere Epicurean worshipper employed established ritual as a means to an end, meantime not surrendering his mental reservations — which were no secret and remained his inalienable right. He denied Providence, to be sure; but he did not deny the existence of gods; he worshipped gods as he understood them. We know of no compulsion in ancient worship. Gassendi held to his own belief in God's control; his supposition that Epicurus and Lucretius were 'atheists' was inevitable; his defense of the Epicurean's worship was untrue — although the mere fact of defense was significant. Gassendi ventured to quote Lucretius and Petronius on the origins of religion in fear, and these beginnings of anthropological speculation, with their heavy debt to Lucretius, constituted a threat to orthodoxy and revelation. The ferment in religious thought is manifest.

Gassendi placed Epicurus before the world as a man of character — a revolutionary view but, now for long, recognized as true. His defense of hedonism remained in seventeenth-century France, to effect later unpredictable and momentous consequences in philosophy, literature, and life.

Voluptatem sine qua Notio Felicitatis nulla est, rem bonam suapte natura esse . . .

was a challenge that renewed an old controversy, and the significance of the argument lies in the fact that controversy could be and was renewed. Were the old antitheses of *virtus* and *voluptas*, of Stoic repression and Epicurean freedom, of Cicero and Lucretius justified? was church-dogma that sought to control conduct, infallible? were duty and happiness irreconcilable? At least Gassendi catalogued Epicurean virtues, and a new understanding of Epicurean ethics was achieved: temperantia, continentia, fortitudo circa metum mortis, iustitia (and a proper explanation of its origin), amicitia were found to reside within Epicureanism. Materialism and sensual ethics were not, of necessity, associate, as a study of the deeper aspects of Epicurean ethics finally revealed.

[311]

Gassendi had gone far in his re-establishment of Epicurean and Lucretian dogmas. While many authorities are cited in Gassendi's work — his knowledge of pagan and Christian literature was very extensive — passages, many of them, of length, are quoted from Lucretius, and they meet us at almost every turn. The Lucretian eulogy of Epicurus, from the first book of the *De Rerum Natura,* verses from the fifth book, prognosticating the ultimate dissolution of the universe, lines explaining the boundless universe, the pessimistic passage relating to the cry of the child, at birth, because of its intuitive conception of the evils of life, passages, even, from the third book on courage in the face of death are but a few of these numerous verses that ring, in the pages of Gassendi, with all of their old authority. No one, before, had dared to raise Lucretius to the eminent level he now attained — a triumph, of which Poggio could hardly have dreamed. Gassendi combined admiration for the poet with rational argument for acceptance of many conclusions of the thinker.

But let no one think that Gassendi's championship of Epicurus was without peril. His audacity brought upon himself charges of libertinism and anathemas of the pious, the experts in eternity. Molière may have been a pupil, he certainly was an admirer, of Gassendi's, and in Lucretius he found his chosen philosopher. The prince of comedy was strangely attracted by the austerity of the tragic Roman; perhaps it was the satirist in Lucretius that drew him. During his lifetime, he had undoubtedly translated much of the *De Rerum Natura*. We do not need to inquire into the extent of Molière's acceptance of Lucretius' philosophizing because that is far from clear, but the Roman left a deep mark on the French genius. But we do know that Lucretius was regarded as dangerous company, so that Molière's discreet editors and publishers failed to include in an edition of all of Molière's works which was in preparation in 1682 (nine years after his death), whatever portions of Molière's translations of Lucretius still remained in existence, in manuscript, at the time. All that is left of his version of the Latin poem is the small, delicious fragment on the blindness of lovers which appears in *Le Misanthrope*.[18] It may give us an idea of the charm of his other versions of Lucretian verses

[18] Act II, Scene 5 (Lucr., IV. 1155 seq.). Ovid (*A. A.*, II. 657 seq.) imitated this passage and Arnobius was familiar with it.

[313]

and leaves us quite unreconciled to the loss of the rest; nor does their fate make us more content with the translations of Molière's contemporaries, Michel de Marolles, the abbé, and Coutures, which have survived the fitful ravages of time.

The *Dictionaire Historique et Critique*[19] of Pierre Bayle (1647–1706) sums up, very fairly, I believe, the opinion of Lucretius held by thinking men, in the seventeenth century, in France. One of the greatest of the Roman poets, — Lucretius' high place in the history of poetry was not questioned by Bayle or any other who knew him. No criticism of Lucretius' atomism — which is probably significant of the wider acceptance of this theory.[20] Not a trace of the old unreasoning criticism of Epicurean ethics — on the contrary, strong and significant defense of Epicurus and Lucretius and their morality. The observation that the *De Rerum Natura* is strewn with moral maxims might, at least, prepare the way for a subsequent critical and correct estimate of Lucretian ethics. Lucretius' vehement denial of providence and

[19] Art., *Lucrece.*
[20] Bayle discusses atomism in his article: *Epicure.*

[314]

of the soul's immortality gave Bayle the greatest pause, as it did others. Lucretius' conception of the nature of gods and of the soul's
mortality was held to rest on insufficient, un-
tenable, and fallacious argument. But *Lucretius' exposition of these views had become
classic.* Even if acceptance of Lucretian conclusions did not follow, *they haunted men's
minds and could not be forgotten.*[21]

Lucretius' progress toward a proper understanding and appreciation was still blocked by
animosities, he was buffeted by prejudice and
hostility, antagonism against him was sharp.
When we consider the translations of Lucretius
into French, which appeared in this century,
in France, as well as the editions, take into account the influence of Gassendi and the adop-

21 Bayle regarded the invocation as a jeu d'esprit — a
mere accommodation to prevailing ancient literary fashion,
not a contradiction or a renunciation of philosophic views,
as some held. The correct interpretation, at the time, was
well-nigh impossible. Bayle's own copious notes, which ac-
company his text, show very clearly that the ' learned ' literature on Lucretius was growing apace. Bayle knew the
ancient literature; he also knew Gifanius, Lambinus, Creech,
Barthius, and many more of the latter-day students of Lucretius; also, the translations of Marolles and Coutures. He
gives and credits the Eusebius (Jerome) *vita* of Lucretius,
and probably most of his contemporaries accepted that
' life,' in the absence of anything better (it appears, again
and again, in the editions).

tion of Lucretian passages into French literature,[22] it would seem that France was leading
in a growing enlightened estimate, and that
England and Germany still lagged behind. Lactantius, long before, had sought to demolish
Lucretius; Ficino, also, with powerful forces
arrayed behind himself, had attempted his annihilation; solemn denunciations were not lacking in this century. Editions [23] of Lucretius

[22] I need mention only Corneille and Racine for un-
doubted parallels, and La Fontaine; the latter made use of
Lucretius' tableau of the seasons.

[23] Pareüs (publ. in Frankfurt) 1631 (accompanied by
Aonii Palearii Verulani *De Animorum Immortalitate,* libri
III);

Nardius (Florence) 1647;

Faber (Salmurii) 1662 (reprinted in Cambridge in 1675,
1686);

Fayus (Paris, in the Delphin classics) 1680;

Creech (Oxford) 1695.

These editions are not critical editions, in our sense of
the word. They display erudition; they carry the *testimonia* and apologies that had appeared in the sixteenth
century. Nardius was distinctly opposed to the L. philosophy and Fayus was strongly Christian and anti-L.
Fayus edited L. for the young prince, because L. was
" elegantissimus poeta." Faber regarded the poet as
" praestantissimus " and he had a high regard for Gassendi; however, cf. the ' sermon ' (before Bk. III. of L.).

Lucretius' text was also printed in Leyden, Geneva,
Lyon, Amsterdam, and Naples.

In 1650, Michel de Marolles' transl. appeared in Paris;
it was reprinted in 1659 and appeared again in 1677 (re-
vised by another hand). M. le Baron des Coutures' transl.
also appeared, in Paris, during this century; it, too, was
reprinted several times. These translations were not successful, perhaps even less so than that of Creech (1682).

continued to appear and he was read in England, France, Italy, Germany, Switzerland, and Holland. The frail fabric of a poem, tossed on stormy seas, survived another century of opposition, until it reached the quieter haven of the nineteenth century.

B — THE EIGHTEENTH CENTURY

The Renaissance had been charmed with the poetry of Lucretius, and the language that had been the subject of barren study on the part of Roman grammarians, before, sprang into life, bright and sharp, quivering with life. But they were, after all, mere words for the sixteenth century — but oh! what words — to clothe an impossible philosophy. The seventeenth century had its deep prejudices against Lucretius and these were sincere enough, but all of the abuse and growing rebellion against his thought was, in part at least, a confession of suspicion that the errors of his thinking might not be, altogether, error after all — as Hobbes and Gassendi were to prove. The eighteenth century

Marolles apologized for his publication; the L. philosophy was wrong but the poem was " heroic "; Coutures called L. the " incomparable " poet who had embellished a poor philosophy; yet he recognized some fine traits in the ethics.

I have not seen a Dutch translation of 1693.

was still in active opposition and we may for our convenience regard Cardinal de Polignac as the focal point of that hostility, which could not ignore the forces that Hobbes and Gassendi had released. Lucretius was the Cardinal's natural foe. Lucretius was the avowed opponent of the ancient belief in *divine Providence;* he therefore appeared to almost all as the enemy of religion. In the eighteenth century, however, Voltaire was to praise him as enemy of superstition — which was a step in the right direction of proper understanding. Lucretius stood before the world as exponent of a *materialistic psychology* and was known by all to have denied the cherished belief in immortality. De La Mettrie, however, in the eighteenth century, was to espouse his methods of reasoning and lead the way to revolutionary views. Lucretius, as Epicurean, still signified to many the defender of an unreasonable *doctrine of Pleasure.* But the hedonism of the Epicurean school was to be judged by fairer critics — after the days of Hobbes and Gassendi and thanks to their influence — than those who had maligned it in the past. French and British philosophy was to find more justification for hedonism than had ever occurred to Epicurus.

Politically, the seventeenth and eighteenth centuries were out of sympathy with Epicureanism. Autocrats could invoke Christianity in behalf of their own selfish ends; but the doctrine of divine right of kings, wars of aggression and conquest were wholly out of harmony with the spirit of Epicurean-Lucretian gospel of man's individual dignity. Epicureanism was not the necessary philosophy for despots and politicians. Political revolution in England, France, and America, leading to the establishment of parliaments and democracies, was more in keeping with the Epicurean doctrine of individualism. However, the earlier Epicurean conception of flight from the world did not meet the needs of this hour, while Lucretius' re-interpretation of individual ethics for the salvation of society had not, as yet, been comprehended. In England, France, and in the American colonies men's minds were engrossed in practical problems of political and social philosophy, and Lucretius offered no immediate, practical solution of these difficulties. Meantime, life was rooted in orthodox religious beliefs and, wherever transcendentalism prevailed, Lucretius could hardly be a favorite, whether in his native Italy or in New England.

The eighteenth century assuredly cherished its prejudices and Lucretius represented no message of vitality to the century at large, either in Europe or in America. Church and State, of course, opposed him. Leaders in government could properly make their appeals to Virgil and Seneca — for defense of imperialism and obedience — to Plato and to Cicero — as witnesses to God's protection — but Lucretius was too much of a rebel, too much an exponent of freedom to win the favor of Church or State. It was in despair that some minds during the French Revolution turned to the Lucretian doctrine of the soul's mortality; the nineteenth century was, finally, to discover the ethical implications of this belief. Lucretius found one of his greatest admirers in Frederick the Great of Prussia who offered asylum to De La Mettrie, to Helvétius, and to Voltaire, and who was enamored of the Lucretian poetry and of the denial of immortality. But his was only a partial and fragmentary understanding of a tremendous doctrine.

In Cardinal Melchior de Polignac (1661–1742) Lucretius found a vigorous and bitter opponent, whose *Anti-Lucretius* was a learned and elaborate refutation, written in Latin hexameters, drawn out into nine books, and, indeed, honored by translation, in part, into English. It represents a resumption of the seventeenth-century animus against Epicurus and Lucretius, and the dread of the Church of these ancient 'atheists.' The Cardinal argued against Lucretius, against *voluptas* which subverted religion, against Hobbes' Epicurean theory of the origins of justice, against Gassendi, and the doctrine of void, against Newton and his theory of gravity, against the theory that atoms were indivisible and immortal, against Spinoza and the belief that motion was inherent in matter, against Locke and his sensation-theories — *a sweeping condemnation of everything that Lucretius stood for and of his growing influence.* The Cardinal staunchly held to his belief that cause exists before matter, that the soul is immortal, and he properly exalted God as the supreme creator. Plato was an "illustrious spirit," while Lucretius, as thinker, was hopelessly in error. But even the Cardinal bowed to the ancient *poet,* upon whose brow he was ready to lay the laurel. The storm of his indignant protest was no accident in the eighteenth century; the war that had been waged against Lucretius in the seventeenth century was continued, and is proof, at once, of hostility against him and of a growing recognition of the validity of some of the Epicurean doctrines.[24] The eighteenth century, before its close, opened wider doors for a deeper understanding of Lucretius.

France [25] was more favorably minded toward Lucretius and the Epicurean philosophy than any other country in Europe, but even there a very considerable tolerance and enlightenment left Lucretius' position an ambiguous one.[26] *Materialism* and a materialistic explanation of sensationalism were not without able defenders: the relation of 'soul' to the bodily organism and especially to the nervous system was discovered; De La Mettrie, Helvétius, and d'Holbach were among those who dared to argue this question, and, of the three, Baron

[24] *Anti-Lucretius sive de Deo et Natura* (published in Paris, 1749, and dedicated to Pope Benedict). George Canning published his *A Translation of Anti-Lucretius* in 1766, in London, and his frankly expressed purpose was " to promote the cause of Religion and Virtue, by overturning the Pillars of Immorality and Atheism." (5 books only were completed.)

[25] Cf. J.–M. Guyau, *La Morale D'Épicure* et ses Rapports avec les Doctrines contemporaines, Paris, Alcan, 1927.[7]

[26] C.–A. Fusil, " Lucrèce et les Philosophes Du XVIIIe Siècle," in *Revue d'Histoire littéraire de la France*, XXXV. 194–210 (1928), and " Lucrèce et Les Littérateurs Poètes et Artistes Du XVIIIe Siècle," *ibid.*, XXXVII. 161–176 (1930).

d'Holbach followed Lucretius to the logical, bitter, and dangerous end that the soul is mortal. *Atomism* and Epicurean physics were, still, most severely assailed: Bayle (before), Voltaire, Diderot, along with many others, rejected the doctrine and, with it, the " hazard " of the atom, as firmly as did Cardinal de Polignac: " ridiculous " and " absurd " were typical of the violent epithets flung at Lucretius, the scientist. Atomism signified a denial of a supreme, intelligent Power, it meant ' atheism,' it destroyed belief in immortality: these conclusions were more than the eighteenth century could swallow. Lucretius, as poet of science, was largely ignored even by haughty sciences of chemistry and of biology which proceeded along their own way, forgetful of their fathers and founders. Meantime, French rationalism was discovering values in Epicurean *ethics*, as Gassendi had done, before; while the Epicurean withdrawal from life was held in reproach, Voltaire distinguished between " true " Epicurean ethics and the conventional interpretation that guided many contemporary ' Epicureans '; Voltaire, indeed, found Lucretius " admirable " in his ethics; and the encyclopedists praised specific Epicurean virtues and the doctrine of happi-

[3 2 3]

ness! Some recognition of the truth about
Epicurean philosophy of *religion* was dawn-
ing upon the minds of a few; while the Epicurean gods were generally held up to ridicule,
Voltaire, at least, discovered in Lucretius, an
ancient Protestant against the evils of orthodoxy and against superstition. Rousseau and
Buffon, meantime, owed a large debt to Lucretius in their studies of primitive man and
his *social evolution;* the *Roman's poetry* also
obsessed their minds. The question was hotly
debated whether didactic poetry — whether of
Lucretius or of Pope — was poetry at all, and
Virgil doubtless was the favorite of the great
majority. But Lucretius had his ardent and
even eloquent admirers, and Voltaire, Buffon,
Diderot, and André Chénier were conspicuous
among his champions who eulogized the independent spirit of the poet, his power and enthusiasm, the flame of his audacity, the grace of
many superb passages in the *De Rerum Natura;*
the invocation, the other prologues, the close
of the third book, the hymn to death, the terrifying close of the sixth book on the ravages
of the plague were repeatedly paraphrased and
imitated — most of the great passages, in fact,
all the way from the appeal to the goddess of

[3 2 4]

love and life who greets us at the opening of the poem to the lines at the close of the last book through which the grim Reaper sweeps his scythe relentlessly. The didactic and philosophic verse of André Chénier (1762–1794) —le poète scientifique — was, in no small part, inspired by Lucretius to whom the author of *L'Hermès* paid magnificent tribute:

Souvent mon vol, armé des ailes de Buffon,
Franchit avec Lucrèce, au flambeau de Néwton,
La ceinture d'azur sur le globe étendue.

Himself a very great artist, his melancholy found exaltation in the sombre flights of the Roman poet; and this outburst was an expression of adoration of freedom that reminds us of the intensity of Bruno's devotion to the spirit of the dead Roman poet.[27]

There was, perhaps, no other man of letters of the eighteenth century to whom Lucretius' valiant spirit meant more than to Voltaire (1694–1778), the chief of European 'heretics' for fifty tempestuous years, the intellectual chieftain of his time. In his attacks on a persecuting and privileged orthodoxy, he often

[27] I ought at least to mention Fontanes, Lebrun, Hesnault, Saint-Lambert, Roucher for their knowledge of and indebtedness to L. in varying degrees.

added to his own irony the scorn-freighted
words of Lucretius. He praised the English for
their freedom of thought; the Greeks came
under his condemnation for their persecution of
Anaxagoras, Aristotle, and, especially, of Socrates; the Romans were praised for their greater
tolerance. Although atheism was ' un monstre,'
although the Epicureans had denied a universal,
divine nature, the great Creator of all, although
Newton had demonstrated God to the sages,
although Voltaire had his deistic reservations,
and although Lucretius' seductive verses on
mortality were erroneus, Voltaire saw, in Lucretius, a champion of freedom. And from
him he borrowed biting satire to make the sting
of his own shafts sharper. Accusing Lucretius
for not reproaching the follies of idolatry, he
praised the Roman for his attacks on superstition, mother of a horrible brood. Voltaire's
indignation against ecclesiasticalism was to
burn its way to a purer religion and, despite
the errors of Lucretius, Voltaire made of him
his ally; their intellectual fanaticism was arrayed against intolerable beliefs of Church and
State. Voltaire had read his Lucretius atten-
tively, he quotes from Lucretius very frequently, and he believed that the verse

tantum relligio potuit suadere malorum

would last as long as the world. Alas for the errors of his physics! but the Lucretian combat with superstition made the Roman poet almost " divine," — one, whose tomb all the nations should crown with flowers.[28] Alas for his physics! which alone prevented this final honor. No one since the days of Seneca had been more chivalrous than Voltaire who, despite his disagreements, visioned this imaginary cenotaph for a brave soldier of Reason. Lucretius had failed in many essentials of philosophic speculation; as poet he was, often, superb; as a leader against the tyrannies of superstition he was immortal.

Lucretius was translated into French by La Grange and by Le Blanc de Guillet and, for the first time into Italian, by Allessandro Marchetti. All three extolled the splendors of the poet, as might be expected; the Frenchmen were lenient with the philosopher but the Italian expressed his detestation of his errors. The repeated reprintings of two of these translations,[29] as

[28] All students of Lucretius should read, at least, *Les Lettres de Memmius à Cicéron* (1771).

[29] Alessandro Marchetti, Londra, 1717 — reprinted 1754 (Amsterdam), 1759 (Lausanne), 1761, 1768, 1779 (Lon-

well as that of Creech of the previous century, the first translation of Lucretius into German, and the numerous editions and Latin texts of Lucretius that were published in England, Scotland, France, Italy, Germany, Switzerland, Holland, and Austria prove how great the demand for Lucretius was and how widely the poet was being read. Of these editions,[30] those of Havercamp and Wakefield deserve special attention.

The Havercamp and Wakefield eighteenth-century editions of Lucretius are monuments to the incredible carelessness and inexact scholarship of their editors. In a century when classical authors were widely known, read, and quoted, when the roll of classical scholars and

don), 1804 (Amsterdam), 1874 (Milan) — M. L. G. = M. La Grange, Paris, 1768 — reprinted, at least 5 times — M. Le Blanc de Guillet, Paris, 1788 — Creech (transl.) 1682 (Oxford), 1714–1776 (London, 5 times). Another transl. of L. into English, done by "Guernier and Others," appeared in London, in 1743. The J. H. F. Meineke transl. (publ. in Leipzig, 1795), about one hundred years after Creech, is the earliest German translation published in Germany; we should recall Herder's marked appreciation of L.; for Lessing, see p. 343. A Dutch transl. appeared in 1701; the transl. of F.–X. Mayr was the first to appear in Austria (I have not seen this book).

[30] I know of 18 such, not including the Creech text which was reprinted at least 4 times, in Europe, in this century. The Tonson and Baskerville publications were very handsome.

archeologists was long and honorable, when parliamentary orators were accomplished in classical literature, when a new interest in antiquities of ancient Greece and Rome was responsible for great collections, Lucretius was being edited by the incompetent Havercamp and Wakefield. Sigebert Havercamp (1684–1742) was the professor at Leyden who produced the variorum edition of Lucretius in two large volumes (1725) in which he included, without taste or discrimination, readings of the text and commentaries of all preceding editions that he could lay hands on. Munro has, for once and for all, flayed Havercamp who failed, completely, to realize the significance of the two Vossian MSS, which were in Leyden and entirely accessible; but Havercamp made the most wretched use of them. Prefaces of the Aldine (1500), of the 1515 Aldine, of the Bologna (1511), of the 1512 Juntine, and of the Lambinus editions are reprinted, with their various *apologies* to prince and bishop for publication of the unorthodox Lucretius; the words of Joan Baptista Pius are typical:

omnia orthodoxae fidei subicio.

The edition includes an array of ancient and later *testimonia* and a 'life' of Lucretius, — everything done without critical judgment. While other ancient authors were affectionately chosen and edited with more sympathy and care, during this century, *Lucretius suffered strangely.* Nor did Gilbert Wakefield's London edition of 1796–97 depart, greatly, from the methods or progress beyond the standards of Havercamp. Accumulation was the aim and passion of both, and Wakefield's edition of three volumes impressed many because of its size and its array of apparent scholarship; it actually deceived competent scholars, until a keener criticism finally established the text of Lucretius and provided a more reasoned interpretation. It was the *poet* who was honored by these monumental editions and, inadequate as they now seem to us, we cannot ignore them or the other editions of this century in any study of the influence of Lucretius. In the poem were embedded brilliant gems of phrase and many astonishing moral maxims — a new discovery — and these considerations undoubtedly entered into the general contemporary attitude toward Lucretius. Poets might use him as a quarry and moralists might find sentiments of value, despite the dangerous gospel of hedonism. The editions are testimony however, chiefly, to the established fame of a great writer, whose place in the history of literature could not be denied.[31] As compendia of information, howsoever lifeless, gathered from many sources, some false, some true, the editions proved important milestones in the history of Lucretian studies.

The *poet* Lucretius appears in eighteenth-century English literature, but I shall limit myself to two important examples. *The Seasons* of the pious James Thomson (1700–1748) was a pioneer literary movement, and, along with echoes of Virgil, there are, too, unquestionably, suggestions of Lucretius. While these are largely verbal in character, they are too important to overlook. Lucretius' diction, quite certainly, but also some minor aspects of his scientific thought appear to lurk in Thomson's mind.[32] But there was far more of spiritual affinity between Lucretius and Thomas Gray

[31] Not one of the eighteenth-century editions of L. was a ' critical ' edition. Neither Havercamp nor Wakefield nor Creech was a Bentley or a Lachmann. Wakefield was reprinted in 1801 (Leipzig), 1813 (Glasgow), 1821 (London), 1823 (for the Delphin Classics).

[32] Cf., *e.g.*, G. G. Cronk, "Lucretius and Thomson's Autumnal Fogs," in *The Am. J. of Phil.*, LI. 233–242 (1930).

(1716–1771), whose characteristic melancholy made the famous debt to Lucretius a natural one:

For them no more the blazing hearth shall burn,
Or busy housewife ply her evening care;
No children run to lisp their sire's return,
Or climb his knees the envied kiss to share.

Both poets [33] felt the tragedy of the terrible immanence of the grave.

C — Lucretius and the Present

The nineteenth and twentieth centuries have been more hospitable: English and French rationalism provided intelligent interpretation and defense of Epicurean ethics. It would be an impossible task to give any detailed demonstration of this, here, nor is that called for. Epicurean thinking has entered subtly and deeply into all of our modes of thought and effort; literature and life bear abundant testimony to the truth of this on every hand. The

[33] Cf., Lucr., III. 894 seq. (and Virgil's *Georgics,* II. 523 and Horace, *Odes,* II. 14. 21). Gray has been called a "refined Epicurean." It is important, too, to recall that the poet Gray attempted a *De Principiis Cogitandi* (its relations to Locke and Lucretius are obvious).

growth of science, with its tremendous emphasis upon the values of this world rather than upon a phantom other-world, and, especially, the influence of the doctrine of evolution have not only released Lucretius from many of the old hatreds, but have even created a new admiration for him. Lucretius had been a dazzling meteor in the sky, whose fall had been predicted either hopefully or with certainty. He has come to be recognized as a planet belonging to the established systems, an essential part of the Graeco-Roman tradition and all that this tradition signifies to literature, rationalism, and idealism.

Lucretius' fame rests on broad foundations. Though not a scientist in the modern sense of the term, his search for the laws that govern the universe and his faith in them established a great position.[34] Though not an independent researcher and experimenter, all too much a follower of Epicurus, as scientist and as logician, he was, none the less, a great adventurer who sought the objective of all scientific inquiry, freedom from Nature's control, freedom

[34] Cf., *e.g.*, John Tyndall, *The Belfast Address*, London, Longmans, Green & Co., 1874. I hardly know of any finer statement in English on the subject of the relation of science to religion.

from a fearful control of ignorance, superstition, and fear. His defense and exposition of atomism placed Lucretius, as scientist, far ahead of the ancient Roman world in physical speculation, and related him to an age 1600 years after his own time — an extraordinary anticipation of modern thought.[35] The same amazing leap beyond the limits of contemporary thinking appears in his vision of a limitless universe. Nature finally justified Lucretius in the person of Giordano Bruno and through the experiments of Galileo and Kepler, — although this doctrine may be questioned today. Biological science eventually proved the truth that lurked in the relatively dim and uncertain speculations of Lucretius. His graphic description_ of a vast, natural experimental laboratory in which atoms were creating, after infinite combinations, at first false forms and eventually the true and permanent genera and species — the inorganic and the organic world, alike: rocks, plants, birds, men, gods, and the stars — is a crude but a genuine theory of evolution. But neither the ancient world nor

[35] Cf. the excellent essay, " The Scientific Significance of Lucretius," by E. N. Da C. Andrade, in Munro *Lucr.*, Vol. II, London, G. Bell and Sons, 1928.

the Christian, for centuries, could grasp the idea that was fermenting in Lucretius' mind — that Nature operates through strange laws of natural selection until, after a fierce struggle for existence, the fittest survive. That the modern science of biology has developed apart from Lucretius and, for that matter, largely apart from Aristotle and Theophrastus, does not diminish our wonder at the intuitive insight of these ancients into some of the obscure mysteries of life. No one would credit Lucretius with knowledge of protoplasm, the amoeba, or of cellular structure revealed to us by the microscope; nor did he know of the variation of species, but, none the less, his three Fates were heredity, environment, and function — as much as they are of the modern biologist. The new biology, and, for that matter, modern atomism and psychology, are not so much in conflict with Lucretius; they, rather, enlarge and transform his theories.[36] Modern anthropology,[37] too, has in large part corroborated the truth of Lucretius' exposition of the progress of primi-

[36] Cf., *e.g.,* J. A. Thomson, *Everyday Biology,* New York, Doran, 1924.

[37] Lucretius is quoted with approval by E. B. Tylor and praised by E. Clodd; cf., also, E. E. Sikes, *The Anthropology of the Greeks,* London, David Nutt, 1914.

tive man, and not the least important discovery has confirmed the Lucretian belief in the origins and evolution of religious thought.

Lucretius firmly and fiercely denied the presence of any Power, outside, to make earth, sea and sky, and all living creatures. This was part of his intellectual integrity and refusal to be traitor to his science [38] and himself. It was a natural universe that he sought to explain, without reference to the supernatural. Few scientists have stood so firmly on what Lucretius conceived to be his scientific ground. We have learned of resentment against him, because of his denial of divine creation, of divine providence, and of divine anger. That resentment has, I believe, often clouded men's minds; and it is only recently that some have grasped the truth of Lucretius' rejection of orthodoxy but his no less tenacious hold on religion. The gods *are* and Epicurean philosophy did not deny their existence. The important fact of

[38] Epicurean science, let us remember, included medicine. Broadly defined, health depended upon a proper arrangement of atoms. Pestilence is discussed by L., VI. 1090 seq. It is maintained by some that the work of Fracastoro (1483–1553), on infections, owes its inspiration to Lucretius' "seeds of disease." Whether true or not, the ancient writer (in a certain sense) and the later Italian (assuredly) had anticipated medical science of the 19th century.

[336]

their existence is proven by the fact of our knowing or imagining anything about them. Epicurean epistemology presupposes the existence of the object, as a necessary antecedent to our knowledge of the object. The Epicurean Lucretius assuredly poured into his new concept of God, his idol of mind and heart, all the idealism of his nature and of his philosophy; and, if the ancient world and the world since his day has scorned his religion, it has been, in part at least, through misunderstanding and largely because of the prejudice that denial of providence inevitably awoke. His religious stand, however, is one of his great claims to fame, because of the courage required for defense of what his reason had taught him.

Three great philosopher-poets, the author of the book of Job, Lucretius, and Omar Kháyyám were all, in their day, regarded as skeptics and heretics, but the faith of heresy is often more profound than that of orthodoxy, and the heroic soul that seeks escape from dogma may find God in finer ways and discover a deeper anchorage. Although a contemporary world may stone its prophets, posterity, sometimes, immortalizes them. Through reason, Lucretius sought the nature of God, as surely as did

[337]

Socrates and Santayana, seeking — if possible
to find it — intellectual justification for his beliefs and a readjustment of emotional values,
as, for example, those of ritual.[39]

If Lucretius had written in prose, perhaps
his fame would have been less great. It was
his verse that captivated, in many centuries,
while his thought repelled men; and, at many
times, his fame as poet flourished while his
repute as thinker suffered. About the distinction of his verse there never has been, relatively, much dispute. The problem whether
Lucretius or Virgil may be the greater poet
has appeared and re-appeared, in time, as we
have seen; but the futility of such argument
has not obscured the essential supremacy of
both poets in their respective fields. Everyone
knows that the Lucretian verse lacks the finish
of the Virgilian; everyone knows that archaisms characterize the *De Rerum Natura* from
beginning to end; everyone knows that Lucretius' white heat of passion made him careless
of minutiae of style and of the finer points of
composition. Lucretius' close relationship to

[39] The Epicurean argument for the true nature of the
gods appears more clearly in Cic., *De N. D.*, I. As for
ritual and its emotional appeal, see L., II. 600 seq.

[3 3 8]

Ennius, one of his great admirations, has long since been recognized; Ennius, Lucretius, and Virgil are the great triumvirate and all would grant that the third transmuted the first into gold. Yet the monotonous music of many long stretches in the *De Rerum Natura* is redeemed by solemnity, the steady march of the Lucretian verses — not unlike the tramp of the Roman army — is relieved by brilliant descriptions, by emotions of exultation and despair; the rhythm is not broken by pretty devices any more than is the music of the spheres. Lucretius himself knew the technical and other difficulties in the way of his verse-composition, but, for the most part, weaknesses of verse vanish in the swiftness and fire of his enthusiasm. At times, the Lucretian poetry creeps but, again, it soars with a majesty that has led many to call it sublime.

The rare combination of philosopher, scientist, and poet has appeared in Empedocles, in Lucretius, and in Goethe. The Roman poet glorified his science by his art.[40] Laboring in the silent watches of the night in order to perfect his medium, to succeed in his high adventure, and to win for himself the prize of

[40] I. 136–145, 921–950, IV. 1. seq.

[339]

the poet's crown, Lucretius was well aware of the perils of travelling a new road, of charting an unknown way in Roman letters. But, eager to make his message more welcome by means of the honey of the Muses in order to win a larger attentive audience, Lucretius, who all but worshipped at the shrine of science and to whose mind Homer was the prince of poets, felt that there was nothing irrational in the marriage of his science and his poetry — so completely were the scientist and the poet fused into one, in his own personality.

It is a proper question [41] to ask, what the poetic motives are that underlie the Epicurean system of philosophy, to which the poetic soul of Lucretius responded with such intense and sure enthusiasm. Poetry is implicit in Nature and her laws, though Dryden did not think so, just as genuinely and as richly as in human action, in spite of Aristotle. Nature and her laws — much profounder theme for poetry than mythology or the vagaries of animism! Not merely a scientific knowledge lies in the poet's mind nor merely the scholar's interest in ab-

[41] Cf. C. H. Herford, *The Poetry of Lucretius* (a Rylands Library Lecture), Manchester (Engl.) Univ. Press, Longmans, Green and Co., 1918.

stractions — but an emotional response that creates a unity between the poet and the majesty of nature, unfolding a vision beyond the reach of scientific understanding. Lucretius, as poet, transformed and transfigured the laws of Nature, a pragmatic world, the atom of matter and its intense creative energy into a universe of tremendous clash and storm, of calm serenity, and of impending disaster; the drama of creation and the tragedy of cosmos' destruction, constantly renewed, strike as deep into the heart of man, and especially of the poet, as the tale of an Oedipus or of a King Lear — for to the poet's imagination nature's epic inspires moods of exaltation and, no less, an enormous sense of melancholy. Lucretius stood spellbound before the spectacle. But, in addition — these larger aspects of the subject aside — Lucretius, as poet, manifests a freshness of feeling in his descriptions of smaller natural scenes that gives his poem a deeper significance for modern times than it had for the ancient, as Sellar [42] has pointed out. Besides — the *poet's* love and sympathy for the beautiful and the *poet's* personification of natural forces tran-

[42] Cf., also, H. R. Fairclough, *Love of Nature Among the Greeks and Romans,* 1930 (in the " Our Debt " Series).

scends all of his scientific wonder, goes beyond the bounds of an ancient mythology, and gives a new vitality to Father Aether and Mother Earth as living powers, whether beneficent or brutal. The poet and the scientist in him have made their peace.

The paralyzing fear of gods, that was a product of the ancient orthodox religion, and the crushing fear of death were large elements in the colossal drama of man's age-long conflict with superstition, caprice, and ignorance — his long struggle through the ages to intellectual and moral victories — and that drama was a worthy theme for the imaginative poet. Lucretius' emotion trembles before the very fear which his logic sought to destroy and establishes the truth of the ancient dramatic theory that the tragic poet must, himself, feel in order to awaken pity in others. It was the drama of human life that stirred the mind of this Epicurean thinker to tragic expressions of great power, as he described the combatants, their victories and their defeats. But it was the poet who caught the eternal beauty of wisdom and happiness in the human world. It was the scientist who comprehended the ephemeral modes of existence, betrayed in the combinations and separations of atoms; but it was the poet who sang of the eternal sacred laws of Nature that govern all — in each case, the permanent behind the veil of passing phenomena. Only a poetic genius could transform science as did Lucretius, and the roll of poets of science is astonishingly brief in the world.[43]

Lessing,[44] to be sure, declared that Lucretius was "a versifier, not a poet," for which he was properly rebuked by Winckelmann, and his philosophy of criticism followed the old dogma of Aristotle's *Poetics*. But the greater genius of Goethe was not bound by the ancient theory that poetry is the imitation of human action and Goethe discovered "a lofty faculty of sensuous intuition" in Lucretius and ascribed to him that power of imagination which goes "beyond the reach of sense into the invisible depths of Nature."[45] This penetrating observa-

[43] Cf. G. Santayana, *Three Philosophical Poets, Lucretius, Dante, Goethe,* Cambridge, Harvard Press, 1910.

[44] There is, however, praise of the great Lucretian passage on the seasons (in book V), in Lessing's *Laokoön;* and Joseph Spence, Professor of Poetry at Oxford, in 1747 recognized Lucretius, as poet, enthusiastically.

[45] Feb. 14, 1821; cf. W. J. Keller, "Goethe's Estimate of the Greek and Latin Writers," in *Bulletin of the University of Wisconsin,* 786 (1916). Cf., also, John Veitch, *Lucretius and the Atomic Theory,* Glasgow, Jas. Maclehose, 1875, on the extraordinary fusion, in Lucretius, of the intellectual and the imaginative.

tion takes into account the scientist and the poet in Lucretius, whose "eternal renown," Goethe believed, was assured; and few men were more competent to judge than Goethe, who frequently testified to his warm admiration for Lucretius in his correspondence with his friend, C. L. von Knebel, author of the first worthy German translation of the *De Rerum Natura* — one that ranks with the best.

Epicurean materialistic psychology had to wait a long, long time for anything like the world's reasoned approval. Lucretius' stand against the Platonists and their interpretation of soul was as brave as his attitude toward the orthodox religious beliefs of his time. The Aristotelians, the Platonists, the Stoics had ruled until Hobbes, Gassendi, and Locke began a rehabilitation, in part at least, of Epicurean psychology. The process of adaptation, of re-interpretation, and of acceptance has been gradual, as science has come, more and more, to dominate psychological laboratories. Our psychology, to-day, is largely naturalistic and materialistic; it uses the mechanism of the body to determine the functioning of the mind and to explain emotions; it is biological in its assumptions, and Lucretius would have felt himself no stranger in the laboratory of Wilhelm Wundt (at least in the German psychologist's early period) or of William James. The conflict between the Platonists and the Epicureans is a fundamental one and will, perhaps, continue forever. But to many minds 'soul' is not what it was considered to be one hundred years ago, and Lucretius might well have subscribed to the doctrine of the immortality of personality or that of influence.

An extraordinary illustration of parallelism and, no doubt, to a certain extent, of direct influence of Lucretius is to be found in the conclusions of the Roman poet and of Ernst Haeckel.[46] The German scholar's pantheism, or a belief in the unity of the world and of God, follows Spinoza far more than Lucretius. But any student of Lucretius will find in Haeckel's discussion of the *mortality of the soul* a re-statement of Lucretius, in the language of the nineteenth-century biologist. Haeckel dismisses the theory of the soul, as a distinct entity within the body, and, so far, he is not in agreement with Lucretius. The word 'soul' is em-

---

[46] Ernst Haeckel, *The Riddle of the Universe*, transl. by J. McCabe, London, Watts & Co., 1900 (the author's preface to the first edition is dated 1899).

ployed as a convenient, " collective title for the
sum-total of man's cerebral functions " and his
psychic phenomena; but, except for that difference, Lucretius, had he lived about two
thousand years later than he did, might well
have written these very chapters.[47] Haeckel's
" physiological " proof that the ' soul ' is not
independent and immaterial, his " histological "
argument, based on a microscopic study of the
brain and a knowledge of nerves and ganglia,
his " pathological " argument that dwells on the
physical infirmities of ' soul,' his " ontogenetic "
argument that stresses the development of
' soul ' in the individual life, the influences of
heredity and of environment, inevitably recall
Lucretius' impassioned array of arguments,
and, one and all, they rest upon the same
naturalistic basis of the human organism, upon
the idea of unity of ' soul ' and body that constituted the inspiration of Lucretius. With far
greater knowledge of physiology, anatomy, and
evolution of the species, of chemistry and protoplasm, Haeckel reaffirms the essential conclusion of the Roman, for whom he expresses great
admiration, on the soul's mortality; and his

[47] Cf. the excellent article of F. B. R. Hellems, *Lucretius and Haeckel,* University of Colorado Studies, III. 3
and 4, 1906.

mature convictions range him on the side of Democritus, Empedocles, Epicurus, and Lucretius, against the dualistic Plato and the Christian dualists, who rest their case on a belief in a divine creation of 'soul,' and on theological, teleological, and moral affirmations, and on a transcendental, emotional craving. The world will choose between the dualists and the monists, but between Lucretius and Haeckel there is a large kinship of spirit; both dared to brave one of mankind's deepest hopes, to stand, unflinchingly, by the laws of Nature, as they understood them, and to claim the highest ethical consequences for their views on one of the greatest riddles of the universe.

Whatever the truth about a categorical ethical imperative or of an ethics of relativity and of individuality, at least we realize, now, that the Epicurean ethics of Epicurus and Lucretius are not what for so long they were commonly and erroneously taken to be — so largely and widely misunderstood that the very word 'Epicurean' was a symbol and a synonym of a vain and frivolous pursuit of selfish pleasures of the senses, a selfish life that found its justification in rejection of the ideas of immortality and of divine providence. On the contrary,

Lucretius' attitude toward life is another one
of his claims to our attention and to fame.
Though he formulated no political, economic,
and social philosophy — which would have been
contrary to the spirit of his Epicurean individualism — he was profoundly concerned with
the problem of the individual man, his intelligence, his happiness, his virtue — as the only
means of redeeming human society. No less
stress, here, upon the supreme value of the
individual than in Christian ethics that seek
to save the human soul for Paradise; but the
Epicurean stress is wholly upon life, here and
now. Temporary inequalities and injustices
that assume a variety of forms, in the years,
but constitute a permanent threat to human
peace, happiness, and justice, were to fade, if
ever, through the perfection of the inherent,
potential capacity of man to attain true wisdom. This was his Utopia — a dream, perhaps, beyond realization, but a dream shot
through and through with idealism. Wisdom,
happiness, and virtue were his stars. Leave
all and follow me was a cry to leave the world
in order to save the world: on the surface, the
old Epicurean gospel of escape; in truth, however, the Roman preacher's and the Roman

patriot's exhortation to redeem the world by means of that revolution in the heart and conscience of the individual man which his philosophy prescribed. Lucretius directed his gaze over the passing forms of governmental and social organization into the heart of a suffering humanity. Christian ideals of faith in man, hope, and charity, democratic ideals of liberty, equality, and fraternity he would have saluted, because of their values to human dignity; but he would, I think, have maintained that their security depended upon the assured victory of wisdom and virtue over the individual mind and heart, and upon recognition of an assured place for human happiness in the temple of life.

Nineteenth- and twentieth-century classical scholarship has not neglected Lucretius. On the contrary, editions of the ancient author, volumes and studies without number that make a formidable library of *Lucretiana,* and translations [48] attest the continued hold he has exercised over many minds that have sought to

[48] I know of translations into English, French, Italian, Spanish, German, Dutch, Portuguese, Hungarian, Russian. The total number since 1800 is very large. It would hardly be possible to give a complete list, here.

establish the text, to interpret the thought, or to reproduce the poem in the language of the translator. Lachmann and Munro, in the middle of the nineteenth century, in Germany and England, Heinze and Giussani at the close of the century, in Germany and Italy, Ernout and Robin, in France, Bailey and Merrill in England and America, in the twentieth century, are among those who have carried forward, with greatest honor to themselves, because of scientific precision, the earlier labors of Lambinus from the sixteenth century. The science of paleography had developed with the years, after the eighteenth century, knowledge of the Epicurean system had grown in accuracy, and, most important of all, an old, lingering prejudice against some of the Lucretian conclusions was evaporating. No more apologies, like that of Aldus in 1500, are printed in editions of Lucretius; no sermons, like an exorcism of the evil one, such as Faber had published in 1662; no futile repetitions of ancient *testimonia* and *apologia,* as had appeared in the eighteenth-century editions of Havercamp and Wakefield. Not that editors and other students of Lucretius were accepting Lucretius' denials of divine providence and of the soul's immortality — which, in any case, is not required of scholarship — but the work of the editor and of all students had become far more exacting and the progress of science in other fields had imposed upon classical scholarship quite a new methodology. Along with an unquestioned sympathetic devotion, which is an essential part of all good exegesis, there is also the unquestioned acceptance of the principle of impartial, scientific appraisal of truth and error, which enables us to understand Lucretius, in perspective, far better than was possible one hundred and fifty years ago. The great editions that I have mentioned are ornaments of true scholarship, they are the tributes of true scholarship to a mind of singular power and independence, they are expressions of a wide interest, on the part of students without number, in Lucretius, whose influence in a variety of ways is beyond computation.

I have, earlier, referred to the "Vossian MSS" of Lucretius. A further word of explanation is required, here. Isaac Vossius (1618–1689) was born at Leyden, but, eventually, in 1673, he established himself in England, at Windsor. He and his father had collected a magnificent library of MSS, including two Lucretian MSS. Bentley endeavoured to secure the purchase of the library for the Bodleian, because of the offer of sale, and Cambridge men hoped to obtain the treasures for their University. But they were bought by the Leyden Academy where they have remained ever since. How Vossius found the two Lucretian MSS or how he obtained them is not known to us; they had been, certainly, the one in Mainz, in the library of St. Martin's church, the other, in the Abbey of St. Bertin, near St. Omer, and Lambinus, in the sixteenth century, knew of the existence of the latter. Although they were secure in Leyden, after 1689, Havercamp did not dream of their significance, in the eighteenth century. It remained for Lachmann and Munro to make the great discovery, which finally placed the text of Lucretius on a sound basis. The one Leyden MS, the one from Mainz, called 'A' or 'O' (oblongus, because of its shape), is a folio of the ninth century; the other, called 'B' or 'Q' (quadratus), is a quarto of the tenth (or, perhaps, the ninth) century. 'A' is written in a beautiful hand and it is very sharp and clear. Corrections of two scribes of the ninth century appear in this MS and the corrections of one of these often agree, very remarkably, with the MS of Niccoli of the fifteenth century, which has been discussed before (p. 254). 'B' is also a finely written MS, though in smaller script, and it has had several correctors, of the fifteenth century. To establish the relationship of these two MSS, their relation to each other and to the original from which they were derived, to discover the values of the fifteenth-[49] century MSS of Lucretius, to determine their significance for the text has been a triumph of scholarship in which Lachmann and Munro, as pioneers, share the honor.

These latter-day editions and innumerable studies, appearing in Germany, England, Italy, France, and in the United States, reflect the intensive study of Lucretius that has taken account of every word and of every idea in Lu-

---

[49] The MSS of Lucretius thus include the following: the two, in Leyden, of the ninth (tenth) centuries; a fragment of eight leaves in Copenhagen, called the Schedae Haunienses (also "Gottorpian"), and another fragment of ten leaves, called the Schedae Vindobonenses, in Vienna (both resembling the quarto); the Poggio-Niccoli MS and its descendants, discussed in chapter XI. For specimens in facsimile of O, Q, Sch. Haun., Sch. Vind., and Florence MS 29 see Émile Chatelain, *Paléographie Des Classiques Latins,* 2 vols., Paris, Hachette et Cie., 1884–1900. Also, De Vries and Chatelain, *Lucretius, Codex Vossianus Oblongus* and *Quadratus* (phototypice editi), Lugduni Batavorum, A. W. Sijthoff, 1908 and 1913.

cretius, with a view to understanding the totality of his poetic and philosophic structure, his
relationship to earlier Greek and Latin litera-
tures, his real place in the world's thought and
poetic creation. These editions possess the vitality imparted by acute and sober scholarship,
and they are treasure-houses of learning, invaluable as long as scholarship may continue.
Yet finality never marks even the most superior
work of this kind, because none of us knows
what information, now hid, may later come to
light, nor would one carelessly prophesy the
attitude of another century toward Lucretius or toward any other great mind of the
past.

We may, in conclusion, recall a few instances
of later direct Lucretian influence upon the lives
of men, remind ourselves of significant contacts
between his mind and later intelligence, observe
some startling examples of admiration, with or
without intellectual approval, and realize, to a
certain extent, the profound influence of his
poetry and discover the deposit of Lucretian
thought in the memory and life of the Western
world. Here I would again remind you of
Haeckel, and I should like to quote the words

of Tyndall:[50] "His [*i.e.,* Lucretius'] vaguely-grand conception of the atoms falling eternally through space suggested the nebular hypothesis to Kant, its first propounder." Byron's misunderstanding of Lucretius' "irreligion" did not dim his eye to appreciation of the poem which he felt to be the first in Latin literature.[51] Wordsworth [52] praises one of the most admirable passages in Lucretius describing natural scenery; a totally different outlook upon Nature did not blind the English poet's recognition of lovely lines that truly describe a typical Italian landscape: the forests, hills and mountains, dales, lakes and streams, meadows, vineyards, olive-groves are there — all remembered with sympathy and sensuous feeling.[53] Mrs. Browning's famous lines in her *Vision of Poets* do justice to the poet, though, unhappily, they express a false sentiment in claiming that Lucretius said "No God." Tennyson [54] has led the unwary astray, in represent-

[50] The *Belfast Address,* p. 10 (see n. 34, p. 333).
[51] Cf. *Don Juan,* I. 43; *Childe Harold,* 4. 51; *Letters and Journals of Byron* (R. E. Prothero), London, John Murray; N. Y., Scribner's Sons, 1898–1901; 5. 554, 564.
[52] A. B. Grosart, *The Prose Works of William Wordsworth,* 3 vols., London, Edw. Moxon, Son, & Co., 1876; vol. II, p. 296 (*A Guide Through the District of the Lakes*).
[53] L., V. 1370–1378.
[54] See p. 6.

ing uncertain legend as truth about the Roman poet's life and death, but Tennyson has not left us uncertain about his high estimate of the splendor of Lucretius, as a poet.

Pontanus [55] had testified to the magic of Lucretius' eloquence, and Palgrave,[56] also, has borne witness to the difficulty of resisting the power of the Roman's charm over the intellect:

" Another time, late over the mid-winter fire, reading the terrible lines in which Lucretius preaches his creed of human annihilation,[57] and, perhaps, those on the uselessness of prayer [58] and the sublime but oppressive fear, inevitable to the thoughtful mind in the awful vision of the star-lighted heavens,[59] so carried away and overwhelmed were the readers by the poignant force of the great poet, that, next morning, when dawn and daylight had brought their blessed and natural healing to morbid thoughts, it was laughingly agreed that Lucretius had left us last night all but converts to his heart-crushing atheism."

The story is told of Gladstone's effective use of verses from Lucretius in what has been called

[55] See p. 260.
[56] *Alfred Lord Tennyson, A Memoir,* by his Son, 2 vols., London and N. Y., The Macmillan Co., 1897 (vol. II, p. 500, Recollections, F. T. Palgrave).
[57] III. 912–977.
[58] The critic was in error, here.
[59] Cf. V. 1194–1217.

"one of the noblest of his orations." As John Morley[60] describes the scene: "The House . . . sat . . . with reverential stillness, hearkening . . . to 'the rise and long roll of the hexameter,'— to the plangent lines that have come down across the night of time to us from great Rome."

Omnis enim per se divom natura necessest
immortali aevo summa cum pace fruatur
semota ab nostris rebus seiunctaque longe;
nam privata dolore omni, privata periclis,
ipsa suis pollens opibus, nil indiga nostri,
nec bene promeritis capitur neque tangitur ira.[61]

Gladstone's audience paid a silent tribute of awed admiration to these verses, though they expressed a sentiment of divine indifference to man to which his audience and certainly the orator could not subscribe. Gladstone paid his audience the compliment of saying that "Many of the members of this House will

---

[60] *Life of Gladstone,* vol. III. 19–20 (year 1883), London, Macmillan & Co., 1903.
[61] II. 646–651 (cf. p. 113, for paraphrase). Gladstone's remarks " You know very well that from ancient times there have been sects and schools that have admitted in the abstract as freely as Christians the existence of a Deity, but have held that of practical relations between Him and man there can be none " (I hardly need to add) do not represent Lucretius fairly.

recollect the majestic and noble lines " — which, then, he quoted.

It was to Goethe that Matthew Arnold dedicated verses that are a reminder, at once, of Virgil and of Lucretius:

> *And he was happy, if to know*
> *Causes of things, and far below*
> *His feet to see the lurid flow*
> *Of terror and insane distress*
> *And headlong fate, be happiness.*

And in his own " Obermann — Once More," there is a notable echo of a famous Lucretian diatribe against the ennui of Roman society and its failure to live life richly and nobly: [62]

> *In his cool hall, with haggard eyes,*
> *The Roman noble lay;*
> *He drove abroad in furious guise,*
> *Along the Appian way;*
> *He made a feast, drank fierce and fast,*
> *And crowned his hair with flowers —*
> *No easier nor no quicker pass'd*
> *The impracticable hours.*

Gilbert Murray expresses, I doubt not, the feeling of many who have thrilled to the majesty of Lucretian poetry without, in the least,

[62] L., III. 1053–1075.

subscribing to the doctrines of mortality, no providence, and hedonism.

" For example, *Omar Kháyyám* consists mostly of dogmatic statements about life which seem to me to be probably untrue and certainly most depressing; but I love the poem and am exhilarated by reading it." [63]

The twelfth-century Persian poem must necessarily come to the mind of all readers of the *De Rerum Natura;* the parallels [64] are too well-known to require recapitulation, here, and Professor Murray's expressed admiration for the one may be matched with many an enthusiastic expression of wonder at the aesthetic qualities of the other.

Strains of Epicurean brooding upon the brevity of life and the finality of death appear in Housman's poetry:

> *Let me mind the house of dust*
> *Where my sojourn shall be long —*

Housman's life, like that of Lucretius, has been the double life of scholar and poet; the two

[63] G. Murray, *The Classical Tradition in Poetry,* Harvard University Press, 1927, p. 253.

[64] The *differences* between Omar and Lucretius are, to be sure, very great; cf., *e.g.,* the *Preface* to the first edition of the *Rubáiyát,* tr. by Fitzgerald, John Lane, N. Y. and London, 1901.

qualities have met in him as they did in one of his great admirations. Hedonism was not foreign to Ernest Dowson, though it was not the refined pleasure of Epicurus, nor the rational happiness of Lucretius; yet all will recall the quality of hedonism that lies in the verses of ' Cynara ' and the Epicureanism of ' Envoy.' The rebellious spirit of Samuel Butler properly reminds us of Lucretius' revolt against established religious institutions, and *The Way of All Flesh* subtly argues for pleasure as a safer guide than duty, sterilized by official prohibitions. The fears of everlasting punishment are condemned with all the vehemence of the ancient Roman, and Butler's sense of freedom goes back through more immediate advocates to those of an older time. To John Davidson's mind, venturing in the awesome vastness of the physical universe and seeking a theology that might be imperative, yet purged of puritanical prudery, Lucretius remained one of the *dii maiores*. The spokesman of ' The Impercipient ' feels himself an outcast from the bright, believing band of orthodox worshippers, and, so far, he is one of that large company of intellectual wayfarers to whom Lucretius belonged; but Hardy's tragic outlook has clothed his speaker in a somber unhappiness that was no part of the Lucretian pride and joy in victory.

In the course of his soul's journey to its mystic goal, Walter Pater's *Marius the Epicurean* had sentimentally pondered the meaning of the "magnificent" *exordium* of Lucretius, had heard the thunder and seen the lightning of Lucretius, had mused on the significance of the brevity of life and on the perfection of the feelings, and had found "the judgment of Lucretius on pagan religion . . . without reproach" at the point of its condemnation of human sacrifice. None knew better than Walter Pater that "every age of European thought has had its Cyrenaics or Epicureans, under many disguises: even under the hood of the monk." Certainly, his Marius was not a Lucretian — although the velvety cadences of the author's prose create the illusion of one type of sensuous Epicureanism.

Leconte de Lisle's surrender to the idea of utter effacement of life in death is Epicurean, and his apostrophe to 'divine Death' is as impassioned as the Lucretian tone, expressed in the phrase *mors immortalis*, a fearless salute to the invincible master; and no less deep in its significance is his discovery of beauty as a

[361]

symbol of impassive happiness. But I know of no more outspoken, ecstatic praise of Epicurus and of Lucretius than that which appears in *Une Nuit au Luxembourg* of Remy de Gourmont — we cannot overlook such expressions of conviction, howsoever extravagant they may appear to us.

Strains from Lucretius, parallels to his thought, echoes from his poetry are found far and wide. Homage rendered to the poet, whose poem enjoys a sovereign status, is found in almost every language of the civilized world. Victor Hugo, Paul Verlaine, Musset, Sully-Prudhomme, Flaubert, Villon, Lamartine, Anatole France; Keats, Shelley, Coleridge, Swinburne, De Quincey, Ruskin, J. A. Symonds, James Joyce, D. H. Lawrence, Rupert Brooke, Andrew Lang, Bertrand Russell; Goethe, Heine, Wilhelm Bölsche; Thomas Jefferson, Poe, Walt Whitman, W. E. Leonard, E. A. Robinson are a few of the many whose tributes of one kind or another are known, presumably, to all scholars. Any adequate account of this infiltration would fill another volume.

The world has accepted atomism, and the dizzy dance of the atoms proclaims the laws of

Nature to us. Acrimony no longer characterizes discussions of a materialistic psychology.
Epicurean hedonism no longer terrifies. A
more enlightened world has recognized the
truth in these doctrines, and our astonishment
grows at Lucretius' acceptance and defense,
in Rome, in the first century before Christ,
of these principles that were long submerged
and only, more recently, have again won favor.
There may be more hesitation in following this
brave Roman in his fearless denial that ethics
are dependent upon a will, outside, and upon
a belief in immortality [65] — his proud belief
that the conscience [66] owes allegiance to no
other tribunal but itself. And the greatest
doubt of all will attend the question whether
worship of God can go hand in hand with denial of divine providence. At least we know,
now, that Lucretius did not mean to demolish
religion's temple but to rebuild it, not to destroy the vessel but to purify it. The old
charge of ' atheism ' need no longer bruise his

[65] All of us are aware of the power of the idea of immortality. It may be well to mention Sir Oliver Lodge,
here. Perhaps a book *What is Hell*, New York, Harper's,
1932, may not be so well known.

[66] Cf. L., III. 1011–1023 (I know of nothing, even in
Maupassant, to exceed in power this passage on the terrors
of the guilty conscience).

fearless soul. The Roman poet's statement of
the relation of science to religion [67] assumes
major importance, to-day, and, far from pro-
voking the bitter diatribes of old, gives thoughtful readers grave and reverent pause. We have
followed the evolution of men's thoughts toward
Lucretius and have discovered a growing recognition of the importance of his *attitude* toward
all of these great questions. Great bitterness
of attacks upon him have yielded to a greater
admiration, as the nature of his mission has
become clearer: to expound the atomic " nature
of things " although real demonstration was
an impossibility in his day; to lay the foundations of science, in Rome, although his own
science was in many respects, necessarily,
grievously faulty; to free religion from superstition, although the very word for superstition
was not even fixed, as yet, in the Latin language
with a definite, accepted meaning; to establish
a new psychology, although ignorance of the
nervous system presented the greatest difficulties; to come to the rescue of permanent happi-

[67] Cf. *Time, Matter and Values,* Robt. A. Millikan, University of North Carolina Press, 1932 (which well expresses
the modern physicist's attitude) and A. N. Whitehead,
Science and the Modern World, N. Y., The Macmillan Co.,
1925 (on science and idealism).

ness in a tortured world. Our debt to Lucretius has become manifest, and not the least debt is that which we owe, through him, to the sacred freedom of thought which was incarnate in him, to that intellectual heroism which scorns cowardice and fear, man's real scourge. The *De Rerum Natura* belongs to the great and grave literature of inquiry and of protest. Although Lucretius believed in the superiority of his message — far more important than that of the dualists or that of the Oracle of Delphi — yet he knew, equally well, that his message was unacceptable to his own age; and it required great courage to believe that this message was not for one but for all the centuries:

> temporis aeterni quoniam, non unius horae,
> ambigitur status . . .

Lucretius, peculiarly free from the emotional entanglements of his own age, was not deceived by the errors of contemporary, orthodox religious thought, was not beguiled by the glamour of Rome's wealth and power, her army and her imperialism; with a love for Rome as deep as any other's, the satirist and iconoclast searched beneath the temporary patterns of religious and ethical behavior, looked beyond the limitations of contemporary science and addressed himself to the long, long future. His march through the centuries has been impressive. His spirit of bold inquiry still rides on:

Haec sei pernosces, parva perductus opella

. . .

namque alid ex alio clarescet, nec tibi caeca
nox iter eripiet quin ultima naturai
pervideas; ita res accendent lumina rebus.

— *eternal vigilance and constant labor; unceasing expectancy, and hope for more light to illuminate the dark mysteries of life* —

He has left us a most precious heritage of freedom — the freedom of reason to explore to the uttermost — and he stands forth from the Roman scene, easily, as one of Rome's most illustrious figures, despite the fact that of his life on earth we know so little — a life and death upon which uncertain legend gleams for a moment. We recognize the errors in his thinking, but, far more important than that, we know, now, more fully than ever before, the truth that lies in the *De Rerum Natura*. It has gained depth and won height through the medium of that luminous poem of which Ovid had rightly said:

Carmina sublimis tunc sunt peritura Lucreti,
   Exitio terras cum dabit una dies.

A BRIEF BIBLIOGRAPHY

I. LUCRETIUS AND HIS INFLUENCE

BAILEY, C., *The Greek Atomists and Epicurus.* Oxford, The Clarendon Press, 1928.

DILL, SAMUEL, *Roman Society from Nero to Marcus Aurelius.* London, Macmillan & Co., 1904.

——, *Roman Society in the Last Century of the Western Empire.* London, Macmillan & Co., 1905.[2]

DUCKETT, E. S., *Latin Writers of the Fifth Century.* N. Y., Holt & Co., 1930.

DUFF, J. WIGHT, *A Literary History of Rome* (from the Origins to the Close of the Golden Age). London, T. Fisher Unwin, 1920.[2]

——, *A Literary History of Rome in the Silver Age.* London, T. Fisher Unwin, 1927.

FUSIL, C.–A., see n. 26, chapter XII.

GLOVER, T. R., *Life and Letters in the Fourth Century.* Cambridge, England, University Press, 1901.

GUYAU, J.–M., see n. 25, chapter XII.

HICKS, R. D., *Stoic and Epicurean.* N. Y., Scribner's Sons, 1910.

JESSEN, J., see n. 11, chapter X.

LABRIOLLE, PIERRE DE, *Histoire De La Littérature Latine Chrétienne.* Paris, Société d'Édition " Les Belles Lettres," 1920. (Tr. by Herbert Wilson; London, Kegan Paul, Trench, Trubner & Co.; N. Y., A. A. Knopf, 1924.)

LANGE, F. A., see n. 17, chapter XII.

LEHNERDT, MAX, *Lucretius in der Renaissance.* Festschrift zur Feier des 600 jährigen Jubiläums des Kneiphöfischen Gymnasiums, zu Königsberg, 1904 (publ. sep.).

A BRIEF BIBLIOGRAPHY

MANITIUS, M., *Geschichte der Lateinischen Literatur des Mittelalters.* 3 vols. München, Beck, 1911–1931.

MARTHA, C., *Le Poëme De Lucrèce,* Morale — Religion — Science. Paris, Hachette et Cie., 1905.[6]

MASSON, JOHN, *The Atomic Theory of Lucretius.* London, Geo. Bell & Sons, 1884.

——, *Lucretius, Epicurean and Poet.* London, John Murray, 1907 (supplementary volume, 1909).

PATIN, M., *Études Sur La Poésie Latine.* 2 vols. Paris, Hachette et Cie, 1914[5] (especially the chapter: " L'Antilucrèce chez Lucrèce ").

PHILIPPE, J., " Lucrèce dans la Théologie Chrétienne du IIIe au XIIIe Siècle," in *Revue de l'Histoire des Religions,* XXXII. 284–302 (1895), XXXIII. 19–36, 125–162 (1896).

SAINTSBURY, GEO. ED. B., *A History of Criticism and Literary Taste in Europe.* 3 vols. Edinburgh and London, Blackwood; N. Y., Dodd, Mead & Co., 1906.[2]

SANDYS, J. E., *A History of Classical Scholarship.* 3 vols. Cambridge, England, University Press, 1903–1908.

SCHANZ, MARTIN, *Geschichte der Römischen Litteratur.* München, Beck, 1909 (vol. with *Lucretius,* in *Hdb. der Kl. Alt.–W.*).

SELLAR, W. Y., *The Roman Poets of the Republic.* Oxford, Clarendon Press, 1889.[3]

SPINGARN, J. E., *A History of Literary Criticism in the Renaissance.* N. Y., The Macmillan Co., 1899.

SYMONDS, J. A., *The Renaissance in Italy.* 5 vols. London, Smith, Elder & Co., 1875–1881 (also published by Holt & Co., N. Y., 1888).

TAYLOR, A. E., *Epicurus.* London, Constable & Co., 1911 (in Series, " Philosophies: Ancient and Modern ").

TAYLOR, H. O., *The Classical Heritage of the Middle Ages.* N. Y., The Macmillan Co., 1903.[2]

——, *Thought and Expression in the Sixteenth Century.* 2 vols. N. Y., The Macmillan Co., 1920.

TEUFFEL, W. S., (Kroll u. Skutsch), *Geschichte der Römischen Literatur.* Leipzig, Teubner, 1916.

A BRIEF BIBLIOGRAPHY

WALLACE, WILLIAM, *Epicureanism*. London, Society for Promoting Christian Knowledge, 1880.

WENDELL, B., *The Traditions of European Literature from Homer to Dante*. N. Y., Scribner's Sons, 1920.

WULF, MAURICE DE, *Histoire de la Philosophie mediévale*. Paris, Alcan, 1925.[5]

ZELLER, E., *The Stoics, Epicureans and Sceptics* (Tr. by O. J. Reichel). London and New York, Longmans, Green & Co., 1892.

ZINGERLE, A., see n. 39, chapter IV.

II. TRANSLATIONS

(A brief list of a few recent translations may be of value, here.)

ALLISON, SIR ROBERT . . . London, A. C. Humphreys, 1919 (verse); 2d. ed., rev. & corr. — Hatchards, 1925.

BAILEY, CYRIL . . . Oxford, Clarendon Press, 1910 (prose).

BERGSON, HENRI . . . Paris, Delagrave, 1913[9] (prose) (extraits de Lucrèce, avec un commentaire, et une étude sur la poésie, etc.).

DIELS, H. . . . Berlin, Weidmann, 1923–24 (verse).

ERNOUT, ALFRED . . . Paris, Société d'Édition " Les Belles Lettres," 1920 (prose) (in the *Budé* Series).

JACKSON, THOMAS . . . Oxford, Blackwell, 1929 (rhythmical prose).

LEFÈVRE, ANDRÉ . . . Paris, Société d'Éditions Litt., 1899 (verse) (originally publ., 1876).

LEONARD, WILLIAM ELLERY . . . London, Dent & Sons; N. Y., E. P. Dutton & Co., 1916 (metrical).

MALLOCK, W. H., *Lucretius on Life and Death*. London, Black, 1901 (in the metre of Omar Kháyyám).

MUNRO, H. A. J. . . . Cambridge and London, Bell, 1891[4] (prose) (often reprinted since its first appearance in 1864).

PRUDHOMME, SULLY . . . Paris, A. Lemerre, 1880 (verse) (tr. of bk. i).

A BRIEF BIBLIOGRAPHY

ROUSE, W. H. D. . . . London, Heinemann; N. Y., Putnam's, 1924 (prose) (in *The Loeb Classical Library*).
VON KNEBEL, C. L. . . . Leipzig, Göschen, 1821 (verse).
WAY, ARTHUR S. . . . London, Macmillan & Co., 1933 (verse).

Readers will have their individual preferences. Blank verse seems to me one essential for successful metrical translation. But, more than that, no translator who lacks a re-creative imagination will ever succeed in the well-nigh impossible task of coaxing this Latin poem over into adequate expression in another language.

III. EDITIONS

(A mere recapitulation of the names of the more distinguished recent editors of Lucretius must suffice, here:
Cyril Bailey, A. Ernout et L. Robin, Carlo Giussani, Richard Heinze, Karl Lachmann, W. A. Merrill, H. A. J. Munro.)

Our Debt to Greece and Rome

AUTHORS AND TITLES

Our Debt to Greece and Rome

AUTHORS AND TITLES

AUTHORS AND TITLES

AESCHYLUS AND SOPHOCLES. *J. T. Sheppard.*

GREEK RELIGION. *Walter Woodburn Hyde.*

SURVIVALS OF ROMAN RELIGION. *Gordon J. Laing.*

MYTHOLOGY. *Jane Ellen Harrison.*

ANCIENT BELIEFS IN THE IMMORTALITY OF THE SOUL. *Clifford H. Moore.*

STAGE ANTIQUITIES. *James Turney Allen.*

PLAUTUS AND TERENCE. *Gilbert Norwood.*

ROMAN POLITICS. *Frank Frost Abbott.*

PSYCHOLOGY, ANCIENT AND MODERN. *G. S. Brett.*

ANCIENT AND MODERN ROME. *Rodolfo Lanciani.*

WARFARE BY LAND AND SEA. *Eugene S. McCartney.*

THE GREEK FATHERS. *James Marshall Campbell.*

GREEK BIOLOGY AND MEDICINE. *Henry Osborn Taylor.*

MATHEMATICS. *David Eugene Smith.*

LOVE OF NATURE AMONG THE GREEKS AND ROMANS. *H. R. Fairclough.*

ANCIENT WRITING AND ITS INFLUENCE. *B. L. Ullman.*

GREEK ART. *Arthur Fairbanks.*

ARCHITECTURE. *Alfred M. Brooks.*

ENGINEERING. *Alexander P. Gest.*

MODERN TRAITS IN OLD GREEK LIFE. *Charles Burton Gulick.*

ROMAN PRIVATE LIFE. *Walton Brooks McDaniel.*

GREEK AND ROMAN FOLKLORE. *William Reginald Halliday.*

ANCIENT EDUCATION. *J. F. Dobson.*